THE ALEXANDER COMPLEX

THE ALEXANDER COMPLEX

THE DREAMS THAT DRIVE THE GREAT BUSINESSMEN

MICHAEL MEYER

Published in the United States by Times Books, a division of Random House, Inc., New York, and simultaneously in Canada by Random House of Canada Limited, Toronto.

Grateful acknowledgment is made to Glad Music Co. for permission to reprint an excerpt from the song lyrics "Where Are You Now When We Need You, Ross Perot" by Clyde Mason and Ken Fairchild. Copyright © 1979 by Glad Music Co. Reprinted by permission.

Library of Congress Cataloging-in-Publication Data

Meyer, Michael
The Alexander complex: the dreams that drive the great businessmen/ Michael Meyer.
p. cm.
Includes index.
ISBN 0-8129-1662-X
1. Businessmen—United States—Biography. 2. Executives—United States—Biography. I. Title.
HC102.5.A2M48 1989
338.092'2—dc19 89-4401
[B]

Design by ROBERT BULL DESIGN

Manufactured in the United States of America

9 8 7 6 5 4 3 2

First Edition

Author's Note

The Alexander Complex is the work of two people. Jennifer Meyer, my wife and an accomplished journalist, assisted me enormously in the editing, writing and reporting. Her contributions, especially for the chapter on James Rouse, were immeasurable. I am the beneficiary of her intelligence, skepticism and tenacity. Without her, the book would never have been written.

CONTENTS

◆

INTRODUCTION

THE ROARING EIGHTIES took us on a roller-coaster ride from skepticism to euphoria and back to skepticism. Perhaps the decade's most positive—and enduring—feature is that it restored our perspective about the role of the businessman in American society. It has always been easy to accept that an Abraham Lincoln or a Dwight Eisenhower could shape history. But it's somehow been illegitimate to imagine that a businessman could. And yet it's so. The history of America, an industrial power above all else, is also the story of farsighted business leaders.

This book is about some of them. They are a handful of modern American visionaries who have done more than amass great fortunes or build giant corporations. By putting together new combinations of technology and economic forces, they have changed the patterns of society, the way we live and see the world. Historians of the future will write of them as our era's empire builders. Everyone has a list of such people. Here's mine:

- Steven Jobs, the upstart founder of Apple Computer, may be the ultimate charismatic leader, a masterful manipulator who leads as much by seduction and intimidation as by the power of his ideas. Described by associates as a "visionary monster," Jobs consumed his own creation—and was consumed by it. When he was deposed in a boardroom coup, he started NeXT, an education-oriented computer company that modestly promises to "revolutionize the way teachers teach and students learn."
- Ross Perot, the eccentric Dallas billionaire who founded Electronic Data Systems, is the Patriarch. He has rescued employees held hostage in Iran, flown Christmas dinners to American prisoners of war in Vietnam and taken on giant General Motors in a personal crusade to make American industry competitive again.

His position, Perot says, obliges him to "speak out," to stand up for what's right. Great wealth creates great obligations—to family, employees and country—and Perot will go to any length to honor them.

• James Rouse, the messianic master builder, is given to such messages as "It's not how many people live in a city; it's how many people use it." In creating the most successful "new town" in America, Columbia, Md., and developing Harborplace in Baltimore and the Faneuil Hall project in Boston, Rouse has become the undisputed godfather of urban revitalization in America. Now, his new Enterprise Foundation is pouring millions of dollars into the nation's inner cities—turning run-down or deserted tenements into affordable, low-income homes—and it aims to do so in a way that everyone says is impossible: by making a profit.

• Robert Swanson, the founder of Genentech, is the Builder. He is the father of modern biotechnology. His latest miracle drug, a heart attack serum called Activase, saves the lives of thousands of Americans a year. He lives to solve problems—problems like AIDS, arthritis and diabetes. His success is a case study in enlightened modern management.

• Ted Turner, the former America's Cup champion, turned an ailing family billboard business into TBS, the first cable television network, and launched CNN, the twenty-four-hour news station. Turner thirsts for fame. He paid millions for Hollywood's legendary MGM studio, partly because it owned his favorite movie, *Gone With the Wind.* That folly almost cost him his empire. Now he's at it again. With his new Better World Society, he hopes to save us all.

• Daniel Ludwig, once the world's richest man, imagined he could corner the world's timber market. He dreamed of "planting trees like corn," and so spent half his fortune to buy and develop a Connecticut-sized piece of real estate deep in the heart of the Amazon jungle. He thought he could tame the wilderness; instead, it tamed him. The humiliation drove him into reclusiveness—but not inactivity. The ninety-year-old magnate recently sank $700 million into a residential and commercial development across the Hudson from Manhattan. He is so excited by its prospects that at the contract-signing he allowed his picture to be taken for the first time in twenty years.

A FEW WORDS about what this book is not. These portraits aren't meant to be profiles. Each explores a particular slant of character that, to varying degrees, is shared by the others. All these men have traits in common: vision, leadership ability, willfulness, extraordinary energy and focus. But that's obvious. This book attempts to catch the essence of their character, who they are, how they think and see the world, how they perform their self-assigned task in life.

As often as possible, I've let them speak for themselves. These are the words and thoughts of Chairmen Jobs, Perot, Turner, Rouse and Swanson. I've tried to capture whatever it is that makes them tick. Why such a thirst to make a mark on history? As with most successful people, there's a strong desire for money, power and glory—the "three great motivators," one analyst calls them. But there's a world of difference between the drives of an empire builder and those of a run-of-the-mill tycoon. When we speak of an Ivan Boesky, for instance, we speak of his haste to get rich and his lust for the reputation and influence that money can give. When we talk about empire builders, however, we're talking about the *ideas* that lift their ambitions above the realm of the mercantile.

Which is not to exempt them from the more basic impulses. The desire for money, power and glory burns just as fiercely for the Alexanders of this world as for the pretenders. It's just that those appetites are channeled so differently. Most public figures—bureaucrats, politicians and big businessmen—are too purposeless—and therefore powerless—to leave a mark on history. They are swept along by events, shouting as they go to convince themselves and everyone else that they matter. It's a deception and a fraud. The men who figure in this book are not among these. They are shaping history, as well as being shaped by it.

As regards my cast of characters, I early on decided to make a game of it. If you wanted to imagine a man with a *pursuit*, a real world-changer, who better to choose than Alexander the Great? If anyone ever lived in the grip of a transformative idea, he did. He wanted to conquer the world and make it Greek. To do that, he built a large organization, a well-trained and loyal army equipped with new weapons and new strategies that he himself designed. Using Alexander as an archetypal model, my associate (and wife), Jennifer Meyer, and I drew up a list of "modern-day Alexanders." And we called the syndrome "The Alexander Complex."

Some names sprang immediately to mind: Perot, Turner, Jobs. We talked to friends, experts, colleagues at *Newsweek*. We spent a month hounding experts up and down the East Coast and, in the process, uncovered a whole subculture of analysts who built lucrative careers around the new cult of entrepreneurship. Some were academics who sought to isolate the qualities that mark the successful entrepreneur. Others were motivational snake-oil salesmen, men Ted Turner calls the "dare-to-be-great types," who jet about the country peddling evangelistic advice to Rotary groups and entrepreneurship clubs.

At each lunch, at each interview, we asked whom we should include in the book. The suggestions were all over the map: billionaire Les Wexner, the founder of the Limited clothing chain. Charles Lazarus, founder of Toys "Я" Us. William Gates, the thirty-one-year-old head of Microsoft, the computer software company. Ray Kroc, the McDonald's king. Donald Trump, the developer. Michael Milken, the beleaguered ex–Drexel Burnham investment banker who pioneered the leveraged buyout and touched off a wave of takeovers that has transformed the corporate landscape.

Some of the ideas were quite imaginative. One friend proposed the rock impresario Gordy Berry, the creator and marketer of the Motown Sound. David Silver, a venture capitalist and author of *The Entrepreneurial Life*, suggested two others: Charles Schultz, whose *Peanuts* comic strip is read and loved by millions of adults and children, and Walter Kemmons, the man who in building the first Holiday Inn sparked America's love affair with the motel.

Kirby Warren, a professor at Columbia University's business school, came up with an especially novel theory. Recalling an old *Star Trek* episode that featured a man who had lived five thousand years—at one point he was Alexander the Great, then Leonardo, then Mozart—Warren suggested that perhaps mankind's greatest spirits are perpetually reincarnated. "There are only so many great souls in the world," he said. "When the Lord gets tired of making them new, perhaps He just recycles them."

As we made the rounds of the experts, a number of things began to bother us. For one thing, the accomplishments of the many seemed dwarfed by those of the few. Malcolm McClean may have invented the container ship and built a shipping empire nearly as large as Daniel K. Ludwig's. But Ludwig never stopped; in the late 1960s, already seventy, he plunged into his Amazon project. Failing in that, he turned over a good portion of his remaining fortune to a Zurich cancer institute. The more we looked, it seemed, the fewer genuine empire builders we found.

What distinguishes the empire builders, in the end, is their passion. They devote their lives to an idea that in time becomes an ideal. More important, they inspire others to buy into their dream. All are out, in one way or another, to change the world. James Rouse, the master builder, is a spiritualist, flat-out determined to make God's word ("Love thy neighbor") his living principle. For him, urban renewal is an instrument of social change; profits are to be used for the public good. For Steve Jobs, an artist of commerce, the computer is less a product than a philosophy and way of life. For Ted Turner, the founder of the Better World Society, reruns of *Gone With the Wind* and *I Love Lucy* are weapons in a struggle against the dominance of the three major television networks. Genuine empire builders are obsessed; they can no more stop following their dream than they can cease to breathe.

A final note. This book makes no pretense to objectivity. I'm a journalist, not a management expert or a psychologist. My stock-in-trade is impressions, gathered in brief encounters and strung together as best I see their significance. And how can I truly pretend to know the people I've met? Even the simplest person is full of contradictions, hidden slants of character. There's a moment in *Lord Jim* where Joseph Conrad's narrator, Marlow, tells of his last glimpse of a man he tried to fathom but could not. Jim is standing on a beach, silhouetted against the jungle, as Marlow's steamer puts out to sea. "[He] appeared no bigger than . . . a speck, a tiny white speck, that seemed to catch all the light left in a darkened world. . . . And, suddenly, I lost him."

If *The Alexander Complex* lets these people breathe on a page, captures a hint of the spark that drives them, then it has succeeded.

CHAPTER ONE

THE CHASE

◆

THE AIR changed color, animals shivered with fear and lightning split the heavens. Or so goes the legend of the birth of Alexander the Great. If mythmakers later suggested that Alexander's real father was Zeus, it is not particularly surprising when you consider how the young king hurtled his way through Greece, Egypt, Persia, Asia Minor and India, capturing all before him and building a united empire, all by the age of thirty-three.

Alexander changed the world in eleven years. Between 334 B.C. and 323 B.C., he harnessed the known world and then discovered others. So dazzling were his conquests that for centuries they eclipsed his real nature. Young, handsome and dramatically charismatic, he was utterly convinced he could not fail. The Greek city-states of the day humored his overarching megalomania. A Spartan decree proclaimed, "Since Alexander wishes to be a god, let him be a god." Medieval Europe and the Orient knew next to nothing of the true Alexander; they knew only the myth, told and retold in a hundred versions and languages from Iceland to Malaya. The Old Testament proclaims him a prophet. Muslims read of him in the Koran. Ancient Celtic manuscripts show him exploring heaven, borne on the wings of griffins. Napoleon called him the greatest general who ever lived, and kept a portrait in his bedchamber. Raphael, Rembrandt and Rubens painted him; so did Ingres, Daumier and David. André Malraux called him the only man with the courage to die of his vices. Richard Burton played him in the movies.

The hero worship continues. Despite a more recent cynicism that has him dying as a drunkard, Alexander's feats defy the skeptics. You can better appreciate the sweep of the man by imagining him in business, arguably the last frontier in today's more circumscribed world. As corporate raiders, Carl Icahn and T. Boone Pickens would be sardines to Alexander's shark. His sprawling holding company, Alexander, Inc., would span a dozen advancing technologies, from supercomputers to bioengineering. Watch him take over NASA's foundering Space Shuttle program and send a man to Mars by 2010. See him negotiate the opening of a Joint Economic Zone in Hokkaido, where U.S. and Japanese partners would build massive electronics and manufacturing plants to export goods to the United States and the rest of the world. Alexander's philanthrophic works might serve as a standard of public-spiritedness for decades, perhaps for generations. So would his reputation for toughness. He inspired men to follow him to the ends of the earth, yet he would fall prey to manic paranoia and turn on friends in an instant. Exhausting one goal after another, he in later years grew so addicted to the adrenaline-rush of risk, adventure and triumph that he sought shortcuts to his thrills. When Alexander died, delirious with fever after a two-week drunk, he was all but burned out.

Alexander has been dead for twenty-three-hundred years, but there have always been people who share his spark. The Greeks called it "divine restlessness." I call it the Alexander Complex. Today's empire builders may not possess Alexander's incandescence, they won't come to be called "the Great," but their divine fires burn fiercely nonetheless. Like Alexander, they cannot stop, nor would they want to. They live in the grip of a vision. Work and career take on the quality of a mission, a pursuit of some Holy Grail. And because they are talented and convinced that they can change the world, they often do.

NOT LONG AGO I read an article about Les Wexner, president and founder of The Limited, one of the country's largest retail clothing chains. He earned about $1 billion in 1987, which makes him no small empire builder in his own right. He was talking about what gives one man the drive of ten, and leaves another at the starting gate. "In his heart of hearts," Wexner explained, "the ploughhorse knows he's different."

Ask any successful businessman what separates the winners from the also-rans, and the answer will most often be a string of clichés: energy, character, integrity, leadership, competitive spirit, tenacity. The traits go on and on, all true and equally unrevealing. They're the same qualities that make for successful managers. Add free-thinking independence and a certain maverick creativity to the list, throw in a flair for the theatrical, and you have the aptitudes of an entrepreneur, artist or symphony conductor. Yet, clearly, empire builders are something more. What keeps them driving and striving when the rest of us, however talented and ambitious, are content with so much less?

Surprisingly, in business, where the profit motive governs, money is relatively unimportant. To be sure, these men are rich. Ross Perot, with a fortune that *Forbes* magazine estimates at $2.9 billion, is the second-wealthiest man in America, after Sam Walton of Wal-Mart Stores. Yet Perot for years drew a salary of only $67,000 from his company, Electronic Data Systems in Dallas, and he lives modestly by a millionaire's standards, let alone a billionaire's. Money, Perot says, is a double-edged gift. It's a wonderful thing to have when you've got something useful to spend it on. But it can be a liability, especially in getting a cash-poor new venture off the ground. If that seems to defy logic, listen to Perot tell it. "When you've got a lot of money to throw around," he says, "you're inclined to let it solve your problems." Has money helped General Motors, one of the the country's richest companies, to beat the Japanese? Perot asks. The answer, judging by performance, is a resounding no.

When Apple Computer was in its infancy, Steven Jobs dreamed of buying a BMW. Now he could buy fleets of them without depleting his $300 million fortune, and money has lost its immediacy. "After a while, you stop thinking about it," he says. "It just isn't important anymore." Ted Turner is emphatic. "Money has never, never been my god," he says, pacing up and down in his office in Atlanta, hammering his point home in a one-man rant on money and power. "One reason I've been successful is that I don't even *care* about money. I care about concepts, variety and adventure. Not money. God, no!"

What would Alexander the Great have thought? It's unlikely he would find Donald Trump, an eighties Midas, to be a kindred spirit. Alexander, after all, is not remembered for his fortune. You could argue that Alexander's territories were his "toys," and that the bigger the conquest, the bigger the thrill. But even amid the excitement and the chaos of a campaign, he never lost sight of his more important goal: to unify Greece and the Eastern Mediterranean. For true empire builders, money is a by-product, not an end. It's a means to build something, an instrument for exploration, extension and innovation, perhaps even of creation. It's not merely a way to continue the game, to "keep score," to create more of the same.

James Rouse, the Maryland developer, might be poor by Ross Perot's standards. He's worth about $75 million, not enough to gain the ranks of the *Forbes* 400. Yet the two men are much alike. They're happy to see their companies grow and prosper. They speak with pride of the jobs they've created and the services they provide. They're excited by the opportunities that money and power create to move on to the next new venture, each usually more ambitious than the last. Ross Perot made his fortune in computer services; now, the Perot Foundation grants millions to fund the Texas school system and promote scientific research. James Rouse was long one of the country's most prominent real estate developers. Today, he has set up a foundation to eradicate inner-city slums. Both men are out to change the world for the better. That's not hyperbole. Scratch a genuine empire builder and you'll discover a drive not to compile riches but, literally, to change the world.

IF MONEY DOESN'T explain an empire builder's drive, what does? Is it lust for power, prestige, fame?

Kirby Warren, a professor at Columbia University's business school, thinks it boils down to a thirst for control and recognition. "Empire builders, past or present, are determined from a very young age to go beyond their current state in life. They often want to become wealthy, and they usually become so," he says. "But the real and vastly more important aim is to control resources that get them recognized. They are extremely bright, extremely energetic men, who like, *really* like, to be in charge, who want to be *famous*." Elaborating on that theme, Abraham Zaleznick, a Harvard psychologist, writes of the need for freedom and independent identity, a form of recognition that translates into rebelliousness and a devil-may-care willingness to take risks. Other motivational experts speak of deep-rooted insecurities, as if the bold, decisive empire builder were really just an overgrown child seeking to recreate—or reinvent—the half-remembered world of his youth.

The notion that childhood insecurity often translates into an adult's drive for control isn't novel. Still, let's trot out some facts as an amateur psychologist might see them. For one, most of these men are short—Napoleon short. Steve Jobs and Ted Turner are the tallest, standing at about 5′9″. Ross Perot, Robert Swanson and James Rouse are all around 5′6″ or 5′7″. Many of them say things like, "I wasn't real good at sports as a kid, but I sure tried hard." All but Perot and Swanson experienced some childhood or adolescent trauma. Jobs was adopted at birth. James Rouse was orphaned and thrown out of his home at sixteen. Daniel Ludwig's parents divorced. Ted Turner's father shot himself, and more than one associate says the shell-shocked, angry son took the blame on himself.

Many psychoanalysts note that the seeds of entrepreneurial success are often rooted in a deep-seated Oedipal complex. They talk of sons who felt close to their mothers and disappointed by their fathers, or who were abandoned by their fathers through death, divorce or devotion to career. This father-son rivalry is often fanned by a strong-willed, assertive mother, who consciously or unconsciously drives the son to outdo his father. Alexander, to draw the historical analogy, was the product of a warring household. His biographers hint that he murdered his father to win his mother's undivided love.

Is it possible that the speed at which a man is running relates directly to whatever he is running away from? David Silver, a venture capitalist and author of *The Entrepreneurial Life*, calls guilt "the most potent generator for entrepreneurial drive and ultimate success." A slippery theory, but one that entrepreneurs (and, by extension, empire builders) must face daily merely by existing. "Brought up to meet traditional expectations and gain approval from society (since not from parents, peers or self), he strikes out on his own. Society still tugs at him, pokes fun, queries him endlessly, questions his sanity, reminds him that he hasn't done what is expected." Guilt forces him to succeed, if only to justify himself and ultimately win acceptance by proving his doubters wrong.

At a deeper level of the personality, writes Daniel Goleman, a psychology reporter at *The New York Times*, some entrepreneurs are prone to what psychoanalysts call "splitting." He sees the interior life of many mavericks as a struggle between two antithetical views of the world: one a "domain of blocks and frustrations"—childhood neglect, parental rivalry, family divisions—and the other "an ideal of freedom." The psyche thus becomes the battleground of an intense inner drama in which the hero seeks to banish the ghosts of his childhood through an act of rebellion.

This shows up in an overpowering drive for liberation and self-reliance. Those destined to succeed learn at an early age that they must—and can—fend for themselves. They set up their own businesses at an early age. Daniel Ludwig salvaged a ship when he was nine; Ross Perot was trading bridles at county fairs by the time he was eight. They're impatient with college and, like Turner and Jobs, often don't finish. They chafe working for someone else; they often quit or are fired, unable to play second fiddle and impatient with the corporate bureaucracy or unwilling to play by the rules. They frequently turn their companies into tight-knit surrogate "families" that they lost or never had in youth. Ted Turner, says a longtime acquaintance, displays a consuming "little-boy need to be loved." Jobs has a manic, manipulative need to be the focus of attention, to be seen as "special" within his self-made corporate "family." Rouse, Swanson and Perot talk of idyllic childhoods, but then they, of all the people in this book, are most content with themselves. Is it coincidence that they put a greater emphasis on the corporate family while building their empires?

Well, maybe or maybe not. Certainly not everything comes down to formative influences. What's interesting about the Alexander Complex is that it's essentially such a positive drive. Ted Turner's office is full of affirming symbols. When he bought MGM Studios, he lined up its nine Academy Awards in a row outside his office, gold and shining with promise. He keeps a cricket on his desk: Jiminy Cricket, that is, as in, "Accentuate the positive. Eliminate the negative." Ross Perot papers the executive offices of EDS with uplifting slogans, ranging from excerpts from the *Boy Scout Handbook* to the sayings of Theodore Roosevelt. So does James Rouse.

Clearly these men aren't *driven* to work for work's sake. They like it. With the exception of Perot, who puts family first, work is the passion of their lives. Every morning, Silicon Valley's highways and hilly country roads are crowded with young electronics whizzes in foreign sports cars, all heading for little environmentally correct, high-tech research centers. They might emerge ten, twelve, eighteen hours later, bleary-eyed and scarcely aware of the time. Workaholic Steven Jobs is among them. Yet these late-night hours are often when he feels most euphoric, the times when he experiences "the most incredible feelings of power," as he once put it, as if he could accomplish anything, that life is full of meaning and purpose, that some divinity is helping him on his way. Rouse, though vastly more phlegmatic, is no less attuned to the cosmic vibes. Sitting in his living room one evening, he takes a call from his son, who wants to talk. They compare schedules. Nothing seems to work. "Okay," says Rouse finally, with a glance at the dining room table loaded with work he wanted to get done that night. "Can you come after ten-fifteen?" This from a man who's seventy-three.

This is work as "fun," as Steve Jobs might say, work with passion. There's excitement, an adrenaline-rush of building or accomplishing great things. "Empire builders are addicted to the exhilaration of the chase," says Silver. Frank Farley, a psychology professor at the University of Wisconsin, makes a study of heroes and the traits that drive them. He categorizes them as "Type T's," thrill-seekers who are "motivated by a passion for novelty, change, uncertainty and risk." Remember Ted Turner. Variety! Concepts! Adventure!

IT'S NO ACCIDENT that three of the men in this book are pioneers in the driving technologies of the last decade. In every era of American business, the greatest fortunes have been made in infant or emerging industries. Steve Jobs figures heroically in this tradition as the popularizer of the personal computer. Ted Turner, says David Silver, was "the first to think of buying real estate in space." He saw that the burgeoning commercial satellite business could be used to challenge the communications oligopoly of the three broadcast networks. Cable television was born. Robert Swanson, almost a decade before anyone else, saw that the fledgling science of biotechnology could be put to immediate commercial use. He is the first and vastly most powerful of the new "gene tycoons."

Opportunity can be seized, or can happen upon one. "Luck is very important," says Ross Perot. "People talk of successful businessmen as being omniscient. They're credited with making decisions that, in hindsight, seem like miracles of foresight. The fact is that most great successes are happy accidents. Someone was in the right place at the right time, and he happened to do things right."

Steve Jobs, for instance, drifted into computers almost as a hobbyist's way of making a little money. He rode the electronics wave, recognizing opportunities and the technology's potential just a few steps ahead of others. Only after the business took off did he begin to think truly innovatively of what the advent of the PC meant for society. Robert Swanson, on the other hand, approached his career much more methodically. He decided in his junior year of college that he wanted to build a large company in an infant industry, and he set course accordingly. He studied venture capitalism at MIT, joined a venture capital firm to learn the ropes and research the technologies that offered the greatest opportunities, opted for the young science of bioengineering and then did all he had to do to "build the first billion-dollar genetics-oriented pharmaceutical company in America."

Jobs falling into computers. Swanson launching into biotechnology with all the deliberateness of a military campaign. Their approaches are polar extremes, yet Swanson and Jobs are strikingly similar. From an early age, each always did precisely what he wanted. Neither followed convention; they went with their own preferences, obeyed their own instincts. Swanson, always deliberate, drew on a childhood interest in chemistry and the excitement of *Sputnik* to make a business of science. Jobs, a free-thinking 1970s-style radical who wore his hair long and bummed around India to find himself, is the artist. If he hadn't become an industrialist, he would have found some other outlet for his creativity—perhaps as a writer, artist or social thinker. For all the differences in style, both essentially act as catalysts.

Their first instinct is to go out and find the people doing the best, most exciting and most innovative work in their field. They bring them together and set goals that they can all work toward, cajoling, cheerleading, guiding, keeping the business on track. They strive to create a special spirit, an esprit that approaches a sense of mission that binds their team, once again, into a "family" that outsiders cannot penetrate. Both Swanson and Jobs were unwilling to let me talk to their employees about them personally. That would focus the limelight on themselves, rather than on the team. Jobs does everything he can to reinforce the impression that his "family" is special; like entering NeXT in a Silicon Valley bike race—on tandems. "We were the only ones to do *that*!" he exclaims. And Swanson? The day I visited him, Genentech was holding a big picnic on the lawn running down to San Francisco Bay. It was what the company calls a "hoho," a Friday afternoon bash where employees get together to celebrate their latest accomplishments. Could I go? "Nope," said Swanson. "It's just for family."

Outside the arts and sciences, very few great things are accomplished alone. Lyle Spencer, a management consultant at McBer & Company in Boston, thinks the empire builder often has more in common with a military commander than a business entrepreneur. The entrepreneur fears large organizations and demands independence. The empire builder, conversely, seeks to build an organization even as he strives to keep key decision making within a close coterie of intimates. "It's not enough to have a brilliant idea," Spencer says. "The empire builder needs to be a charismatic evangelist who can rally people to his cause and then lead them. He has to be a savvy politician, an inspiring coach, a good manager and a technical whiz. It doesn't hurt to be an actor with a flair for the dramatic." Not all men can be all this, not even the men in this book. Hence the emphasis on teamwork. They extend themselves through others. "The great entrepreneurs, the genuine empire builders, know what they stink at and make up accordingly," says Xenas Block, director of New York University's Center for Entrepreneurial Studies. "They instinctively know how to build a team and recruit people who have the skills they lack."

It all comes back to vision. The great entrepreneur inspires people with his drive and vitality. By the sheer force of personality, he is the center of attention in his social and business life. His desire to be the best, to be different, to make a mark in the world, goads him to project himself to the head of the pack. And how better to do that, ultimately, than through the superiority of his ideas?

What emerges from a study of the people in this book is that empire builders above all think of themselves as *visionaries*. They are endowed with a singular, *transformative* idea, perceived in total detail as if it were a reality before them and not just a dream. And they succeed brilliantly at communicating their vision to the team that ultimately makes it real. It is this clarity of ultimate goals that holds a team together and keeps the empire builder's "army" on course as it makes its everyday marketing and production decisions.

CHAPTER TWO

THE VISIONARY

◆

IT WAS a weird encounter, that first meeting with Steven Jobs.

It's a bright Monday morning in May in Palo Alto, the heart of Silicon Valley. I'm sitting in a conference room at NeXT, the renegade computer company Jobs founded after being fired from Apple Computer. Dan'l Lewin, the marketing director, a lean, tanned, clean-cut young Californian who the next day would be swimming in a "senior Olympics" at Stanford, is wrestling with the "easy pop" top on a bottle of all-natural fruit juice as he briefs me on the company's efforts to build a revolutionary new computer. A supercomputer for the masses.

Jobs is the essence of the entrepreneurial empire builder: a brilliant, charismatic leader in a pioneering technology. He was only twenty years old in 1976 when he co-founded Apple in his parents' garage. When the company went public four years later, it was a $2 billion corporation. Silicon Valley has many impressive success stories, but few to rival that. It was Jobs, after all, who *popularized* the computer, who put the word "personal" into the PC and made it accessible to ordinary people. Before Jobs, the computer was an alien and hostile machine, something that bleeped and whirred in science fiction movies and loomed silently behind closed doors in multinational corporations and secret government offices. Now, with cozy vanilla-colored desktops sitting in half the homes and offices in America, it's hard to remember that it was any other way. Yet only a decade ago, cartoons in *The New Yorker* featured angry workers booting their computers out of the workplace. Then came an eerie spell when computers started booting the humans out; then computers booted out other computers. Like many things not understood, the computer assumed the talismanic qualities of a religious icon that could be approached only by the initiated, high priests of a high technology who spoke obscure languages like FORTRAN or BASIC.

Jobs changed all that. He was the first to see that by demystifying a technology that baffled most of the rest of us, he could build a product that would change people's lives. He envisioned a need where there was yet no need, a market where there was no market. And he not only had the vision, he saw how to make it real. Jobs recognized that recent advances in the transistor and the microchip suddenly made it possible to miniaturize the computer. He prodded his partner, technical whiz Steve Wozniak, into adding a video monitor that showed the user what he was doing and, along the way, made high-resolution graphics possible. The pair devised a keyboard, a memory and a disk drive, and hired fancy designers to come up with a streamlined casing. The Apple II was born, the first bona fide PC. Apple was on its way. Its rise is one of the modern legends of American entrepreneurship.

Now, at NeXT, Jobs is trying to repeat the triumph. It will be a year or more before the new computer is introduced and Lewin won't divulge any operational details. Only that there has never been anything like it, and that it has "something to do with education." "Education in America is a mess," he says. "We want to help change that by capturing the new wave of technology and putting it in the classroom. We want to revolutionize the learning process. History shows it only takes a few people to make a difference in society. It only takes one Steve Jobs."

It only takes one Steve Jobs. The NeXT computer had yet to make its debut, but Silicon Valley was already buzzing with rumors of the Second Coming. The excitement was fed by reports of its unsurpassed capabilities: graphics of video quality; sound that would do the Talking Heads proud; hardware and software of a sophistication normally found only in the most well-funded scientific research labs. But most of all the excitement surrounded Jobs himself. He is at once the *enfant terrible* of the computer world and its high priest. His publicist likens him to a rock star. Clearly he's taken on the aura of a folk hero—brilliant, unpredictable, controversial. Admirers think he walks on water. Detractors claim that he's a manipulative opportunist, a fraud who's taken credit for the technological wizardry and management skills of others. But the skeptics only goad Jobs on. If he succeeds big at NeXT, they will be silenced.

"Hi!" As Lewin expands on NeXT's vision of the future, Jobs bursts into the room. He plops into a chair and swivels his feet onto the conference table. He's in uniform: blue jeans, white button-down shirt, no tie. Peering at me over the tops of a battered pair of suede running shoes, he skips the usual pleasantries and machine-guns me with questions. "Who are you? What are you doing here? I don't know anything about you. I mean, you just showed up on my calendar. I don't really like talking to journalists. Why should I agree to be in your book?"

It wasn't the reception I had expected. Before leaving for California, I'd had doubts about scheduling an appointment on a Monday, let alone 9:00 A.M. on a Monday morning, when any industrialist worth his dictaphone would be organizing his week and getting his troops deployed. The last thing Jobs would want would be a reporter asking questions about his life, worldview and the future of NeXT and the computer industry. And so the Friday before, I called to confirm the meeting and express my reservations. "Oh, yes," said an aide. "We went over your proposal with Steve this morning. He's expecting you."

The words echoed in my brain. *He's expecting you.* What's he up to? I wondered. Why this feigned ignorance of our appointment? "That's a classic Steve-ism," an Apple graduate later explained. "It's his way of taking control of the situation, of putting you in his debt so that maybe you'll write nice things about him."

I think the real reasoning goes deeper. Jobs may have wanted me in his debt, but more than that he wanted the relationship to begin as unevenly as possible. As another associate told it, it was his way of "sliding a sheet of ice under your feet," of throwing me off guard and casting the interview in doubt. Jobs didn't give a hoot whether I liked him or not. He wanted only my respect and my subservience. He wasn't interested in a "relationship." He wanted control.

Control. Jobs is good at getting it. Control over his subject matter, control over the future, control over his image, control over his employees and situations. As I made the rounds of the Valley, I heard lots of "Steve-isms."

As in his reputation for browbeating "bozos" who don't measure up to his exacting standards.

As in his legendary impatience. (Jobs has been known to tell traffic cops to "hurry up" and give him a speeding ticket, so that he can get on to where he's going.)

As in his almost willful lack of tact. (One technician at Apple tells how Jobs once stopped by and asked what he thought about a particular supplier's software. "It sucks," the employee replied, amplifying his opinion in expletive-laden detail. Jobs laughed, then introduced the technician to the visitor at his side: It was the manufacturer.)

If I'd had an inkling of this darker side to Steve Jobs, I would have been better prepared when he bullied me. Who else would I be talking to? he asked. I mentioned Ross Perot, the Texas billionaire who founded Electronic Data Systems and had recently invested $20 million in NeXT. Jobs nodded his approval. Then there was Robert Swanson, head of Genentech. "I have a lot of respect for him," said Jobs. Finally I said I was thinking of including Donald Trump, the New York real estate mogul.

"Donald Trump?" Jobs winced, shook his head, jerked his feet off the table in a paroxysm of pained incredulity. "I don't want to be in a book with Donald Trump! What's he ever done?"

I replied that, among other things, Trump planned to build the world's tallest building on Manhattan's Upper West Side.

"So what?" interrupted Jobs.

So, he wants to give New York a building that would be, as he puts it, a "great, true, vital symbol." A visual reminder that New York is the best, most vibrant city in the world.

"Bullshit," said Jobs. Are gambling casinos in Atlantic City heroic? Is Trump Tower on Fifth Avenue a monument to architecture? Trump's buildings are "junk"—garish, badly designed, big gold initials all over the place, a blight on the city. All Trump wants is money and power, Jobs declared. "He'll never do anything good."

The meeting ended with Jobs telling me that he had jury duty most of the week and might not be able to "fit me in." "You didn't fly all the way from New York just to see me, did you?" he asked, smiling.

JOBS WAS PROBABLY RIGHT about Trump. But I dwell on the incident because I've come to see it as an emblem of sorts. "To understand the entrepreneur, you have to understand the psychology of the juvenile delinquent," says Harvard psychoanalyst Abraham Zaleznik. Jobs has a streak of rebellious adolescence that is integral to his charm and his dynamism. He deliberately sets out to break rules and jar people with his iconoclastic chutzpah.

Jobs fears growing old, becoming less receptive to the world about him and resistant to change. "You see very few people in their thirties and forties doing anything really creative," he says. Revolution is the province of the young, and the future lies in revolution. Remember the television commercial that Jobs commissioned for Apple?

It ran only once, during the 1984 Super Bowl, but it became one of the most talked-about TV spots ever. It showed a cavernous, blue-lighted hall, where rows of uniformed, zombielike workers sit mindlessly on wooden benches as an Orwellian "Big Brother" preaches at them from a giant television screen. Then a pair of double doors at the back of the room spring open. An Olympic runner bursts in, a beautiful, full-color, full-bodied Amazon who strides masterfully up the aisle. As the runner nears the screen, she whirls a great sledgehammer around her head and lets it fly. It arcs upward in slow motion, then down, smashing through Big Brother's bloated image and smashing it to pieces.

I thought it was one the best commercials ever made, but it led to excess the next year. Seeking to go itself one better, Apple and its advertising czars, Chiat-Day in New York, came up with a Super Bowl extravaganza still known on Madison Avenue as "The

Lemmings." It featured a line of dispirited businessmen, carrying briefcases and straggling across a dismal plain in somber Execu-Suits. They're chanting a tuneless dirge, faintly familiar. After a moment you recognize it: Walt Disney's "Heigh-ho, heigh-ho, it's off to work we go." And off they do go, across the plain and toward a cliff, marching in lockstep and toppling, one by one, off the precipice.

Now, that's *gloomy*. Jobs thinks it might have been a mistake because it was so profoundly alienating. But there's no denying the power of those ads. They cast IBM (popularly known as Big Blue) in the role of oppressor and made Apple seem the liberator. Don't be a drone, they said; think for yourself. And that idea—liberation—is what Steve Jobs is all about. In his secret mind's eye, Jobs sees himself a bringer of light to the world. The personal computer is not just a product. It is a way of life. Work is not a job, it's a calling. Success and profit are not ends. They are a way of changing the world.

That's the positive side. The negative side shows up in Jobs's screed against Donald Trump. The outburst hinted at more than a willful immaturity; it was an upwelling of overpowering ego. Jobs was horrified at the chance of being associated with someone he doesn't see as an equal. Jobs thinks Trump won't be more than a blip on the screen of history. Jobs wants to be far more.

Why this curious blend of insecurity and superiority? By nature and inclination, Steve Jobs has an overwhelming need to dominate, to be recognized as the best and the brightest of his times. He's out to change the world and remake it, partly in his image. His vehicle is power—the power of ideas, embodied in what he calls "insanely great" products on the leading edge of the next great technological wave. He disdains the word "entrepreneur" because it connotes "smallness." He prefers to be thought of as a "leader" or a "visionary." Maybe even a prophet. But to lead, to be visionary, presupposes a superiority of ideas and an ability to inspire, to inflame others. That means the ideas have to be special, futurist, unified. They have to be avant-garde, ahead of everyone else. Jobs has thus become a seeker. What distinguishes him above all else is the quality of his questions and, ultimately, his answers. "The journey is the reward," he says, enshrining that bit of Eastern philosophy as an informal corporate slogan. Work, again, is a calling and a way of life. And to play his self-assigned role in life, Jobs has created a vision—alluring, uniquely his own, different in all ways from all others.

A seeker, a challenger. Jobs accepts nothing at face value. His is a focused, hungry intelligence, eager for the confrontation that, in his experience, produces insight. Jack Dudman, dean of students at Reed College in Oregon, where Jobs took his only formal college courses, recalls Jobs as a teenager. Jobs was flunking out, and Dudman tried to take him under his wing. Even then it was impossible to toss out an idea or an offhand remark without Jobs playing devil's advocate, peppering Dudman with questions until he was persuaded or dissuaded of its merit. At NeXT, he's apparently little different. The company has lost only five of its eighty-five employees, but at least two left partly to escape the stress. "Steve fosters an environment where he questions everything," one ex-NeXTer told *USA Today*. "You can question him, but you damn well better be right because he's good at making you look foolish."

He certainly tried to make me feel foolish. Jobs kept me dangling all week until finally, on Friday, the day before I was to return to New York, he squeezed me in. We hopped into his black Porsche convertible, and as we cruised over to nearby Stanford University, a few minutes' drive from NeXT, I got a glimpse of the Jobs brilliance. "Our goal," he says, "is to change the way teachers teach and students learn."

The phrase pops out so effortlessly, but it's not just a slogan. To change the way teachers teach and students learn. How do you do that? As Jobs tells it, the NeXT computer (as in what's next in technology, what's next from Steve Jobs) will be the "neatest," most "incredible" PC ever, more powerful and more versatile than anything the competition (read IBM and Apple) could possibly imagine. The idea is to build sophisticated computer *simulators*, the sort of real-life replicators that air force fliers train on and biochemists use to model DNA. NeXT is going to put them in classrooms across the nation. These workstations, as they're called, usually cost between $100,000 and $250,000. Jobs wants to chop the price down to $4,000, so that everyday college students will be able to use the same equipment that's now available only to the nation's top scientists. And not only will he make the technology available, he'll make it accessible—perhaps as easy to use as the Macintosh, the ultimate "user friendly" PC.

Jobs projects a palpable sense of excitement as he talks about his work and the technology behind it. I remember once, long ago, listening to him discuss the future of computers. Someday in the future, he had said, we will build a computer so powerful, and program it so thoroughly, that it will be able to replicate human thinking. A philosophy student, for instance, could tap into "Aristotle," a program that captures everything about Aristotle's life and times and worldview, the underlying principles of his philosophy. He could "ask Aristotle a question." He could debate the great Greek thinker. You might not get the right answer, Jobs went on. It could be all wrong. But maybe not.

NeXT isn't about to give us all that. But it's taking a big step. "You wouldn't believe this stuff. If someone had told me about this product even a year ago," Jobs says, "*I* wouldn't have believed it. I would have said it's impossible, technically impossible." His energy level rises as he contemplates the possibilities of the impossible. He subconsciously steps on the accelerator, and the Porsche leaps ahead. Before long, we're barreling toward Stanford at eighty miles an hour; the lush countryside flashes by in a blur. It's a great ride, and a great vision. But it didn't come to Jobs overnight.

MAY 1985. A sullen, downcast Steven Jobs just lost a power struggle to Apple president John Sculley. At one point, the two men were so close that *Time* magazine reported they "finished one another's sentences." Sculley is the marketing whiz who created the "Pepsi Generation" ads that broke Coke's near-monopoly in soft drinks. Slated to become Pepsi's new chairman, he was lured to Apple by his budding friendship with Jobs, who saw him as both a personal mentor and a brilliant manager who could help guide

Apple's expanding business. Jobs gave Sculley a hard-sell challenge that has been written up in every account of their subsequent rift. "Do you want to spend the rest of your life selling sugared water, or do you want a chance to change the world?"

It was a very public love affair and an equally public and nasty separation. Accounts vary. Some say Jobs tried to fire Sculley, fearing that he was usurping his role. Others say Sculley decided to unseat Jobs in the belief that he had neither the experience nor the discipline to handle Apple's increasingly complex affairs. In his autobiography, *Odyssey*, Sculley writes that Apple's board of directors prodded him to oust Jobs for the good of the company, and that he wept a "flood of tears" when he did so. That may be more than a little self-serving, but there is not much disagreement about the result. "I was fired," says Jobs.

He wasn't just tossed out the door. After all, Jobs was Apple's founder, its guiding spirit and an icon of the computer age. But Sculley made Jobs's life so miserable that he simply had to leave. Sculley announced, through the newspapers, that Jobs had been relieved of all operational responsibility within the company—a public rebuking that, Jobs says, kicked the wind out of him. He was moved to "Siberia," a distant block of offices empty of almost all staff but himself. No one returned his phone calls. No one consulted him. No one seemed to care.

Jobs is reluctant to talk about the experience. Even as he walks the placid, blissful Stanford campus, the memory darkens his mood. He gropes for words, as if fighting for air. He once compared the experience to losing a child. "You work for years on something, and then it's taken way. . . ." He pauses, frowns. "I didn't have anything to do. I mean, they took my office away, everything. . . ." Another long pause, a shrug. "But life goes on."

Jobs left Apple four months later, but not before the Great Moment. One day in August of 1985, Jobs had lunch with Paul Berg, a Nobel Prize–winning molecular biologist at Stanford. Friends describe the period of Jobs's exile in almost biblical terms. It was a quest, a search for identity. Jobs is the prodigal son wandering in the wilderness, miserable, depressed, searching for a role and meaning in life. If others saw him during this time in less flattering terms, something like a disappointed kid kicking through the gravel in his sneaks, no matter. Salvation was at hand, in the person of Berg.

That lunch, Jobs says, was a turning point. Restless and at loose ends, he was at home one day "reading up on some biochemistry." Never mind that Jobs hadn't graduated from college; he spent one desultory year at experimental, radical-chic Reed College in Oregon. Never mind that Berg is a Nobel Laureate. Jobs, just sitting around *reading up on some biochemistry*, calls him up. "I had a lot of questions," he explains. "So I asked if we could have lunch."

Jobs sensed an opportunity. As it turned out, this was to be the transition from Apple to NeXT. In his reading, Jobs had learned that a few large chemical companies and universities were starting to use computers to aid their research in the new field of recombinant DNA. Such experiments, normally done in sophisticated wet labs, are enormously complicated, time-consuming and expensive. Berg was already using a big mainframe computer to accelerate the process; he and his team would simulate experiments in such a way that they could see how human genes and proteins "fold" at the molecular level. Why aren't more people doing this? Jobs asked. They're trying, Berg replied, but the equipment is still very experimental—and horrendously expensive. How expensive? Jobs wanted to know. A few hundred thousand dollars. And the software needed didn't exist at all.

Jobs was at first intrigued, then elated. He had already made a hundred connections. Could he build the computer that Berg and others needed in their work? A little research showed that maybe he could. Better yet, he could build it and bring it to their students. The possibilities were endless. Properly handled, the nascent technology that Berg was using so haphazardly could accelerate the learning curve in scientific education. "If we could just bring some computational horsepower to this problem, and some software, there could be a revolution," Jobs enthused. "The field would explode. All these graduate students and undergraduates would get to participate in state-of-the-art research, not just a few specialists off in a corner somewhere."

Jobs had already been thinking a lot about education. Several months before his meeting with Berg, confused about what to do next, he put himself through an exercise that management psychologists employ with clients unsure about their life's goals. It was a little thing, really. It was just a list. A list of all the things that mattered most to Jobs during his ten years at Apple. And The List, like the lunch with Berg, was also a moment of epiphany.

"Three things jumped off that piece of paper, three things that were really important to me," says Jobs. The first was the Apple Education Foundation, set up in 1978 to give computers to schools for use in kindergarden through twelfth grade; the second a program called Kids Can't Wait. Jobs tells me how he used to dream of donating a computer to every school in America. Figuring that would cost more than $100 million, vastly more than Apple could afford, he tried to get a tax bill through Congress that would permit companies donating the computers to deduct 80 percent of the cost of the equipment. "I helped write the bill," he says with pride. "We didn't hire a lobbyist, but I spent three weeks walking the halls of Congress. Met about half the House and a third of the Senate. And it was fantastic! I mean, it passed the House, 237 to 60—the largest majority a tax bill has ever gotten!" It never became law. It died in the Senate during Jimmy Carter's lame-duck session. But California passed a version of the plan, and to Jobs, half a loaf was better than none: "We ended up giving away ten thousand computers in California. One to every school in the state. We called the program Kids Can't Wait. The kids can't wait for Washington to come around."

The third thing on the list was the Macintosh, the computer that had a helpful little "mouse" to walk you around the screen, that offered friendly directions whenever you were stuck, that boasted the most advanced graphic capabilities of any PC of its generation. "Making Mac was highly pleasurable, probably the neatest thing in my life to date," says Jobs. But better than making Mac was seeing it used in certain ways. "When I walk into a Fortune Five Hundred company and see a Mac on a manager's desk, that's nice," Jobs says. "But when I walk into a dorm room and see a Mac, that makes me feel even better. Not that I like one person more than another. But I sort of see the student using it and know he's never going to be the same. He's never going to put up with an IBM PC again. He's going to go through life expecting a better class of tool. It's a permanent change."

The message, Jobs says, was obvious. "I thought about all the things we did at Apple and at Macintosh, and what those three things meant, and I said to myself, 'Life is trying to tell me something here. What I really like is education.' "

IT SEEMS SO PAT, so convenient, this image of Steve Jobs moping around the house, making lists, searching for truth, meaning and identity—and then, lo, the Message, like an omen from the gods. Education! Computers! Purpose! Yet management psychologists say such soul-searching is an important aspect of the process of discovery and innovation. "Successful managers," says Charles Garfield, head of Performance Sciences, Inc., in Berkeley, "go with their preferences." They search for work that is important to them, and when they find it they pursue it with passion.

After that meeting with Berg, Jobs found his passion again. The computer he would build would be the neatest, sleekest, most truly awesome computer ever. And Jobs would sell it for less and make it available to more people than anyone thought possible. But that was two years ago, and NeXT isn't just an idea anymore. It's a block of low, modern buildings on Deer Creek Road, overlooking horse pastures and the distant, blue-hazed Santa Cruz Mountains. It sits beside Hewlett-Packard, the company that brought electronics to the Valley. You can bet the choice of site is no accident. Symbolism is big with Jobs, like parking his 1967 BMW motorcycle in the atrium of the Macintosh complex at Apple as a model of quality engineering and design. The proximity to HP suggests a godfather and godson, side by side. The pioneer of yesteryear, the pioneer of tomorrow.

The NeXT team has refined its goals. "When we started the company," Jobs says, "we went out and talked with lots of educators. 'Focus on learning,' they said, not on teaching. Focus on learning. And when do people learn best? They learn best when you put them in an environment where they can interact with their subject. Ideally you would like to be able to give every freshman biochemistry student a DNA wet lab. You would like to give every student of French history a time-travel ticket back to the age of Louis the Fourteenth. You would like to give every nuclear physics student a linear accelerator.

"Well, we can't give people time-travel tickets. We can't afford to give every biochemistry student access to a five-million-dollar wet lab or a thirty-five-million-dollar linear accelerator. But with a very powerful computer, we can *simulate* these things. We call them simulated learning environments. And if we can make them cheap enough, and provide breakthrough software that allows the world's best professors to write programs that can recreate these simulated environments, then we can make a real difference in the learning experience."

Yet stating the goal has proved easier than reaching it. It's May 1987. When Jobs started the company in September 1985, he wanted to have the new computer ready by now. Marketing surveys told him it should sell for no more than three thousand dollars, if it was to be affordable to students, and that his best "window of opportunity" would be the summer of 1987. Since students and universities normally do the bulk of their buying during the summer when school is out, Jobs feared that missing the target would delay the project a whole year. It could cost NeXT its head start against the competition and make it more difficult to grab a dominant share of the market.

That deadline was now upon him. At the time of my visit, potential buyers had not even seen a test prototype of the machine—a critical first step in marketing any new computer. Jobs told colleagues at the outset of the venture that he didn't think NeXT could survive if the deadline slipped. But it is now apparent that he has no choice. He would have to set a later target: the summer of 1988. Even that, it turned out, would be pushing it.

That explained a great deal of the urgency in the air at NeXT. There was still so much to do. A marketing staff had to be hired. There were hitches on the manufacturing end, and technical problems with the hardware. New and sophisticated software had to be written. And money was becoming a problem.

Jobs launched NeXT with $12 million of his own. The core group of founders was six people, Jobs and five associates who left Apple to follow him. All took substantial cuts in pay. All put some of their savings into the venture. But now, with shipment delayed, the seed money was running out. Worse, major universities, NeXT's prime potential customers, reportedly wanted a heavyweight financial backer behind it and on the board of directors before they committed to buy thousands of still-untested computers.

Enter H. Ross Perot, the Texas billionaire who founded Electronic Data Systems. Like the U.S. cavalry, Perot galloped to NeXT's assistance in the moment of need. "Steve Jobs is the most extraordinary young man I have ever met; there's no one else like him in American industry," Perot told me at a meeting in Dallas, months before I talked with Jobs. That's high praise, considering that Perot himself was also just thirty-two years old when he quit a job at IBM to set up EDS. "But by the time I started my own company," Perot says, "Steve was already on his second."

If NeXT succeeds, the story of their partnership will become legend. As Perot tells it, he was sitting at home one night, flipping channels during the intermission of a televised football game, when he came across a PBS documentary on entrepreneurs. There was Steve Jobs, brainstorming with his team at NeXT. Perot was impressed. So impressed that the next morning he phoned Jobs out of the blue. "Let's talk," he said. Perot flew up to Palo Alto and spent a day with Jobs and his employees. Later, three of his associates made a closer inspection. They "put the company under a microscope," one said, and their report was sterling. Perot soon offered to put $20 million into NeXT—in exchange for a 16 percent share of the company—and happily took a seat on the board.

The confidence Jobs inspires is extraordinary. Twenty million dollars is a lot of money, even to America's second-richest man. Yet it wasn't the specifics of NeXT's business that sparked Perot's enthusiasm. It was the *aura* that counted, the climate at NeXT—the commitment, the idealism, the employees' faith in their work and the worthiness of the goal.

Jobs is at his best in any brainstorming session, and PBS captured that. The show was filmed at a retreat early in the company's start-up, a tradition begun by Jobs at Apple and continued at NeXT. A core group of eleven employees is discussing what its goals should be, how best to build up the company. Jobs dominates the room. Even when he's not talking, he is moving, exuding energy, guiding the discussion through sheer body language. When he hears something he doesn't like, he squints, furrows his brow, shakes his head. When he likes something, he gets visibly excited. His eyes light up. He bounces in his seat, paces, gestures.

He talks about what NeXT will be like—greater than Apple was at its best, which was "insanely great." Action must be taken on this or that problem, Jobs says. They must speed up development of a certain component. They must pinpoint their best potential markets. Jobs shows himself a master at defining priorities, exciting others with his vision of what NeXT can be, clarifying the company's ultimate goals as they move from research through production to the actual marketing of the new computer.

"IBM had its day," he says. NeXT is next. He uses phrases like "slicing into the future," riding the "crest of a wave." Perhaps most important, say the PBS narrators, he plants the seeds of a corporate culture and evokes a sense of mission. "More important than building a product," he says, "we're architecting a company that will be more than the sum of its parts. And the cumulative effort of the twenty thousand decisions that we're all going to make over the next two years is going to define what our company is. One of the things that made Apple great was that in the early days it was built from the heart. One of my largest wishes is that we build NeXT from the heart. And people that are thinking about coming to work for us, or buying our products or who want to sell us things, feel that we're doing this because we have a passion about it. We're doing this because we *really care* about the higher educational process, not because we want to make a buck. Not because, you know, we just want to do it to do it."

Perot, watching that performance, likened it to "listening to fine music." Football was forgotten. This was something he knew about. This was about building a company, targeting a market, communicating a vision and enlisting a following. Jobs is hypnotic.

He paints a future so vivid and alluring that everyone *buys into the dream.* A motivational chain reaction begins. "I was finishing their sentences for them," Perot later said in admiration.

HEAR AN ECHO? That's what people had said about Jobs and John Sculley. Perhaps the difference this time will be that there's no schism between two warring psyches—the soul of the visionary against that of the corporate manager. Perot and Jobs share a way of looking at the world. Both identify education as vitally important to their goals. Both took risks to build their companies. Just as Perot drew on his experience at IBM to scope the market and identify a gaping need for computer services, so has Jobs scouted his potential market and come back with the highest-quality response: a product that not only satisfies the customer today but taps into his desire for an ideal product of the future, one that will help him expand his own frontiers.

Jobs isn't taking credit for a new idea. Air force pilots have long trained on flight simulators; scientists are increasingly using computerized workstations to simulate everything from atom splitting to genetic engineering to the functioning of the human brain. Nor does he claim to be advancing the technology, strictly speaking. As at Apple, Jobs's mission is to take the very latest and very best technology, combine it in unusual ways and *democratize* it, to give it to you and me.

Among those who know him, that ability is legend. "His amazing talent, his genius, is to take very advanced and very expensive technology and put it on people's desks," says Alain Rossman, a former software designer at Apple. "He's a consummate popularizer." Dan'l Lewin makes a similar point. "Steve is always looking right at the edge of the technological horizon. What can be done now? How do we make the next great leap? How do we make a product out of this? Steve's goal in life is to build great products by combining technologies in a way that no one else has. That's the essence of creativity. He is an artist whose medium happens to be technology."

The artist in Jobs shows up in his attention to details. One of his first acts in founding NeXT was to pay designer Paul Rand, who created corporate logos for IBM and Exxon, $100,000 to come up with a trademark. The result: a small 3-D cube, white lines on black, with the letters N-E-X-T blocked one to a side. Except that it's spelled NeXT, with that one lowercase *e*. Very high-tech. Very late eighties. Very hip. It's Rand's idea, but Jobs loves it. It's one of the thousands of small but distinctive details that add up to the vision of Steven P. Jobs.

The lens of that vision focuses as widely as it does narrowly. Last year Jobs bought a company called Pixar, set up in 1986 by filmmaker George Lucas, the man who a decade ago used computers to generate the stunning special effects of *Star Wars*. Pixar is the world's pioneer in photographic-quality computer-animated images, and at a convention of computer specialists in Dallas last year the company strutted its stuff. On a giant screen, Pixar's technicians projected a video of a landscape that looked like an interplanetary backdrop for one of Lucas's science fiction films. A gigantic fiery red star sat low on the horizon, glittering over waves that lapped rhythmically on a beach in surreal slow motion. A second sequence depicted a beach chair scampering across the sand, dipping a metal "toe" into the water and timidly dashing away. A third featured two desk lamps batting a rubber ball back and forth with their springy, cone-shaped heads. The lamps were utterly mobile, as if they were alive and on film. In fact, they were simulations generated by Pixar's computer.

Pixar's technology is now at the point where technicians can take a single photo of a landscape, then resurrect it as a living field of vision. Trees blow in the wind, the sun rises and sets, the sky changes color—as if a whole day had been filmed. And Pixar now belongs to Jobs. By engineering Pixar's microchips into the NeXT computer, Jobs has combined the most dramatic visual capabilities available with some of the most potent hardware and software around. The result, in time, will be a desktop computer combining the graphic and audio quality of a color television with the analytical and manipulative power of an advanced mainframe.

You see here the same vision that originally drove Apple: Take the most advanced technology available, chop it down in price and bring it to the people. Pixar's computer, two hundred times more powerful than current desktop computers, costs more than $120,000. At NeXT, Jobs hopes to sell a somewhat less powerful but vastly more versatile computer for $4,000. At an affordable price, people will be able to buy a computer that was formerly available only to the nation's top scientists and corporations. Students will be able to learn from visual experience. Amateurs will see how pros handle real-life situations. Engineers, artists and scientists will be able to simulate reality, play with it, experiment with it and, in the process, transform it. They will save time in their research, for the computer will help eliminate many of the false leads and missteps that are normally detected only through painstaking laboratory tests. There could be a revolution in American education.

"That's what NeXT is all about," says Jobs. "That's what we're trying to do."

IF EMPIRES WERE only as large as the idea behind them, Jobs would qualify as a visionary of the purest form. He's at his best talking about ideas. He exudes a seemingly careless and carefree energy that makes him look even younger than he is. Coming down to meet me in the lobby of NeXT, he took the steps two at a time, then jumped the last four. Playing the guileless innocent, he says that starting NeXT "is the hardest thing I've ever done. You wouldn't believe how hard it is to start a company. It's really, *really* neat. I like it."

You would think it easy to like this man, but it's not. Jobs plays people like an accordion, squishing and expanding them. As we talked over lunch, he apparently decided it was time for another mind game and waited, stone-still and silent, for nearly a minute (I counted) before answering a question. Maybe I was supposed to buckle, get nervous, start babbling. But I didn't feel like playing and waited him out. The interview ended the way Jobs should have liked. I respected him; his ideas excited me. But did I like him? Did I want to write nice things about him? Not very much.

Jobs inspires ambivalence as much as he does admiration. "You don't want to do a puff piece on Steve Jobs," said one key associate at Apple. "A lot of negative baggage comes along with this guy." The stories are legion. Of Jobs being perfectly charming one day and screamingly abusive another. Of dropping friends, girlfriends and colleagues because, as one former friend puts it, he suddenly decides they're "unimportant." Of his walking into the middle of meetings, listening for a moment, then telling everyone that they're all wrong, that their ideas are "bullshit," and that *this* was the only way the project could go.

As with many strong leaders, ambition and megalomania often drive Jobs to the edge. John Sculley once described him as a visionary "monster." Steve Wozniak, Jobs's partner in history, expresses a similar ambivalence. "His ego is just tremendous," says Wozniak. "He has to be accepted as the brightest person in the world when it comes to computers. No one else can be his equal, no matter what the environment." Wozniak believes Jobs's drive to dominate turned him into a tyrant at Apple, even though he's quick to say that Jobs never turned on him. "He'd create very bad feelings in the company because of the way he treated people. He always felt he was so important, so far above them, that they really didn't matter." Wozniak also chafes at Jobs's willingness to take credit for the achievements of others, and to go back on his commitments. "Steve always put his own interests first, and will use anyone to his advantage."

How can this man have done all he has if he's what Wozniak says: a brilliant egomaniac who fosters ill will among employees and cannot be trusted? Isn't this contrary to what we accept as basic leadership? If Jobs uses and abuses people, if he whimsically selects an "in" crowd within his company, how did Apple rise so far in a market that demands so much from its product and therefore its creators? To be sure, Jobs had exceedingly able management help along the way; in fact, he never, not for one day in the life of Apple, had operational control of the company. He was a vice-president to a succession of hired top guns: first Mike Markkula, then Mike Scott and finally John Sculley. His loftiest title at Apple was vice-president and, briefly at the end, chairman. Yet not even Jobs's critics deny that neither Apple nor Macintosh would exist without him. Jobs was always the key—the innovator, the visionary, the driving force in the company. And why?

Because, as one former employee puts it, he is the "Electric Kool-Aid Acid Dream Machine." Jobs doesn't offer security, a fabulous benefits package, a steady career path up the corporate ladder. Nor is he interested in people who want such things. Jobs offers *dreams*. He looks for and attracts the few good men and women who, like him, can burn in the night. They are young mad scientists, searching for answers to the list of "impossible" questions he poses. People come to Jobs because they want to test themselves. They are far more interested in a challenge and the thrill of discovery than a job. You hear it again and again. Jobs promises people the chance to do their very best work. He stretches them, often brutally. After all, doing the impossible isn't easy. It takes hard work, unbelievably hard work. And time. And sacrifice: of personal freedom, of family, of friendships, of all interests outside of the office.

This is a bunker mentality. If you survive and succeed in the Jobs pressure cooker, you come to know and respect yourself. You do it because you love it. Work becomes a mission. But if you fail, if you can't hack it, you burn out and are cast aside. Jobs, then, comes to be seen as someone not to be trusted. He's a monster whom there's no satisfying. You are filled with resentments.

Is it any accident that insiders talk of a messiah complex? Leader Jobs takes on the aura of the supreme evangelist, so excited by his ideas, so convinced that they are doable, that he infects others with the same raging fever. But when he isn't there anymore, when the project is over and the "high" has died down, he leaves an aftertaste. Christ's apostles saw Him as God incarnate; His detractors saw a deluded egocentric who incited unrest. Granted, the apostles—with one glaring exception—stayed around longer than most of Jobs's disciples. But the analogy works. When you're on the inside, Jobs is the thrill of a lifetime. Like going to the moon, knowing you can never repeat the experience.

Just look at Wozniak now, the guy who really designed and created the Apple computer. He has started his own company to manufacture his own inventions, none of which have anything to do with computers. Only a couple of people work with him, a number that "Woz" (as he is called) already finds bureaucratic. And the scope of their products? Almost embarrassingly small. His main device is what he calls a "universal remote control," a souped-up version of the little box you keep by your bed to switch television channels. Except that Woz's box lets you tune right into HBO or your video, without first turning on the TV.

You have to wonder. If Wozniak hadn't had Steve Jobs in the garage with him—goading him, stretching him, showing him the future—would Apple ever have been? I doubt it. "Steve saw," says Wozniak. "I didn't."

STANFORD UNIVERSITY likes its MBAs to schmooze. So, a couple times a week, it hosts "brown bag" lunches, where executives from leading corporations come to brainstorm with the students.

"I hated those lunches," says Michael Murray, a Stanford grad and the former head of Macintosh marketing. "These New York investment bankers and *Fortune* Five Hundred executives would stand up in their nice suits and say, 'Come work for us. We're really neat.' But they weren't really neat. They were boring."

Then, in the spring of 1980, Apple showed up. Murray was sitting in the back of the auditorium where the lunch was being held, reading a newspaper and keeping half an ear tuned to the proceedings. "The Apple execs were making their pitch, all in suits and sounding just like every other company. But then something strange happened. A guy about my age came in, dressed in jeans, a button-down shirt, no tie, and wearing a suit vest underneath a quilt ski vest. He looked like just another student. But instead of taking a seat, he walks down to the front, hops up on the desk where his people are sitting and folds his legs under him like a Buddhist guru. 'Hi!' he says. 'I'm Steve Jobs. What do you want to talk about?' "

Apple, at the time, was still so small that many in the room had never heard of it. But there was Jobs, looking like anything but a nine-to-five *Fortune* 500 exec and, Murray says, "talking about how he's got this incredible company called Apple that's going to change the world." And he wants some interesting people to help him do it. "The effect was electric, like a message from the messiah. 'Come help me change the world.' "

Murray wasn't aware of the corporate politics behind Jobs's mission. Apple had recently begun work on a successor to the Apple II. It was to be called Lisa, a high-grade desktop for business buyers. Jobs wanted to run it, but to his surprise the board wouldn't let him. They wanted a more experienced manager. Jobs was shunted aside. Apple's top brass wouldn't listen to him; neither would the engineers. Jobs was startled to find that his comfy little counterculture company had grown into a corporation, with its own agenda and own values. It had become a place where most people wore their suits dark and their hair short. Jobs didn't like it. He was convinced that Lisa was going to ruin Apple, that new management bean-counters would turn Apple into a mini-IBM. So he fought back with a project called Macintosh. Nobody at the top cared about that. Mac was just some designer off in a corner somewhere. Jobs grabbed it. He wasn't sure what it would amount to. Mac was anything but the sophisticated desktop publisher the world knows today. But Jobs believed that this small project could somehow, anyhow, become the next "metaphysical garage"—a small, ideologically pure team building a big, ideologically pure product. Pulling together the best, most "really neat" people, he would build yet another "insanely great" computer that would displace Lisa and save Apple from itself. It would change the world. It would put Jobs, a man who needs purpose above all else, back at the helm of his company.

But Murray knew none of this. What drew him was the call to change the world. That very afternoon he called Jobs and asked for a job. "I don't want a regular job," he told him. "Have you got something different, something really creative?" Apple attracted lots of people like that: people who wanted to do something "different," something "really creative." Murray in time became Jobs's "right-hand man," handling Mac's marketing drive, working, in his words, as an "evangelist" for the cause. He joined the cult with all the unreserved enthusiasm of a Moonie or an *est* convert. He bought into the dream. He knew that Apple II had indeed changed the world in a very short span. How could Mac fail to do so? "This was the psychology of Mac. This was its passion," he says. "We believed fundamentally that we were changing the world. We honestly did. What Apple represented was the democratization of technology. Putting this enormously powerful thing called technology, which can be so scary, into the hands of the people."

If that sounds like the language of revolution, it was. "Most of us were in our late twenties and early thirties," says Murray. "We missed the Beatles. We missed the civil rights movement. We missed Vietnam. Macintosh was our social revolution. We threw ourselves into it." And Jobs fueled their fervor. He was the Pied Piper, who played his role so well that many of those around him had no idea they were being led. They were carrying the banner alongside him—in some cases, they believed, almost independently of him.

Murray, himself a dynamic, driven man, is talking Commitment. Unlike many settlers in Silicon Valley in the seventies, he was married and had children. Almost alone at Mac, he managed to integrate and thrive in his two spheres. Yet his loyalty to Jobs, and of course to Apple, became complete. He and the rest of the Mac inner circle worked like men possessed. The boundaries between work and nonwork broke down. Work became the source of all joy and purpose in life. It became the very essence of life. Hundred-hour weeks were common. "Every night at six o'clock," says Murray, "it was as if a little invisible telephone would ring in your head. 'Why don't you stay just another half hour?' it would say. 'Think how much more you could get done.' Then, at six-thirty, the little phone would ring again. Why not another hour? Before long, it was ten. Then you would go eat with Steve." You would talk about what a great product Mac was going to be. You would talk about the vision and the amazing high of working together to create something that had never been done before. And maybe afterward you would go back to the office. Just to polish off a few odds and ends. Maybe you'd never go home.

People kept this up for months, even years. Home life suffered. Marriages broke up. People rarely discussed the outside world.

Ronald Reagan's election was almost ignored. But no one cared. No one questioned. "We didn't push as hard as we did because Steve asked us to," says Murray. "We did it because we wanted to. We loved it! It's why we came to the Valley. We were changing the world!"

Where does obsession leave off and reality begin? All this sweat, and fever and fury, and for what? Macintosh was a remarkable machine, but did it really change the world? Not really. And what does it mean, anyway, to "change the world"?

"We'd ask ourselves that from time to time," says Murray. "Great. So we're going to change the world. How? 'I dunno,' we'd say. 'It's got something to do with this great computer called Macintosh, and it's going to change the world.' Yeah, well how? 'Beats me. We'll make it up as we go along.' " Management experts sometimes rationalize such behavior as "goalless planning," a kind of entrepreneurship by intuition, and they may be right. But at bottom we're not talking management here; this is evangelism, a business-world Praise the Lord movement. And you have to wonder. Could idealism alone push these people to work as they did? Surely there must be more.

Murray hints at a deeper explanation. Call it the younger-sibling syndrome, a condition peculiar to the late 1970s. Many in Jobs's inner circle were born around 1955, as was Jobs himself. They were a cusp generation, too young for Vietnam or the civil rights movement (the symbolic divides of the fevered late sixties) and too old for the money-oriented seventies and eighties. Envying the passion of their older brothers and sisters, the argument goes, they plunged into causes of their own. They blended the idealism they yearned for with the glamorous capitalist opportunities their own times suddenly offered. They went to work for companies like Apple.

Well, yes. Clearly Jobs placed the cause above all else. So, probably, did Murray and hard-core technical types who wanted to do pioneering research. For them, the dream lived. Yet how many others at Apple lived to "change the world"? Not many, I think. The reality of Apple, as it grew, was the nine-to-five routine of any large organization. Even the "passion" of the elite Mac group was confined to a clique of twenty or thirty key people. The thousand or so other employees might just as well have worked for General Widget. Even within the clique, the passion was impure. Among the believers were opportunists. Many gravitated to Jobs because he was "hot." Just as a presidential candidate attracts talented, ambitious young men and women hungry to be White House aides, so did Jobs draw the most ambitious computer whizzes. Association with him meant success, money and recognition. Like winning a Rhodes scholarship, it was to be anointed. And so it's proved. Debbie Coleman, a financial manager at Mac, is Apple's chief financial officer. Alain Rossman is a top executive at Radius. Michael Murray helped start Convergent Technologies, a big California-based computer manufacturer. Dozens of others went out on their own, propelled by their moment of glory with Jobs. "Do Best by Me" was as much Apple's banner as "Change the World." The idealism as often as not was camouflage for life in the Steve Jobs jungle.

Does that matter? After all, it's the beliefs of the moment that drive an enterprise. Those closest to Jobs unquestionably worked with total wired-in commitment. They embraced the vision, so far as they were able. Yet that's a key phrase: *so far as they were able.* Was anyone at Apple able to believe as intensely and see as far as Jobs? Not likely. With few exceptions, the role of visionary was his alone.

JOBS HAS BEEN alone for most of his life. He shuns intense emotional relationships. He doesn't join organizations. He was a phantom at Reed College, making few good friends during his year there and managing, later, to alienate most of them. He bought an apartment in New York for $2 million, then commissioned I. M. Pei to redo it at a reported cost of $15 million, complete with twelve-and-a-half-foot nickel-and-bronze doors and Pacific Coast floor-planking that requires its own climate-control system. All this attention to detail, yet he's never lived in the place. At home in the Valley, he rattles around in a big, near-empty house near Palo Alto and sleeps on a mattress on the floor.

Romances tend to be brief and inconclusive. His latest girlfriend left him, complaining that they had "no life together." Jobs shrugs off such things. To accomplish anything great, you have to sacrifice. Yet there's something sad in his devotion, and even cruel. Jobs rarely speaks of his personal life, and one thing he's especially secretive about is the daughter he all but ignores. Her name is Lisa, and she was born twelve or so years ago, when Jobs was a teenage hippie sharing a group house with a girlfriend he later outgrew. Jobs has left Lisa without a father, just as he himself was left without his natural parents.

Those who know Jobs well say it's impossible to understate the importance of his origins. It's not only a wellspring of his drive, but also of his originality and uncanny effectiveness as a manager. It's also a key to his often brutal megalomania and manipulativeness.

Strictly speaking, Jobs wasn't an orphan. He was adopted as a baby, the eldest in a family of three children (his siblings were not adopted), and grew up securely and apparently happily in a working-class family in Cupertino. An adopted child is by definition a wanted child. He has parents who are "his" and who generally love him as if he were their natural child. Yet even in the best of circumstances, to be adopted is to be special. Most people think of themselves as different from everyone else in one way or another. But adopted children must struggle especially hard to create their identity. They are conscious of their status and often feel apart, as if something were not quite right in their past. They spin out secret fantasies, in which they might figure as "lost" princes or princesses, occupying a position in life far more glamorous than their present station. And sooner or later they show a natural inclination to search out their biological parents, both to discover themselves and, psychologists say, to shed a subliminal anger at the real parents who "rejected" them in youth.

Jobs was no different. Michael Moritz, in his book *The Little Kingdom*, tells how Jobs's adoptive father would buy used cars that he and his son could fix up together. As often as not, Jobs would be more interested in the car's history than its mechanics. He would daydream about the family that owned it: how many children the parents had, where they lived, what the father did for a living, whether they were happy. When he grew older, he tried hard to learn more about his roots. "He was very insecure about himself," says Dan Kottke, a software designer in Palo Alto who describes himself as Jobs's best friend at Reed and later helped him start Apple. That didn't extend to any insecurity about his abilities, because he was, Kottke says, "absolutely brilliant, smart enough to just think his way through whatever he needs to do." Nor did it reflect any lack of support at home. "My parents instilled in me a certain optimism about the future, a certain confidence in one's own abilities to slowly but surely sort things out," Jobs says. Yet deep down there always seems to have been a flicker of doubt—of uncertainty about his origins, who he was, what life might hold for him.

At Reed, for instance, Jobs was the recluse, always standing hesitantly at the fringe. "He was this quiet, lonely guy, whom I befriended partly because I felt a little sorry for him," says Kottke. "He was very introspective. Totally different from the way he is today. He was searching for himself, as if he always felt a little off-base because he didn't know who his parents were, because he was insecure about his roots. He felt he had a particularly powerful connection with his [biological] mother. Not his father. It was his mother."

Jobs didn't spell out that connection. But he once told Kottke that he felt he had to find out more about her: who she was, where she lived and where she came from, what her life was like. So one of the first things he did after Apple began making money was to hire a private investigator. Jobs doesn't seem to have told many people about the results. "Steve was always very secretive," Kottke says. "He told me only that his father was an American serviceman stationed overseas, and that his mother was of Middle Eastern origin—and very, *very* beautiful."

I tried, without much result, to find out whether Jobs ever met her. But I did discover an interesting subtext to the story. A friend of mine later went to a book party in New York honoring Mona Simpson, a twenty-nine-year-old critical sensation who had just written a novel, *Anywhere But Here*, loosely detailing her own search for identity in a broken family. As Simpson stood talking to a guest, a short, shaggy-haired guy came up and stood beside her. "Oh, I'd like you to meet my brother Steve." As it turned out, shortly before Simpson's book was to appear, she got a phone call out of the blue. "Hi!" the voice said. "This is your long-lost brother!" Some years after his adoption, it seems, Jobs's mother married a college professor (who himself left home when Mona Simpson was thirteen, not to return). Just as Jobs sought out his natural mother, so, too, did he seek out his sister.

Perhaps it was the uncertainty about his roots that made Jobs the seeker and the questioner he is. When you're never quite sure who you are, or where you came from, appearances will always be deceiving. Most of us as children at one time or another harbor fantasies that our parents don't love us, or that we're really orphans—psychologists call this syndrome the "foundling fantasy." It's a chance to imagine that we are special, set apart by some secret and glamorous past—princes and princesses, again. But if you really are an orphan, and if you're as talented and willful as Jobs, you might act out those dreams. Jobs clearly sees himself as special, as among the "vital few" destined to do great things. He's constantly trying to prove himself and persuade the world that he has the inside track on all the right answers. But what actually sets him apart from other emotionally immature and insecure people is the vividness of his imagination, the quality of his questions and the breadth of his answers.

This may explain his obsession with work. It's a form of escape. He throws himself into his job because personal relationships, far from being "unimportant," are so potentially threatening. Jobs failed as an infant to convince his mother to keep him. Now, helpless no longer, he uses all his adult wiles and persuasive gifts to manipulate people into a corporate "family," the only family that he can control, where he will always be the center of attention and cannot ever be given away.

This is important, because it's the heart of the phenomenon psychologists call "splitting." Like other industrialists in this book, Jobs's interior life has been a struggle between two worlds: one of blocks and insecurities, often rooted in childhood, the other an ideal of freedom. The result is an overpowering drive for liberation, control and willful self-assertion.

Jobs found his own path early. Raised in a nonacademic household, he dropped in on classes at Stanford and enrolled in science seminars sponsored by Hewlett-Packard. He insisted on going to Reed College against his parents' wishes, and while there was drawn to Eastern philosophy. He meditated, experimented with drugs, went barefoot, traveled in India and had his head shaved by a guru. (Or so goes the myth; Kottke, who went with him, says the "guru" was actually a crazy Frenchman . . . but then, back home in Cupertino, a shaved head was a shaved head, and that was pretty weird). He briefly joined a commune and faddishly embraced the virtues of special diets and fasting. Friends remember his lectures on the evils of meat, his readings from a book called *The Mucusless Diet Healing System.* He flirted with the notion of going to Japan and joining a monastery. Even now, he says, the fascination with Eastern mysticism lingers. Joining a monastery, building a corporation: In some ways, he says cryptically, the two paths aren't that different.

People talk of Jobs's brilliance and vision, but perhaps more important is his sense of unbridled freedom and the will behind it. Jobs has "split." He is one of those who knows no boundaries. "Most of us place blocks on ourselves. We perceive all the reasons why something can't be done," says Michael Murray. "We get trapped in the bureaucracy of living: Can I meet the mortgage, will I get promoted, how can I find the time to do this? Jobs for some reason has never fallen into these traps. At Mac, when we were stuck, he could think freely, without the concept of limits. 'Whoa,' he'd say. 'You guys are thinking in traditional patterns. Stop. Here's what we're going to do.' "

That could rub people the wrong way. Remember Wozniak's complaint that Jobs always seemed to be "trampling" on other people's ideas, that there was "only one possible solution" to a problem, and that was always his. Yet Jobs's one universally admired trait is his ability to see and act independently of normal barriers. "The thing about Steve's vision was its purity," says Wozniak. "He rarely let anything compromise it, never allowed obstacles to bump him off course. He kept all the creative people at Apple working on the same track. His vision went one way all the time." Others talk of his conceptual flair, his ability to combine dozens of different technologies and juggle a hundred different elements, from keyboard and hardware design to marketing, manufacturing and software. It was almost as if he could see at the outset what the product would look like when it was done, down to its smallest details.

Not to know boundaries. That was only reinforced by Apple's phenomenal early success. "Steve's path was unorthodox, even for the times," says Murray. "He experimented, broke with the established order, learned to thrive on chaos. And it paid off, more handsomely than he could have imagined." At twenty-five, when most people are hemmed in by the constraints of first jobs and meager finances, Steve Jobs was free. Apple did more than make him rich. It validated his whole worldview and gave him license to *keep* breaking the rules. If Jobs was by nature a challenger, success made him even more so.

It also made him even more willful, more autocratic. "If there's anything more important than his vision, it's his will," says Murray. "Steve has a very forceful personality. Nothing can wait. He insists on the unique quality of his vision and his beliefs. He pushes, he pulls, he drags. For Steve, the ends totally justify the means. He does whatever is necessary to get where he wants to go. And when you get there, everyone says, 'This is great.' You forget all the pain and all the frustration." You forget the broken marriages, the burned-out careers, the personal hardships. Because it's been such an incredible journey.

JOBS NEVER FORGETS that others don't feel the passion as deeply as he. They're mostly followers who must be goaded, prodded and pushed to greatness. And so he manipulates. He uses people in ways that help them best use themselves.

People are at a loss to say precisely how he does it. He has so many devices, so many artifices. Where does leadership begin and personality leave off?

Trying to find a clue, I had dinner one night with Guy Kawasaki, an ebullient, open, hard-core Californian who describes his past job at Macintosh as a "software evangelist" specializing in "reality distortion."

Something clicks. *Reality distortion.* "What's that?" I ask.

"It's where you went out and got people to bet their company on Macintosh. We'd persuade them to write software for us without any money up front, and without any certainty that Macintosh had a future or that the project would survive. We got otherwise sober businessmen to make huge, even irrational financial commitments, with no guarantee of a return. Our fervor and zeal distorted their sense of reality. This was not sales. This was evangelism."

Kawasaki says this with appealing gusto. He's a tanned, healthy Asian-American, another smart, ambitious young Stanford entrepreneur born, you guessed it, in 1955. Just like Jobs, just like Murray, just like almost everyone else on the Macintosh dream team.

I suggest that "reality distortion" might be a metaphor for the whole climate Jobs fostered at Apple, and Kawasaki laughs. "No question. As a pure charismatic leader, Steve Jobs is the best. He's the greatest! He can lead people through concrete walls, and he does it by distorting reality."

He gestures out the window of the restaurant. It's about ten in the evening, and people are strolling under the palm trees lining Palo Alto's main drag, enjoying the balmy darkness. "If I told you the sun was out, would you believe me?" Kawasaki asks.

"Sure. Maybe it's shining in Peking."

"No, right here in Palo Alto. Well, there are people out there right now who would believe it's daylight if Steve Jobs said so. It's an amazing thing. Quite fascinating."

I didn't get it. Jobs distorts people's reality, Kawasaki explained, by turning their views around. By confusing them. He leads by manipulation.

"So that men may see, I throw dust in their eyes," wrote James Joyce. But that was only a flickering of understanding, so I asked Kawasaki for an example. "Do you mean he harangues people into excellence? Or he slides ice under your feet, to keep you off balance?"

"Both. But the closest metaphor is that he spins you like a top. He takes you in his hand, twirls a string around you and winds you up, then throws you. And then you spin for a while. And when you fall down, he picks you up and spins you all over again."

"So how does he wind you up?"

"He'll tell you that you did something great. Listen: praise by Steve Jobs is the highest praise there is."

"Because he can be so critical?"

"Hostile. Absolutely hostile."

Hostility, Kawasaki says, is also integral to Jobs's leadership. "It's leadership by intimidation. Leadership by taking away your sense of direction."

And replacing it with his own direction?

Yes, Kawasaki said, but that comes much later. The first step is intimidation, a sort of boot camp of the soul, a mind game of motivational psychological warfare.

This was getting interesting. Mind games. Boot camps of the soul.

"Steve has a way of testing you," Kawasaki goes on. "It's very interesting. He'll come up to someone and say, 'Guy is shit. He's not working well with the developers. They're not doing the software on time. I talked to so-and-so, and he thinks Guy is shit, too.' The game begins when the person Steve is talking to tries to figure out what he is really saying. You don't know whether Jobs really thinks Guy is lousy, or whether he's testing you. And it's a dangerous game. If you think Guy is great, and Jobs genuinely thinks he's lousy, and if you stand up for Guy, then Jobs may think you're all wet and mark you as a 'bozo.' On the other hand, if Jobs secretly thinks Guy is great, and you agree with his line that Guy is lousy, you're a bozo again."

"This is a way to motivate people?"

"Absolutely. Because the worst thing that could ever happen to you is to be labeled a bozo by Steve Jobs. Because he never forgets and he never changes his mind."

But I still didn't understand why this helps get people working at top pitch.

Well, says Kawasaki, this is just one of a "zillion" mind games Jobs uses to push, pull, intimidate and manipulate people into looking at things *his* way, into joining his metaphysical "family." "Steve creates a climate where you lose touch with your own reality." Your way of seeing the world gets turned upside down. You're no longer confident about your place. You lose your balance and start spinning like a top. "When that happens, you become clay in his hands." The old reality is distorted, a new reality is born. Not only do you begin to see the world Jobs's way, you become a little Steve Jobs clone. You become a monomaniac. You buy into the dream.

That can be very exciting, Kawasaki says, because that's when life becomes intense and full of passion. Work takes on the quality of a mission. *Change the world!* The appeal is particularly seductive for people weaker than Jobs, who can't find the same passion and purpose on their own. Yet a trip with Jobs can also be very destructive, not least for its addictiveness. "Make no mistake," says Kawasaki. "You are being used. You are being abused. Steve Jobs is a drug, and you're hooked once you've got his needle in your arm. He may not be heroin. He may not be methadone. But Steve Jobs is a drug. I guarantee you that."

IS JOBS STILL that way at NeXT? After all, he's older now and presumably wiser. For the first time he's running his own show, which means that he no longer has to fight for leadership as he did at Apple. Logically, except for his mania for work, you would think he'd become more relaxed, easier to be around, less manipulative in managing and motivating his staff.

There are signs that he has changed. Perhaps the most persuasive is that Jobs himself wants to change, or at least seems determined to learn from past mistakes. In building NeXT, Jobs wants to instill in it the spirit he believes was lost at Apple. Passion, purity, commitment—the watchwords of Chairman Jobs. But how to ensure that the past won't repeat itself, that NeXT won't grow into another behemoth full of unimaginative nine-to-fivers who won't give themselves over to the dream of working on "really, *really* neat" projects? How to create the perfect corporate culture, the sort of company ("built from the heart") that prompted Ross Perot to open his checkbook for $20 million? The sort that keeps people working with passion and never, never burning out.

The answer, Jobs explains, is what he calls "management by values." "You read a lot about management systems. You know, management by objective. Different ways of measuring people. Well, I've found through the years that none of that stuff works.

"The problem is that in a very fast-moving situation, such as at NeXT, where we're trying to develop a whole new technology, after-the-fact measurement is deadly. Let's say you set some objectives for someone and they fail. What happens next? You're dead. So, what you want is during-the-fact or, even better, before-the-fact measurement. And how do you get that? Well, what I finally came around to was 'management by values.' You want people in your company to make decisions according to the same values as you yourself would."

And how do you find out whether people share those values? Lists, naturally. You put them through the same soul-searching exercise Jobs went through after he was fired from Apple. "You ask people to list what they care about most in their jobs and in their work. Obviously you want that list to resemble your own. For example, I feel strongly that you shouldn't worry too much about the bottom line. You're much better off worrying about the top line: clarity of vision and strategy, hiring the best people, giving them the tools to do their job. That sort of thing. If you pay enough attention to the top line, the bottom line will take care of itself."

That sounds suspiciously like one of the maxims that got Jobs into trouble at Apple: inattention to costs, to operational details, to deadlines. But wait. Jobs is just warming up. We're still talking about The List.

Jobs is big on values because of his experience at Apple. As he sees it, the company went through a profound but fundamental shift as it grew from a fledgling start-up to a major corporation. It wasn't just a matter of scale, he says; it had a lot to do with outlook and philosophy. "During the first few years at Apple," Jobs says, "our goal was simple: to make the best computers in the world. We realized we had to make a profit to accomplish that goal, so we said, 'Okay, let's make a profit.' But our goal was still to make the best computers in the world."

After a time, Jobs believes, those values changed. "The goal at Apple today," he says, "is to make lots and lots of profit. And, oh, if we have to make a decent computer to do that, okay, we will. That's a subtle but important flip, because it changed the whole incentive structure at Apple. The people who came to make great computers began to leave. They found they were working with people, or for people, who didn't share their values, who because of their focus on the bottom line couldn't justify the cost of some improvement, even though in their heart they might have known it was the right thing to do.

"The six of us who started NeXT," Jobs concludes, "all want the same thing. We all really want a company where really bright young people can come and be given substantial responsibility very early, before all the idealism is beaten out of them. We want a very free climate of discussion, where we can all be flat-out honest and tell each other what's wrong with something and not hold any punches. Perhaps most important, we all share the same goal. We want to make a major contribution to the educational process in the next five to ten years, through the use of the computer. That's our number one goal. The size of our profit comes second."

And Jobs's own role? "To keep the team together. To recruit the best people. To reiterate and keep up our confidence in the long-term vision. To set the level of excellence by saying, 'No, that's not good enough. Let's do it better.' "

This is the language of moderation and balance. Or is it? It's easy to talk about "shared values," the importance of the "top line" over the "bottom line." It's more difficult to act out the theory. Certainly Jobs will never compromise technological purity. His goal will always be to build the best computer possible, whatever the costs and to hell with compromise. But will he find a style of leadership that's less manipulative and less vulnerable to burnout? I'm skeptical.

We're back in that conference room at NeXT, and I've just had that first off-putting encounter with Jobs. Dan'l Lewin has taken me aside. He's trying to dispel Jobs's reputation as a driven and abrasive boss. "I don't think there's anyone here who is uncomfortable about their relationship with Steve," he says. Jobs has grown from his experience at Apple. He is much more relaxed and open. "We're not trying to sprint," says Lewin. "This is a marathon, and we're pacing ourselves. This is a fundamental difference from Apple." The work week at NeXT is sixty or seventy hours, not a hundred. Lewin even speculates that Jobs might one day "drop out" and devote a few years to a family, if he ever has one. "He has changed totally from the way he was at Apple."

That is to say, obsessive, compulsive, rude, inconsiderate, unpredictable and, often, nearly impossible to work with.

I've broached this prickly topic by way of an article I read on the flight out from New York. A writer for *Esquire*, Joe Nocera, had visited Jobs ten months earlier. No one doubts Jobs's brilliance, but Nocera, for one, was uncomfortable with the way it sometimes seemed to show up. As in Jobs's propensity to show off his intelligence by humiliating others. As in what Nocera called his "almost willful lack of tact." As in his "inability to hide his boredom when forced to listen to something that doesn't interest him, like a sixth-grader who can't wait for class to end."

Which, as it happened, was the way Jobs behaved in front of Nocera. The scene was this same conference room at NeXT, where Lewin happened to be giving a marketing presentation. It was about delegation of responsibility and lines of authority, all mapped out in complicated diagrams. Jobs squirmed, fidgeted, got more and more restless as Lewin droned on. Finally, Nocera wrote, Jobs could endure no more. "I think these charts are bullshit," he interrupts. "Just bullshit." Lewin is thrown, but Jobs has already moved the discussion on to another topic, apparently deepening the marketing director's embarrassment. "Can we do something *really* important?" Jobs asks. "Can we get that electric outlet fixed?"

Lewin has gone out of his way to tell me that things didn't happen quite that way. The real story, he explains, is that a long discussion got compressed into a couple of magazine paragraphs. That distorted the train of events, he says. Jobs was not as impatient or abrasive as it appeared. The discussion did not die with electrical outlets. Lewin was not cowed. The incident was out of context. Jobs *has* changed. Really.

At almost precisely this instant, the door of the conference room pops open. Jobs sticks his head in. "Hi!" he says, smiling that tight smile. "I don't want him to tie you up all day," he tells Lewin, jerking his head at me with scarcely a glance. "We've got a product to ship!"

" 'Bye," I say. But Jobs has already turned and is out the door. Lewin picks up where we left off, but a second later Jobs is back.

" 'Bye. That was my line for you."

Poor Dan'l. He's looking stressed. The *Esquire* nightmare is happening all over again. Through the window in the door, you can see Jobs pass by a couple more times, perhaps huffing and puffing, perhaps not. Who knows?

Lewin shrugs. "See, I block that out," he says.

Maybe so, but I notice our conversation winds up pretty quickly now. Lewin is no wimp, but neither is Steve Jobs a changed man. He's every bit as driven and impatient with distractions as he was at Apple. Work is still a calling. Time is wasting. The world awaits. There's no respite for the chosen.

CHAPTER THREE

LIVING THEATER

◆

PLACE A call to Apple, and the reception is polite, impersonal, cool as day-old spaghetti. "Apple Computer. May I help you, sir?"

Then put in a call to NeXT. "Hello, NeXT Incorporated. This is Christine. Just a moment, Michael, and I'll direct your call to Alex." You haven't met or asked for Alex, but never mind. Here he is, bouncy as a teenage gymnast. "Hello, Michael. Alex! How can we help you?" *Boing!*

It's easy to overplay such differences, yet they go to the heart of entrepreneurial leadership. People who build companies, let alone empires, do so in their own image. Their ventures are the expression of their dreams, shaped by symbols.

Steve Jobs is big on symbols. He focuses on every detail of NeXT's image, as if to say, This is what I have built; this is who I am. There's the Rand Logo, for starters. One of Jobs's first acts was to commission a book recounting its creation, printed on expensive vellum and sent to any journalist who happens to misspell the visionary NeXT as a humdrum "Next." The subtext is obvious. This is a first draft of history; NeXT is important and its birth should be celebrated.

Then there's the car Jobs drives: a top-of-the-line Porsche that mirrors his view of his product. NeXT, his people say, builds the Porsche of personal computers; Apple and IBM, by implication, are content to sell Fords. Finally there's the NeXT computer itself. Like the logo, it's an obsidian cube, a striking standout in the vanilla world of personal computers. Because the machine takes some time to warm up, an intriguing rumor circulated through the Valley as the date of its introduction approached. Jobs, reportedly, had asked his favorite rock group, the Talking Heads, to compose a song that will issue forth during the interval. I was skeptical; a duet between Yehudi Menuhin and the NeXT computer would be more in tune with the market these days. But even so, it was a *symbol*. The Talking Heads are the ultimate in avant-garde rock—sophisticated, intellectual and ultrachic. Like the band, like the machine. NeXT, the insider's choice.

Jobs's subliminal image-making sometimes goes overboard. Take the Silicon Valley Four-Man Bike Race, a cycling invitational for the Valley's techies. Jobs and three associates participated, and snapshots of the event, bound neatly in a little album, *just happened* to be lying on the receptionist's desk the day I visited. Jobs shuffled through them with me looking over his shoulder. There were the NeXTers, all in biking togs and perched on sporty two-man tandems. Everyone else in the race rode normal ten-speeds, of course. But not the NeXTers. They rode twosome, a distinctive team. Jobs gloats, pointing out his people. "That's Bud. He did great! That's Rich. He really rode hard." But Jobs isn't really thinking about how great Bud did or whether Rich rode hard. Nor did it matter that the race was fun. What made Jobs happy was that NeXT rode tandems and no one else did. The symbol counted above all: NeXT is special, better and more creative in every way than anybody else.

You could think of these as props in a living theater. The black computer, the Talking Heads, the eye-catching high-tech logo, the tandem bicycles—they're all devices to set the scene, paint a backdrop, create a mood that persuades people they're about to experience something that will enchant, inspire or move them. But as with any theatrical production, the result is only as good as the material and the director and actors who interpret it. In a corporation, that means the product and the people who make it. At NeXT, that means Steve Jobs and the computer. A nice logo and a perky staff are nothing without him.

No one is more aware of this than Jobs. He is the author, director and leading man in the ongoing production that is NeXT. He delivers his lines with studied perfection. "The reward is the journey," he says, to the admiration of his staff and the audience.

His choreographed entrances and exits are part of the show. When he bounces down the stairs, two or three at a time, he's just following the stage directions. His blue jeans, tennis shoes and white button-down shirts are a costume, a uniform with a message. We think differently, it says; we don't fit the mold, we break it. And what better image to cut when you're out to *change the world*?

Jobs plays himself up as deliberately as any rock star. As his publicist says, he *is* a rock star, as big on the American scene as the Talking Heads. Everyone knows who he is. Pretty girls wink at him as he walks the Stanford campus. *Newsweek, Fortune, People, Business Week*—just about every national publication in the country has featured him on its cover. He's a media darling, one of the rich and famous. He hobnobs with Nobel scientists; he goes out with Joan Baez. When the king of Spain was introduced to Jobs at a San Francisco party, says Ross Perot, the two were soon "eyeball to eyeball, talking computers." In no time at all, Jobs has "Juan's" personal phone number—and a sale.

Jobs and his associates somewhat cynically call this the Camelot Effect. Jobs is the young king coming into his own. His cadre of elite young mad scientists are his Round Table, the Knights of High Tech. But this mystique, this winning charisma, is as manufactured as it is natural. Jobs is the sorcerer as manager. He seduces with his oratory and evangelical passion. He uses symbols to build his myth and project his dreams. He shows himself to his public and his colleagues only through his role, a mask that is carefully crafted to mark him as a man of his time and place.

JOHN KEEGAN, a prominent military analyst and author of *The Mask of Command*, has made a study of leadership through the ages. Great leaders, he writes, are many things besides commanders of armies. They may be diplomats and, like Eisenhower, excel at conciliation as much as organization and strategy. They may be intellectuals in the style of Woodrow Wilson. They may be evangelists who lead with missionary zeal, such as Joan of Arc, or they may be demagogic, like Hitler or Napoleon. Most likely, however, they will at one time or another be all of these things.

Keegan considers this chameleonlike gift to be the heart and soul of leadership. Such qualities as courage, integrity, intelligence, energy and persistence may be taken for granted, he says. But to lead requires an ability not just to command but to inspire—and to inspire requires the general to appear to his followers in whatever guise they want and need at the critical moment. The great leader is thus a great actor. He assumes what Keegan calls the "mask" of command, "made in such form as will mark him as a man of his time, so that his men know him as what they hope for and require." They make themselves "stars" in the theater of the real. They become seducers. Their passion overrides logic.

ROSS PEROT, the Dallas billionaire, would hate to be called a seducer. But that's what he is. Like Steve Jobs, he promises dreams. He's a spellbinding illusionist in the theater of the real.

You have only to visit Perot's office to understand everything about the man—and nothing about his company, Electronic Data Systems. *Electronic data systems.* Does that sound interesting? Decide for yourself. Descend into the bowels of EDS, far below Perot's penthouse offices, and you enter a world straight out of *1984*. Banks of giant computers, looming in cavernous acoustic-tiled rooms, are busily processing insurance claims, payroll accounts and inventory records for companies and government agencies around the country. The minutiae and pace of the work are boggling to the layman, the subject matter unutterably boring to almost anyone. Yet consider this: Perot's people, too, count themselves among the chosen. Every day they come to EDS, enter the windowless, humming hive of computers and glue themselves to a terminal that spits out data (the same kind of data, day after grueling day) for eight to ten hours at a stretch. And they do it with excitement. They do it with unbending vigilance. They think of their work as a calling and themselves as a crack team on a mission of high purpose. They believe, wholeheartedly, that data processing is *fun*!

Let's return to Perot's office. Nothing here suggests the subterranean hell below. The rooms are large and light. The windows look out on the rolling greensward of the company golf course. And there are the Symbols.

Perot's office is a trove of patriotic Americana: There's the flag that flew over the Capitol the day the first *Apollo* astronauts landed on the moon. And there's a tattered banner that flew over Fort Sumter, a fighting man's flag. A giant bust of John Paul Jones dominates the lobby below: "I have not yet begun to fight." And everywhere there are eagles: soaring imperiously in paintings, carved above doorways, sitting bronze and life-size in Perot's office, holding down papers, in miniature, on EDSers' desks.

It's hardly a surprise, then, to learn that Perot served in the navy. It follows that he's the man who once tried to fly a planeload of Christmas dinners to American prisoners of war in Vietnam, and who later rescued a pair of EDS employees imprisoned in Iran. Insiders joke that EDS is the only company in the world to have its own paramilitary capability, except that it's no joke. The symbols are eloquently truthful. EDSers are computer commandos, an elite "SWAT team" that travels the country troubleshooting other people's computer problems. They do the work that few others can understand. They fight in the trenches of a baffling and often boring electronic war, a daily struggle against "glitches" and crippling data-processing snafus. They make the information age run smoothly. They are its unsung honor guard.

The military imagery is no accident. EDS puts a premium on military virtues: instantaneous responsiveness, a committed "can do" ethic, uncompromising attention to detail, integrity. Even so, it's an illusion. EDS is a corporation, not a Special Forces unit. Data is at stake, not national security. Instead of death and danger, EDSers face down only boredom. Why, then, do they rally around Perot's flag? What's the magic formula?

Perhaps it's that Perot draws out the best in people, because he draws out the best in himself. He sets a relentless example. As the next chapter will illustrate, Perot early in life embraced a code of conduct as idealized as it was personally compelling. He, too, wears a mask. The elements of the code are part military, part Boy

Scouts, part biblical. Treat others as you would have them treat you. Respect and value your fellow men. Be truthful, honest, courageous. Never, never give in.

The code has come to permeate the whole of EDS. There's a dress code; blue suits and short hair. There's a cultish commitment to loyalty and family values. Perot went to Iran himself, where he might easily have been arrested and jailed, out of loyalty to his employees. Perot's dedication to his people is legend. When someone gets sick, he's been known to fly in just the right specialist from anywhere in the world. Those who do well by him do well themselves. Last year he paid one young manager of the Perot Group, his family holding company, a bonus of $5 million.

Perot's rigorous allegiance to a rigorous code rubs off. He attracts a supporting cast. At EDS, living by the code becomes an end in itself. The actual work, data processing, becomes the path to truth and self-knowledge. That's the secret of EDS—the theater made real, work as a kind of morality play that lets otherwise ordinary people be heroes. There's a purity and heady freedom in taut command and taut moral fiber. Perot's troops are battle-ready, fit and proud. And make no mistake: EDS runs on pride—the pride of the pro, the pride of belonging. For the barriers to entry are high. EDS recruits are chosen carefully. They're tested every nine months, and their ranks are weeded unsentimentally. There are standards to be maintained and rewards along the way. Perot and EDS have been so successful, the reputation of EDSers has soared so high within the industry, that it becomes a privilege to *serve*. That EDS is merely a company gets lost in the theater. The illusion takes over, yet that doesn't matter. It gets results. It has worth in its own right. *Semper Fi.* Live by the code, and count yourself among the chosen, the strong and the free. The journey is the reward.

The journey is the reward. That's Steve Jobs's line. Compare the way Jobs and Perot use theater, and the similarities are striking. So are the differences. Both are uncompromising, willful men who lead by the power of their ideas and the seductive sweep of their vision. Yet where Jobs is the often petulant manipulator—using people, manipulating and confusing them so that they buy into *his* dream, burning them up and casting them aside—Perot is the mirror opposite. He leads mainly by the strength of his example. The code by which EDS lives is his, yet it's apart from him. By living the code, Perot's employees embrace an impersonal set of values. This is no cult of personality, thinly veiled. EDSers, however much they may look alike, are not clones of Ross Perot in the way that Macintoshers, or presumably NeXTers, are of Jobs.

That's an important distinction, best seen when the work is done. An astonishing number of people who once worked for Jobs speak of a sense of loss or dispossession. It's not just that they miss the drug, the adrenaline-rush that accompanies any association with him. Rather, they miss the passion, the total commitment. Somehow, everything they do afterward pales by comparison. Those who leave EDS, on the other hand, don't experience the same feeling of loss. That's not necessarily because EDS's goals are less lofty. Instead, it has more to do with the fact that their sense of self-worth isn't so closely linked to Perot personally. When people leave EDS, they take the code with them. They continue to live it. The dream doesn't die.

CHAPTER FOUR

THE PATRIARCH

◆

ROSS PEROT won't come right out and say it. That would spoil the surprise. Worse, it would look like he's grandstanding (which he is, sort of) by building up interest and then jolting his listeners with the little secret.

The secret is the slender red book he's waving in the air as he strides around his ballroom-size office. It's a tattered little volume, as well-worn as a Bible, and marked with paper clips, Xeroxed inserts, penciled inscriptions and turned-down pages. "Ross," as he likes to be called, is exuberantly reading off its principles:

" 'Speak politely.'

" 'Return everything you borrow.'

" 'Do not take liberties with women.' "

Nose in the book, finger in the air, Perot circumnavigates the room. He's surrounded by the symbols of his life and values. Bronze sculptures by Frederic Remington—cowboys busting broncos and eagles soaring. Paintings by Norman Rockwell. Photos of his wife and children. The American flag that flew over the Capitol on the day the first men landed on the moon. An enshrined copy of *A Boy Scout's Code.*

" 'Do not hit or swear at people.'

" 'Do not burn crops.'

" 'Do not pretend to know what you do not know.' "

A note from Ronald Reagan lies not-so-casually open on a side table. The cherry-paneled room, furnished with American Colonial replicas, looks like it's straight out of the Smithsonian. And dominating all is the famous painting: Archibald Willard's "Spirit of

'76"—the one of the three fife-and-drum players marching home from war, the picture that once hung in the White House.

"You don't know what this is?" Perot exclaims, raising the little book high, his Texas accent twanging like a broken ukulele. "Why, you gotta know what this is. It's the Little Red Book. By Mao!"

As in Mao Tse-tung, the Chinese revolutionary leader—after Marx and Lenin, the top commie of them all. And this from Henry Ross Perot, Mr. Red, White and Blue himself. The man who's been called the "Commando of Free Enterprise," "the Billy Graham of Business," "the Promethean Patriot," the "Jug-eared Juggernaut of Industry." The man who built a computer services company from scratch and compiled a personal empire worth $3 billion. Who's used his wealth to ransom Americans held by terrorists, to upgrade the Texas school system, to fund scientific and medical research, to give his family, friends and country a helping hand in good times and bad.

For Ross Perot is a family man, and he lives by family virtues: honesty, loyalty, fidelity, caring. There are many rich Americans, but Perot is something more. He has a code, written in some mythic past, as if he were the Last Real Texan in the mold of the Alamo and the Texas Rangers.

More than that, he's the closest thing we have to a national patriarch, urging us, his adopted American sons and daughters, always to "do the right thing." When two of his employees were seized and imprisoned in Iran in 1979, Perot personally went to Teheran and organized a jailbreak. The exploit was celebrated in Ken Follett's best-seller *On Wings of Eagles*. Later it was made into a five-part television series. *Esquire* once lionized Perot with a snatch of verse from a pop song:

Where are you now when we need you, Ross Perot?
Who else can we turn to?
There ain't no real-life heroes
Throughout this wretched realm.

When General Motors bought out Perot's company in 1985, he passed out copies of *Eagles* at a welcome dinner. The message was clear. GM workers were now his family. Perot would do anything—anything—to help them in a pinch.

For Perot, money is not just power. It's a summons and a moral claim, a way of extending his will and doing "the right thing" in the world. "Now that I've got it," he says, "I have to figure out what to do with it."

But . . . if Perot is all this—Superpatriot, Family Man, Ultimate Capitalist—why is he standing tall against the backdrop of "The Spirit of '76," waving the Red Book and spouting the sayings of Chairman Mao?

Because, he says, "this is timeless leadership." And in these trying times, we Americans could use a little leadership like Mao's.

Listen, he commands: " 'Persuasion, not compulsion, is the only way to convince people.'

"Now that's especially true in business," Perot says. "Persuasion is key. It sounds simple, but it's amazing how many people forget that. Often as not, managers in America don't consult with their employees. They don't treat people with dignity or respect, don't really even *care* about them. They just order them around. They hire experts to do 'strategic studies' without asking the opinions of the people who actually do the work. What do you think that does for morale and motivation?"

Perot reads again:

" 'On a blank sheet of paper, free from any mark, the most precious and beautiful characters can be written, the freshest and most beautiful pictures can be painted.' "

A long pause.

"Now that's fascinating. You see, the thing about China's six hundred million people in Mao's time was that they were all poor and 'blank.' This may seem like a bad thing, but in reality it was a good thing. Poverty gave rise to the desire for change, the desire for action. That was how Mao was able to coalesce and motivate an entire nation. He created one China, for the first time. Everyone said it couldn't be done. But Mao did it. And he did it because he gave his people a doctrine that they could all buy into."

I suggest that Mao's Red Book was also a way of manipulating the masses, that his rule led to the excesses of the Cultural Revolution, but Perot swats the notion away like an errant gnat. "We won't think about that," he says. Perot isn't as interested in the consequences of Mao's creed as he is in its effectiveness. Mao led because he used his creed as statistics are sometimes used: to give moral backing and purpose to whatever it is you want to do. Is there a similarly ominous note in Perot's own love of slogans?

"Hey, I've got something else for you," he says, jumping out of the rocking chair where he has momentarily alighted and disappearing through a door behind his desk. He reappears a few seconds later.

"Here. I'll give you the best of them all. *Leadership Secrets of Attila the Hun.*"

Attila the Hun? Perot is laughing, a chortle that squinches up his eyes as if he's been stung on the nose by a bee.

"Yeah! I had five hundred copies printed up one time to give out at a General Motors dinner. The title's sort of tongue in cheek. But it's there." Perot is very emphatic. "Everything you need to know about management and leadership is *there.*"

It wasn't an easy job, apparently, being the Scourge of God. It took leadership, courage, organization and, above all, a code—a code not unlike Ross Perot's.

Later, in my motel room, I leafed through Perot's gift. Perot has so many copies left because GM chairman Roger Smith wouldn't let him hand it out at that fancy dinner; it was just too irreverent, too . . . well, just too *everything* for stodgy GM. Like the Red Book, it's a slender thing, chock-a-block with dandy little management sayings. *Tough, provocative* and *useful* management sayings. If nothing else, Attila left a legacy of collected wisdom, written down fifteen hundred years ago by the conqueror's scribes and rescued from obscurity by a scholar of Perot's acquaintance.

Like: "A good Hun will be loyal."

Like: "You must be willing to remain your natural self and not take on an aura of false pride."

Like: "A good Hun does not lie, cheat or steal. . . . He must hold a profound conviction of duty over all other ambitions."

When it came time for Ross Perot to draw up a code of conduct for his own company, Electronic Data Systems, he knew where to go. The result was an odd mixture of Mao, the Ten Commandments, the *Boy Scout Handbook* and *Semper Fidelis*, the marine corps' pledge of honor. There was a dress code. EDSers were the white-collar commandos of the computer industry, decked out in identical dark blue suits and white-shirt uniforms. "They have to parachute into their clients' offices and work there for weeks or months at a time," Perot explains. "They have to blend in. A blue suit is camouflage for the corporate jungle." The boss's moral code is equally stern. If a married employee was found to be having an affair, for instance, he'd be fired. "He's got a lifetime contract with his wife," Perot once said. "If she can't trust him, how can I?"

Perot has been criticized for treating employees like children—*his* children. He's been accused of creating a corporate culture more closely resembling a private militia or medieval fiefdom than a modern multinational business. He's been called a dictator, intolerant of those who don't share his Methodist, idealized values. But that's unfair. The "family" atmosphere he sought to create at EDS was simply *his* view of family values and virtues. It was *his* way of building a company, whose winning edge would come from its sense of mission and high purpose. After all, you don't have to work for him.

At its simplest, working for Perot means buying into his invincible "can do" ethic. It means uncompromising attention to quality, service and, as leaders from Mao to MacArthur would call it, duty. And if you're building a company and those are your aims and values, you have to surround yourself with like-minded people. If that sounds familiar, it ought to. It's "management by values," as practiced by Steve Jobs and virtually all exceptional leaders.

"You've got to create the right environment," Perot is saying. "You've got to have high standards of quality and excellence." Perot makes it abundantly clear that, at least in the early days of EDS, you either bought into that corporate ethic or you didn't buy in at all.

"Let's start with the question: What is EDS?" says Perot. "EDS delivers the finest computer services in the world. Nobody beats us in quality or price.

"Now," Perot continues, "that sets the stage for the next question: What's an EDSer? Basically an EDSer is someone who does whatever needs to be done to reach that goal. He's a person who goes anywhere twenty-four hours a day, seven days a week, to serve a client. Sometimes people say, 'If I wanted to work those hours, I'd be a doctor.' I say, 'That's tough. Doctors get Thursdays off.'

"The point is this: If you don't want to be part of an organization that's willing to go the last mile to be better than anyone else, don't come to work for EDS. Go find a quiet pond. Nobody gets paid for staying around here. Everything's based on excellence. People who do the most get paid the most. People who make the greatest contribution get promoted. That creates a dynamic environment."

Ask Perot about his purpose in life, and he'll get a little impatient, a little uncomfortable. "I create jobs," he says finally. "I create jobs. Good jobs. And so I keep doing it."

It's an interesting answer. I've never met anyone who saw his role in life as *creating jobs*. Perhaps it's Perot's way of saying he cares for his fellow men, which in many ways is obviously true. A good job, after all, is a gift, conferring a sense of self-worth, belonging and achievement. Perot could also mean it in the sense of taking care of people, which might be a form of control as much as fellow feeling. Whatever, Perot doesn't create just any old jobs. They're his kind of jobs, performed his way. He has little patience with people or lifestyles he does not understand. Seldom have I been more conscious about my hair being a couple of inches too long, or the stubborn spot on my travel tie.

Perot cuts off further speculation about his inner compass with a laugh. "That's too cosmic. My mind, it goes on overload." Then, suddenly, he's all energy and decisiveness:

"Hey. Did you ever read Genghis Khan?"

As a matter of fact, no.

"Well, read him now," says Perot. "That's a guy who understood leadership."

Perot is clearly enjoying his chance to startle. He trots out three notorious villains—Mao, Genghis Khan and Attila—and passes them off as men of principle. Perhaps they were, though on one level that's beside the point. Perot is very aware that these were forceful leaders who knew how to seduce their followers and maintain discipline—self-discipline and, more important, spiritual discipline and allegiance to the cause. Perot is no different. His code is an exhortation to do the right thing: for the individual, for EDS, for the nation. It's all one and the same.

DOING THE RIGHT THING. It is the great constant in Ross Perot's life. When he was young, growing up in the little East Texas border town of Texarkana, his mother snipped a Norman Rockwell print out of a magazine and tacked it above his study desk. It was a Boy Scout at prayer, Perot once told the *Washington Post*, and it was "everything I strived to be."

This may not have been the true beginning of the code, but it's as good a departure point as any. Ross Perot grew up to be an Eagle Scout. He built the Ross Perot Scout Center in Texarkana. His *Boy Scout Handbook*, his hatchet, his merit badges, are there, under glass, carefully preserved as icons of the man, his way of life and worldview.

You can't help but wonder if the embalming of these emblems indirectly protects the owner from worldly wear and tear. Perot, a man who believes in openness, communication and unpretentiousness, exhibits much the same righteous certainty as Mao, Attila or Genghis Khan. It's inconceivable that anything could shake his basic values. Perot's conviction that he has a corner on the truth, that what he is doing is Right, is both a strength and a weakness. It is by definition a source of inflexibility; yet it bolsters Perot when his course is fraught with personal or corporate danger.

Doing the right thing. Perot first sprang into the public eye in 1968, when he worked what *Fortune* once called "the greatest single personal coup in the history of American finance." Taking his five-year-old company public at the height of the boom market, he became a billionaire virtually overnight. Then, in 1969, he began using his wealth in the manner that's since become his trademark. Learning through the Defense Department that American prisoners of war in North Vietnam were being brutalized, were dying of disease and malnutrition, he developed a plan for embarrassing Hanoi into providing more humane treatment.

And so, a few days before Christmas, Perot chartered two red-and-green Braniff 707s, loaded them with medical supplies and Christmas dinners and flew to Vietnam. The North Vietnamese didn't let him in; he didn't expect them to. "The point was to embarrass them, and it worked," he says. "We spent two million dollars and got sixty million dollars' worth of publicity. That was enough to elect a president then, and it was enough to help change the treatment our boys were getting in the north." Mission accomplished.

Since then, Americans in distress around the world have been able to count on Ross Perot. In 1979, after Perot sprang his employees from a Teheran prison, the White House asked his help in gathering intelligence for its own mission to rescue fifty-two U.S. diplomats held hostage in Iran. "I sent my people back in," says Perot. "The only intelligence gathered on the ground for that mission was gathered by my people." When the attempt failed and several U.S. servicemen were killed, Perot set up a scholarship fund for the children of the victims.

In 1981, when Italian terrorists kidnapped Brigadier General James Dozier, the State Department asked Perot to pay a $500,000 ransom. Years later, an EDS employee found himself next to Mrs. Dozier at a dinner party. He asked her about the incident. Neither she nor her husband had ever heard about Perot's efforts to help them.

In 1986, Perot was identified as the secret money behind five unsuccessful attempts to ransom U.S. hostages in Lebanon—among them the former CIA station chief in Beirut. Perot's White House contact in the affair: former national security aide Oliver North, a central figure in the Iran-contra scandal. Perot also traveled secretly to Hanoi that year, at the invitation of the Vietnamese government, to pave the way for a visit by army general John Vessey. The two sides were to meet on Americans still missing in action, but the talks went nowhere. Perot takes setbacks philosophically. He has a motto to suit: "It's better to try and fail than not try at all."

Perot isn't at all hesitant to talk about his public role. In fact, his responsibilities as a civic leader, philanthropist, diplomatic emissary and political gadfly long ago began to supercede his role as a businessman. He seems to relish being a sort of national conscience. "I like to stir things up," Perot has said more than once.

In stirring things up, his guide is always how to do the right thing. But what is the "right thing"? For Perot, it's always personal—family values writ large. When Perot was considering whether or not to launch a rescue mission for his people in Iran, he had to think about the corporate impact. What if he himself were taken prisoner? What if the mission were bungled and some Iranians or EDS employees were killed? The potential penalties, in the form of legal liabilities and lost profits, could conceivably have meant the demise of EDS. Yet Perot had only one thought uppermost in his mind: These are *my* people and I've got to get them out. And he was *there* in Teheran.

Clearly when Perot confronts an issue, he moves with boldness, agility and determination. In the early 1980s, when Texas governor Bill Clements asked him to lead a statewide campaign against drugs, Perot spent more than $1 million of his own money on the effort. New laws were passed that permitted authorities to seize drug runners' assets; penalties for possession were stiffened. Perot even hired his own security detachment to guard undercover agents testifying against drug dealers in court.

More recently, when he was named head of the Texas Governor's Select Committee on Public Education, Perot picked a fight that would make him enormously unpopular. In football-crazed Texas, where it's not uncommon for a school of two thousand students to have as many as five football coaches, Perot prodded the legislature to enact a "no pass, no play" rule for high school athletes. Students are in school to learn, he said, and football in particular was interfering with that basic mission. The outraged chairman of the board of education called Perot a "dangerous man." Others branded him "un-American." Texas bumper stickers proclaimed: I DON'T BRAKE FOR ROSS PEROT. But as Perot sees it, the academic requirement is just plain good sense. In speech after speech, he has charged schools with wasting billions of tax dollars. "At a time when we're losing to international competition," he says, "why do we spend all our time worrying how much we play?"

In October 1987, during the stock market crash, Perot was a one-man Greek chorus of catastrophe. Perot himself had gotten out of the market months before, mainly because he could no longer understand the forces driving it. As the Dow Jones Industrial Average plummeted, *Newsweek* invited five world financial leaders (including Helmut Schmidt, former chancellor of West Germany, and Harvard economist John Kenneth Galbraith) to assess the damage. "It's outrageous that our elected officials say the fundamentals of our economy are sound," Perot declared. "*None* of the fundamentals are sound." There were dozens of radio and television appearances. "The market crashed because we're spending beyond our means," he told viewers on CNN's *Evans & Novak*. "The typical American spends all he makes, borrows all he can and has no safety net. If he lost his job, he would be an overnight pauper."

"How long can we continue our debt-spending binge?" he wrote in a *Washington Post* editorial. If we don't get together and raise taxes, improve productivity and lift ourselves up by our bootstraps, he warned, "we will be the first generation to take more than we gave, and fail to pass on a stronger country and a better life to our children."

Perot seemed to be everywhere, speaking out. Much of what he has to say sounds like common sense, and it probably is. But you wonder if things might not be more complicated than he thinks. Sometimes, listening to Perot talk, you feel you're in the presence of a marine corps Ronald Reagan—stern as steel, to be sure, but folksy and anecdotal, as if he lived in an idealized world as often as the real one. Implicit in Perot's worldview, as in Reagan's, is the notion that if he could raise himself by his bootstraps, so, too, can others, if only they would adopt the same values and the same positive outlook on life.

It's a wonderful way to be, but perhaps a merciless one as well. Perot's way of life is for the strong. Not everyone is or can be that way. Perot often seems on the verge of dismissing others who don't share his views, even as he so obviously cares for others.

* * *

DOING THE RIGHT THING. Speaking out. Thinking of our children. That Norman Rockwell print pinned over Perot's desk when he was a boy.

It's dangerous to overplay symbolism, but with Ross Perot there's no escaping it. The Rockwells that line the walls of the executive suite at EDS headquarters are personal and eloquent metaphors. Perot bought them, at great cost, not just because they represent an idealized America, but because they are *his* America. Or at least he thinks they are.

Perot's giving me the tour. Many of the paintings are famous, the stuff of Christmas catalogs and holiday cards. If the Museum of Modern Art in New York were to put aside its snobbishness and build a Rockwell wing, the collection would be full of gaping holes—unless, that is, Ross Perot lent some of his.

There's the painting of the young marine just home from war, regaling his friends at the local garage with tales of valor and showing off a captured Japanese flag. There's another of a sailor on leave, strung out in a hammock in his parents' backyard, his old dog asleep nearby. And then there's Perot's favorite, "Breaking Home Ties." A farmer and his son are sitting on the running board of an old jalopy. The boy's in a new suit; Dad's in his work clothes. It's a moment of parting. Junior is off to college. His suitcase is plastered with a big STATE U pennant. The father has his arm around the boy's shoulder; he's sad, the son's excited and expectant. To complete the picture, the family collie has his head on the youngster's knee. It's pure homespun 1940s, recession-era chic: families worn by hardship but united and happy. "That's the world I grew up in," says Perot, hands clasped behind his back, rocking on the balls of his feet as he looks at the painting. "I'm a product of that time."

For Perot, that's almost enough to explain why he is what he is. It's all right there: in the Rockwells, in the Boy Scouts, in Perot's devotion to his family and his country.

"I don't spend a lot of time thinking about myself," he says. "I'm not introspective. It's a terrible disappointment to people who interview me. They keep looking for these hidden meanings." They want to know what *really* makes Ross Perot tick. "But the truth is simple: 'What you see is what you get.' That's all there is."

You hear that refrain from almost everyone who ever knew him—his friends, his family, his associates. *What you see is what you get.* They use that exact phrase, as if it were a verse in the ballad of Ross Perot. It's tempting to accept that testimony at face value. But what do you really see when you visit Ross Perot? He is, after all, a man enthralled with folksy mottoes, slogans that come out so easily and lend themselves so perfectly to inscription in polished wood. He's enraptured by the prospect of challenges and overcoming adversity, preferably through adherence to a noble code. Yet, again, it had better be his code—or else.

People have different strengths and talents, which is one reason why it's so important to know yourself. Perot long ago learned who he was. His particular genius is in organizing and motivating others. As a leader, he is loyal and expects loyalty. He cares about issues that include drugs and education. He cares about families whose fathers, sons or husbands could be dying in faraway Vietnamese jails or enduring torture by psychopathic Red Brigaders. Yet if the people who are suffering were not in some way connected with Perot, the United States or some cause he holds dear, would he spring to their assistance with the same eagerness?

The Rockwells, again, hold the key. They are a mixture of sentimentality and austere morality. Perot likes the pictures for the very things that put off upscale art critics: their meticulous attention to realistic details, their idealized subject matter, their folksy accessibility. The paintings tell a story that we all can *share*, instead of posing questions that challenge our values or that can be interpreted individualistically. Perot believes in one way of life, one God, one form of government. He's a companionable absolutist for whom the real world, like Ronald Reagan's, is partly a world of his own making.

WHERE DID THOSE values take form? How did Perot come upon his code? If pressed, he will credit his parents and his upbringing in Texarkana, the dusty little town straddling the state line between Texas and Arkansas.

Bette Perot, Ross's older sister, sits in an office down the hall from her brother's at EDS. All the Perots work together, handling the family's fast-growing business interests. Young Ross Junior has an office not far away, where he deals with the family's land and oil ventures. His sister Nancy sits in another cubbyhole, buying and selling U.S. Treasury bills and liquid securities for her father's portfolio. Bette directs the Perot Foundation, channeling hundreds of millions of dollars into causes she and her brother deem suitable. She's direct, warm and no-nonsense. With her navy blue skirt and jacket and her white blouse, fastened at the neck with an antique brooch, she looks more a high school principal (which she once was) than a manager of one of the country's largest fortunes.

"Did you notice the motto on the wall?" she asks. "Ross and I chose it together."

A MAN IS NEVER MORE ON TRIAL THAN IN A MOMENT OF EXCESSIVE GOOD FORTUNE.

"We truly believe that. We truly feel we have a great responsibility to administer our resources in a responsible and intelligent way. To do that, we give grants to groups that will help the largest number of people. We want to help those who help themselves, but we also want to help those who cannot help themselves. We never just give money away. That doesn't work. That only makes the situation worse."

Like welfare? I ask.

"Like welfare. We are certainly not into that."

What the Perots are into is education, medical research, the arts—projects that they can control, that have an ultimate and concrete return. They have built hospitals, sponsored cancer research, donated land, buildings, libraries and study centers to Texas universities. Years ago, when New York's mounted police couldn't afford to keep their horses, Perot stepped in with a hefty check. More recently, Perot donated $10 million for a new symphony hall in Dallas, another $8 million for the Dallas Arboretum.

"We try to do a lot in the field of human needs," says Bette Perot. Especially for children. Bette says Ross is particularly proud of a program he sponsored in the Dallas public schools. Like many self-made men, he believes education is the key to opportunity. And he worries that minority students in Texas are becoming a permanent underclass, partly because they tend to fall behind white students early in the educational process. His solution, Bette says, was to spend $2.5 million to develop a curriculum geared specifically toward the needs of inner-city children in kindergarten through sixth grade.

"Most inner-city children start school without the rudiments of an education. They don't know their colors, or the alphabet, or how to count. They're at an immediate disadvantage. So you've got to get them up to speed. You've got to help them while they're very, very young, because by junior high school it's too late."

So how does this fit in with growing up in Texarkana? As Bette sees it, it *all* goes back to Texarkana.

"Ross believes our parents gave him the basis of his character, of his integrity," she says. "We grew up surrounded by grandparents, aunts, uncles, cousins. Everyone knew our parents, and everyone knew us. It couldn't have been a happier way of life for a child."

Ross agrees. "Everyone knew us," he says. He's sitting in his office, leaning comfortably back in his rocking chair, his place of repose for casual conversation.

A few years ago, Perot was quizzed by some management experts from the U.S. Navy. They wanted to know what sort of background and upbringing produced the best leaders. "It was an interesting phenomenon," says Perot. "Most of the fellas who rose to leadership positions—at least in the navy—came from small towns and small school systems. Now, logically, they shouldn't have done as well as people from larger cities or more privileged backgrounds. But they did.

"It's hard to generalize about these things, but the obvious conclusion is that you're better off growing up in a small town. Everyone knows you. Everyone knows your father. You're an individual. You're one hundred percent accountable." Failure cannot be hidden. Moral lapses cannot be concealed. Hard work and integrity are recognized. Achievement is rewarded.

What memories of his folks spring most immediately to mind? The answers are like snapshots from the family photo album, sepia-tinted but from the heart. Perot talks about his parents the way you hope your children will remember you. The way Rockwell sees family.

"They always loved me. They always encouraged me. They never pushed me," he says. "They were wonderful examples in how they lived their lives. They taught me that everyone is worthwhile, that everyone is equal.

"You see, during the Depression a steady stream of people came through Texarkana. They were just drifting around the country. We called them hobos. Today, they'd be called homeless. Most of them were pretty scruffy; some may have been dangerous. They were all hungry. Well, my mother always gave them something. She wasn't afraid of them. She was tiny, but she would always feed them and take care of them."

Ross Perot, Sr., sold cotton for a living. "Lots of people worked for him—most of them blacks—and he took a very personal interest in them. When they were too old to work, he took care of them. It was more than just sending money. Every Sunday, after church, he and I would go visit them, make sure they were all right. We'd sit on the front porch, side by side, and talk.

"That was a wonderful thing," says Perot. And it was, for in those days, in East Texas, blacks and whites didn't mix. "Dad didn't care what people thought," says Perot, and he's clearly his father's son. Taking the elevator up to Perot's office at EDS, I notice that he goes out of his way to greet employees by name, or at least give them a cheery hello. He disdains the perks that men in his position often lavish on themselves: the limos, the personal parking spaces, the private corporate dining rooms. "Feed the troops first," says Ross Perot. "The officers come second."

The mother and the hobos. The father and his employees. Lives of paternalism, concern and a willingness to lend a helping hand. "Those are very vivid memories," says Perot. "You see that as a child and you remember."

There are other images, other memories.

"Everybody worked in those days," Perot recalls. "I started

working when I was seven. I worked four hours a day after school, and twelve hours on Saturday."

When he was little, his father would take him to the fairgrounds every Saturday. There he would trade bridles, buying for four dollars, selling for five dollars. One of his first lessons in business, it seems, was watching his father in action. Ross Senior was a tough trader, skilled in dickering for the best price for his cotton, but he never pushed too hard. Buying cotton is a seasonable business, he told his son. If you squeezed a farmer too hard, he wouldn't come back to you the next year. It was the *relationship* that counted, the sense of mutual *trust* that developed between you and the people you did business with. Without trust, without mutual fair play, you couldn't build a business.

As he grew older, Perot helped his dad break horses. He sold garden seeds door-to-door and magazine subscriptions to the *Saturday Evening Post* (filled, of course, with the illustrations of Norman Rockwell). He delivered newspapers, on horseback, to the worst of Texarkana's slums. Characteristically it was a special deal he worked out with the managers of the local *Gazette*. Because the route was dangerous, and no one had delivered papers to that part of town before, Perot got to keep two thirds of all the money he collected, not just the customary third. When his boss complained that he was making too much money and tried to cut his commissions, Perot went straight to the publisher and demanded that the paper honor its commitments.

It did.

Perot pauses for a moment, and I ask about a story I'd read on the flight out to Dallas. It was not long after Christmas, and perhaps for that reason it struck a chord. Ross Senior worked hard, but the family was never wealthy or even especially well off. And so one Christmas Perot's father sold a favorite horse so that he'd have enough money to buy Christmas presents and a Christmas dinner. The story had all the elements of Charles Dickens's *A Christmas Carol*—love of family, fellow feeling, sacrifice. Even in the larger-than-real-life world of Ross Perot, it sounded a little too good to be true.

"It's true, all right," he says. "We all knew my dad loved that horse. It showed how much he loved us."

It's the same love Perot shows to his own family. It's the Norman Rockwell father scraping and saving to send his son off to State U. It's the principle on which Perot founded EDS and built it into a business giant.

THE LUNCHTIME RUSH is over at the EDS cafeteria. Only a few small groups of well-dressed workers hunch over healthy meals. Most eyes are fixed on Ross Perot. His are fixed on the lettuce-and-raisin salad on his plate. He stirs it with a fork.

No doubt about it. That's one *pathetic* salad. The leaves are brown around the edges, the carrots soft and soggy. Suddenly Perot is up and on his feet. He's making a beeline for the salad bar. The guy behind the counter sees him coming. Uh-oh. He ducks his head. Gets busy with his knives and forks. But he's lost. Nothing can save him. The founder is on the warpath and heading straight for him.

"Hey. Can you rustle up some more salad?" Perot's pointing at the wet, limp, pitiful remnants stuck to the sides of a big plastic bowl on the counter.

He's not giving orders. He doesn't sound mad. He just looks it. There's that expression of pained incredulity that says, "I can't *believe* I have to do this. I don't *want* to do this. I just want to eat my raisin-and-lettuce salad. But it's *terrible*. And if I don't do this, then everybody else will have to eat this crummy stuff. No way, José."

And of course the guy rustles up a new salad. Like, right away. Pronto. And it's a great big salad. A huge, beautiful salad, overflowing the bowl, crisp and cool and green and just full of big, juicy raisins. Trouble is, by this time hardly anybody's around to eat it. It's 2:30 P.M. Lunch is over. EDS is back at work.

Does that matter? No. For Perot, it's the principle that counts. Dagnabbit! For however long this cafeteria is open, my employees will be able to get a good salad!

That, in a nutshell, is the essence of Ross Perot's leadership. No detail is too small, no problem too inconsequential, to be undeserving of the boss's attention. Not that Perot doesn't delegate (he does, and extremely well), or that he's a busybody. (He isn't.) It's just when he sees a problem that needs attention, however small or large, he attends to it. Pronto. When he has to act, he acts.

There's a plaque outside Perot's office, yet another inspirational motto. Except for Perot, it's not just inspiration; it's a leaf from his daily operations manual:

EVERY GOOD AND EXCELLENT THING STANDS MOMENT BY MOMENT ON THE RAZOR'S EDGE OF DANGER AND MUST BE FOUGHT FOR.

Business associates are used to being phoned at home at three or four in the morning. They're accustomed to being summoned to Perot's home on Sunday afternoons. For all his folksy, down-home style, the urgency Perot injects into his work is palpable. He literally exudes energy; he glows with it like some human light bulb. When he's relaxed, sitting in his rocker as he is now, the glow is cozy, like being next to a warm fire. But woe betide those who get in his way when he's on the warpath. They get burned up.

"Ross isn't ever uptight," says his sister Bette. "He just makes everyone else uptight."

"I like to stir things up," says Perot. "My strength is in getting things moving."

"The most important thing about him is his determination," *On Wings of Eagles* author Ken Follett has said. "He's smart and charming and funny, but he's the most strong-willed man I ever met. I. suppose that's the reason he's such a successful businessman."

Perot and I happen to be talking about the secret of success.

It's not intelligence, he says. "Now this is theory, not fact. But the smarter people are, the more sensitive they are. And the more sensitive they are, the more they feel pain. I think people who are not as smart can endure a lot more pain and a lot more discipline.

They have this ability to lock onto a problem and pursue it through many difficulties. Perhaps *the* most common trait among very successful people is their ability to endure and persevere. Again and again, you will find brilliant business careers are built squarely on the rubble of early failures. Why, if you're looking for common traits, that just leaps off the page at you!"

That might sound like a rationalization, but I think of Dean Acheson, Truman's brilliant secretary of state, making a similar point to Winston Churchill in *Present at the Creation.* Academic or intellectual distinction, at least at the undergraduate level, was a poor index of ability, the two men agreed. Leadership lies in the bottom half of the class, was how Acheson put it. Tenacity and strength of heart were what counted.

In truth, extraordinary intelligence can be a liability. Someone of brilliance sees shadings that elude others. But by the same token, says Perot, he's troubled by ambiguity. He often sees too many sides of an issue to be decisive. He loses focus and strays from his objective. That saps his ability to lead, befuddles the vision. And when a business leader is not clear in his own mind, how can he be clear to others?

"I'll tell you one thing about Ross," says Bette Perot. "It's a trait that makes him very hard to work with at times, but it also allows him to be successful on very hard programs. He has what I call 'tunnel vision.' When he's working on a drug program, you can't get his attention on any other subject. He immerses himself totally. He will not let you pull him out. He will not dilute or disperse his energy on other things. He just has this tenacious appetite for the task at hand."

I ask Perot about patience.

"You won't find much."

Luck?

"A lot of that."

Creativity?

"A great deal of creativity."

Perot tells how he was once poked and prodded by a group of researchers studying the sources of creativity. "These people were probably dead wrong," he says, "but their theory was that there's a direct correlation between creativity and children who had to create their own entertainment."

I have a sudden vision of what's to come. Norman Rockwell couldn't paint it better. Little Ross at home, playing on the floor with makeshift toys of his own devising, building huts and forts and Indian encampments on a rug that his parents and grandparents made themselves as a fire burns in the hearth.

Well, not quite, as it turns out, but not too far wrong, either.

"When I was a boy, there wasn't anything I would passively watch," says Perot. (Translate that as TV.) "I built stuff. My mother would give me spools, bits of this and that I could make things with." Inevitably, as with most other things Perot feels strongly about, you get the feeling this will be summed up in a pithy little saying. And sure enough, here it comes. Ross just can't help himself.

"The creative part of the brain is like a muscle. If you don't use that muscle as a small child, it may be too late to join the weight-lifting team in college."

There was something I wanted to ask Perot. If he hadn't gone off on his own, if he had stayed at IBM, where he started out, how successful would he have been?

"Oh, not very," he says, with complete and disarming surety. "Thomas Watson [the founder of IBM] asked me that once. I told him I'd be somewhere in middle management, being asked to take early retirement. He laughed and said, 'I hate to say it, Ross, but you're probably right.' I would not have been successful in a big corporation. I'm too direct. Too purposeful."

"So success is in large measure a matter of knowing yourself?"

Perot swats this softball with relish.

"That's the most important thing in any management position." He's leaning forward in his chair to emphasize the point. "Know yourself. Know your strengths and weaknesses. Be realistic. If you fantasize, you're in trouble."

Perot's back on the link between intelligence and leadership.

"The most effective leaders are people who are not blessed with all the gifts of the world, because it's natural for them to reach out to other people and give them responsibility for tasks they themselves cannot perform. You'll find a lot of very smart people, even geniuses with truly great ideas, who never realize their potential because they don't know how to extend themselves through people."

And who's done that best? Who does Perot think are the most remarkable business leaders in the country?

He waves the question away.

"Oh, I don't know. Let's go to . . . Look, all leadership is treating people the way you'd like to be treated. You've got to treat people as individuals. You've got to treat them with dignity and respect. You've got to create a working environment where people feel needed and worthwhile and part of a team with a mission they can buy."

In other words, a vision.

"It's so simple. We teach a leadership course here at EDS. I wrote the book."

The book, as it happens, is an unpretentious little pamphlet called *Success in Business*. It's a compendium of "Rossisms," not to mention Maoisms, Bible-isms and Attila-isms.

Here's Ross on the meaning of success: "Success is doing something you enjoy and doing it well. The teacher, minister, elected official, military officer or missionary who is tops in his or her field is every bit as successful as the person who makes a great deal of money."

Note the absence of several hot jobs of the eighties. Like investment banker, currency trader or management consultant.

On pacing yourself: "Young people have to remember that a career is not a hundred-yard dash. It's a cross-country run, requiring you to produce consistently over a period of years."

On the importance of people: "The sooner you realize how insignificant you are, the brighter your career will be. Only when you surround yourself with men and women of greater capabilities than your own will exciting things really start to happen."

On leadership: "Leadership is trust. And never forget: trust is fragile. It can be lost in an instant. It must be re-earned each time you have contact with another person."

On failure: "Failures are skinned knees—painful but superficial."

On self-discipline: "Something in human nature causes us to start slacking off at our moment of greatest accomplishment. As you become successful, you will need a great deal of self-discipline not to lose your sense of balance, humility . . . and commitment."

For Ross Perot, success is never securely won. There can be happiness and completeness in life, but never satisfaction. There is that abiding restlesslessness that the Greeks called divine. There is that plaque outside Bette Perot's door:

A MAN IS NEVER MORE ON TRIAL THAN IN A MOMENT OF EXCESSIVE GOOD FORTUNE.

ROSS PEROT BEHAVES as if he were always on trial. As if all that he has built and all that is important to him might suddenly come tumbling down. It's not that he's paranoid, because he isn't. He's happy, at ease with himself, perfectly capable of leaving his work and his cares at the office. But somewhere, at the back of his mind, he is constantly on guard, less against some unseen threat than against a possible moral failing, or that first glimmer of inattention that is the sign of complacency.

Where does that constant readiness come from? Maybe it's the Texarkana upbringing. Maybe it's genes, an inbred determination never to let up and never to give in. Perot himself would probably call it a habit of wise vigilance. He insists that his life, like most, has been largely influenced by luck, which can go for you or against you.

"Life is a cobweb," he says, borrowing a metaphor from a speech he likes to give to local high school students. "The lines cross at funny angles. Whether you're successful or not doesn't depend on how good your plans are, especially those five-year 'strategic plans' business schools teach. Success depends on how you react to unexpected opportunities."

But what determines *how* you react when opportunity knocks? There's a classic anecdote that figures large in Perot's "myth," as he cheerily calls it. After graduating from high school, Perot enrolled in Texarkana Junior College and promptly got into a spat that would foreshadow the rest of his career.

As Perot tells the story, the college board had just voted to move to a new facility that would be built at a one-square-block site elsewhere in town. Perot, then student-body president, thought it was a mistake. How could the college grow? He looked into the decision and discovered that the land was owned by a crony of one of the board members. Perot never went public with the information, but he threatened to. He got beaten up in the process, had his teeth kicked in, as he puts it. "But I had 'em," he says, "and they knew it."

The college soon after bought a hundred-acre parcel of land outside the city. Today, Texarkana Junior College boasts a verdant campus and an enrollment of two thousand students, instead of the two hundred in Perot's day. "I took on the establishment," Perot says. "I took on the board, and I won."

Now that's a strange statement from a man whose ambition at the time was to secure an appointment to the U.S. Naval Academy at Annapolis. Never mind that this kid from a parched and landlocked little town in East Texas would yearn for the navy. What's odd is that this firebrand who got his kicks challenging authority would hanker for the regimented authoritarianism of the military. Equally odd is how Perot came to choose the academy. Even as a youth, he seems to have followed his own counsel. Yet in making that early key decision, he was swayed by the example of another.

"There was a boy I admired who lived down the street from us," Perot explains. "A brilliant, outstanding young boy. Came from a wealthy family. He had gone to MIT for a few years, then won an appointment to the Naval Academy. He told me all about it. I wanted to go.

"And I did go," Perot says with that swift, cocky smile of a man who has always known how to get what he wants. But what did he want? The navy, or the challenge? Or was it the recognition, not only that Perot was among the academic elect, but also the social equal of that wealthy boy next door?

Getting into Annapolis wasn't easy. Perot had been badgering Texas congressmen for an appointment to the academy for several years. Then, in 1949, a retiring senator was cleaning out his office. He asked whether any last things needed to be done. "Well, sir," an aide replied. "There's an unfilled appointment to Annapolis."

"Anyone want it?" the senator asked.

The aide remembered Perot.

"Well, give it to him."

The story is told and retold in the press, often as an example of what you might call "made luck." But Perot isn't quite sure it's true. He got the story through the senator's aide, he says, but once the senator's daughter wrote him a letter, saying that her father's decision was hardly so casual. "I always make it a point to tell the press both versions," Perot says with a laugh. "They always tell the old one."

But that's hardly the point. What impresses me is Perot's punctiliousness.

Perot thrived at Annapolis. "I loved it. It was a good education. I liked ships. I liked everything about it." He was president of his class in both his junior and senior years. Though no whiz academically (he finished in the anemic lower middle of his class), he excelled by another measure. Annapolis in those days had a system where midshipmen were evaluated three times a year by their peers. "Your classmates would evaluate you, your instructors would evaluate you, military officers of the academy would evaluate you," Perot says. In all twelve of those evaluations over four years, Perot was ranked first out of a thousand every time but one.

Then came another of those tests, another choice of whether to speak up or shut up. Perot was chairman of the honor committee when the son of a famous and enormously influential man ("I can't tell you who") was caught stealing, a clear breach of the academy's code. Because of the cadet's father, there was pressure to let the charges slide. Perot marched into the superintendant's office to complain. "Anyone else, and he'd be expelled," Perot said. He then announced he would resign if the academy didn't uphold its principles.

"You know you're right, don't you?" the superintendent replied.

Perot acknowledged that he did, and so did the academy.

"The guy was gone," Perot says. "I did the right thing."

Perot went to sea on the destroyer *U.S.S. Sigourney* in 1953 as a fire-control officer and "just about everything else you can think of," he says, including ship's chaplain. But by 1956 he was looking to get out. "It was a great experience. I got to see the world, twenty-two countries, seventeen seas and oceans. But I had trouble with the promotion system. It was based almost entirely on seniority. I wanted a situation where the more I did, the more I got."

As it happened, Perot was then an assistant navigator on an aircraft carrier. "My job was to coordinate all the activity going on around the ship. We'd have maybe twenty escort ships. There were submarines beneath us, destroyers all around us, ammunition ships. All day and all night there was this incredible activity. Ships coming alongside, aircraft taking off and landing, radar surveillance. This all had to be coordinated on the bridge, and I happened to be the guy who was doing it."

Because aircraft carriers are big and comfortable and the center of fleet activity, it was common for groups of traveling VIPs to helicopter in for a visit. And it was while Perot was on duty one day that some brass from IBM came aboard. Perot was working his razzle-dazzle and caught the man's eye.

"Who's that?" the captain was asked.

"Oh, he's just someone who's leaving the navy," he replied.

And so, Perot says, the man came over. "How would you like to interview with IBM?" he asked.

Perot looked at him a little blankly. "Mister, I don't even know what IBM is. But you bet. Sure, I'd like to come talk to you."

IBM was then just getting started. The computer age had barely dawned. Though Perot's knowledge of computers was limited to the relatively unsophisticated electronics used in the navy, that was enough for IBM. "It was like signing on with the Wright brothers," says Perot. "In those days, anyone who had ever touched an airplane was a pilot. It was the same with computers. I didn't know much, but in the land of the blind, the one-eyed man is king. I was at the right place at the right time."

Perot made the move from the navy to IBM with barely a break in stride. The jobs were similar. Both were highly regimented. There was a dress code: blue suits and ties simply replaced a uniform. There was the same sort of crew-cut, team-oriented esprit. There was hierarchy, for even in its relative infancy IBM was big, with full divisions of trainees, second vice-presidents, assistant vice-presidents and so on up through the ranks. Yet there was also a critical difference: IBM offered incentives for high performance. Execs who remember Perot tell of how, almost from day one, he marched in and asked to be assigned to the toughest accounts. He figured if he could handle them, he'd earn more, get noticed and move up fast.

He was right. Move up fast he did. He logged in commissions so quickly that he began meeting his annual sales quota earlier and earlier every year. By his fifth year, in fact, he managed to sell it out by January 19, scarcely three weeks into the new year. That was a mixed blessing, for while it demonstrated Perot's salesmanship, it also made the company less willing to assign him any additional accounts. He was already earning more than many of his bosses, which at IBM was not done. As a result, Perot's only reward for showing his mettle was to be able to sit around and contemplate the THINK signs scattered around the office. Perot would occasionally bring a bathing suit to the office. He had plenty of time to stroll over to the YMCA for a dip.

Some people might find that relaxing, even consider it a reward for a job well done. Clean desks, efficient minds. But Perot hated it. He hated to stroll. He hated even more the idea that your work could leave time for a midafternoon swim.

Perot wanted out, and he had the germ of an idea. The computer industry was maturing quickly. Technology was getting more sophisticated, and computers were being used for more and more complicated tasks. Things were getting to the point that IBM's customers wanted something more than just hardware. They wanted help in using it. They were asking for software tailored to their needs. They wanted people who could train them to use their equipment and set up integrated computer systems. They were looking to *rent* their expertise. In short, they were talking computer *services*.

Perot proposed that IBM set up a new division to do just that. He would set it up. He would run it. But Big Blue demurred. Not our market, they said. Too risky. That was it for Perot. He was down, depressed. He went into a psychological tailspin. One day, working off some of that spare time he possessed in such abundance, he went to have his hair cut.

In the pantheon of American business, that haircut ranks with Steve Jobs's lunch with Paul Berg. It was a watershed. For as he sat there leafing through a back issue of *Reader's Digest*, Perot came across a little filler quote that he says changed the course of his life. It was from Thoreau's ode to self-reliance, *Walden*, and of course it was made to order as a slogan: "The mass of men lead lives of quiet desperation."

There's nothing inherently inspirational in that. In fact, it's one of the most pessimistic sentiments ever to seethe on paper. But Perot didn't see it that way. For him, it resonated with hope. You can be sure that if Perot hadn't stumbled across Thoreau, he would have seized upon some other, equally well crafted slogan. But at the time, *Reader's Digest* gave him the courage to be different, to do the right thing and find new purpose in life. It crystallized the idea to go out on his own and found EDS.

EDS HEADQUARTERS in Dallas. The castle of the computer commandos. Rolling lawns and hills, screened in by fences and shrubbery. It looks more like a country club than a multinational corporation. There are tennis courts, a pool, a golf course—all for the exclusive use of EDS employees, Perot's corporate family. They are encouraged to use the facilities during the lunch hour, after work, on weekends. Aggressive inclusiveness, in the cosmos of Ross Perot and EDS, is a virtue and no liability.

Visitors arrive along a sweeping drive, past the security forces at the main gate, past the guard dogs, past the pathways blooming with flowers and the satellite dishes beamed at the sky. And then the citadel itself: a soaring monolith of white stone and black glass. Flags snap at a battery of mastheads, one for every state and foreign country where EDS does business—seventy-five of them. There's a reflecting pool and an unending expanse of greensward, as if EDS were the nerve center of a government intelligence agency in Washington.

That, at least, is the impression. It's not unlike CIA headquarters in Langley, Virginia. The same imperious white buildings. The isolation amid the greenery. The flags and the telecommunications apparatus. The great seal in the cavernous, echoing lobby, and the motto: THE TRUTH SHALL MAKE YOU FREE.

The resemblance doesn't end there. The double glass doors slide open, and there's the same sleek marble lobby. A huge bronze statue of John Paul Jones stands on one side. On the other, a great eagle, the company bird, alights on a mule or some other hapless beast—it's hard to tell what. But there's no ambiguity about the motto emblazoned in bronze letters on the wall: EAGLES DON'T FLOCK; YOU HAVE TO FIND THEM ONE AT A TIME.

Welcome to EDS. The home of the free, the brave and the hungry.

It's an interesting contrast—Perot the compassionate family man and corporate provider, Perot the corporate commando. EDS may be the only company in the world with a paramilitary capability, whose commander in chief gets calls from Oliver North and has a voice in U.S. security councils. EDS no longer hires heavily from the military, as it did in the days of Vietnam (partly because Perot believed it was incumbent on the company to help vets who helped their country). But the squeaky-clean image of the services remains.

Brisk young men and women, neatly groomed in navy suits and charcoal pinstripes, stride through the lobby. No one ever seems to stroll. They're energetic, snappy heartland Americans. They keep their hair short; not a mustache is to be seen.

Perhaps that's why EDSers have so often been called clones of Ross Perot. They aren't really, for this is as much a function of their job as the founder's example. EDS has been entrusted with secret, proprietary information. Not national secrets, or anything like that, but everyday *personal* information, very important to you and me and the country. It therefore helps to look like the family banker.

EDS is a computer services company. That means, for a fee, it acts as sort of a nationwide data-processing department for literally thousands of U.S. and foreign companies and government agencies that don't want to buy their own computers or train a staff to use them. EDS furnishes the computers, programs them, operates them. EDS employees work full time on the premises for the life of the contract. The customer's employees need only to be taught to prepare records and make good use of the information EDS subsequently provides.

And what kind of information does EDS process? All sorts of sensitive things: payrolls, for one. Bank savings and loan accounts. Insurance claims. Pensions. Medical benefits. Disability payments. Social security. Medicaid. Medicare.

Electronic Data Systems, a $4.4 billion behemoth employing forty-four thousand people, handles between a fifth and a quarter of all Medicaid and Medicare claims. It handles virtually all such benefits in some states, Texas and California among them. The company maintains the personnel and pay records of more than 11 million U.S. military men and their dependents. It practically runs London's public transportation system. It has been a pioneer in computer-aided engineering and plant-floor automation. So who benefits from EDS's efficient operation, and who gets hurt when there's a hitch? You and me, pretty directly. Ross Perot is not merely a symbolic patriarch of the nation; he's got a father's duties in fact, right there in the bowels of EDS.

Art Trevino, a short, compact young man bristling with factlets about EDS, has been standing by to give me a tour. The Dallas regional operations center is a three-story complex next to the main building, all white stone and arches, a sort of mini–Kennedy Center. And it hums. An almost inaudible but persistent trembling as billions upon billions of bits of information flood into the center via telephone and satellite from around the world.

The place is *full* of computers, all busily chewing up the information as it comes in and spitting it back out in a microsecond. Dispatching the okay on Aunt Matilda's wages in Peoria so she can go out and buy the week's groceries. Processing Uncle Joe's Medicaid application so that he can have that hip operation in Los Angeles. But it takes an act of faith to imagine these flesh-and-blood transactions. The humming, thrumming EDS operations center looks like nothing so much as a set for Stanley Kubrick's *2001*.

Scarcely any human attendants are needed. In the basement of the complex, twenty mainframes, guarded by a security man in a Plexiglas booth, whir away in an empty room, white acoustic tile from floor to ceiling. The computers are blue and gray, IBM's colors. "They hold at any one time seventeen-hundred-billion bytes of information, the equivalent of twelve libraries of Congress," Trevino says in hushed, tour-guide tones. "They are kept cool by twelve twenty-ton air conditioners that maintain the room at forty-eight percent optimal humidity."

We ascend to another floor and . . . *it could be the War Room at the Pentagon.* In half a dozen glassed-in, darkened amphitheaters, the computer commandos strut their stuff. A huge electronic map of the United States dominates one wall. Batteries of computer terminals glow dimly in the semidarkness. Squads of commandos sit at the controls, zapping data across the country, watching vigilantly as EDS's computers work silently and swiftly.

This is what Trevino calls the Network Service Center, linked into 150,000 EDS terminals at similar operations centers in 49 states. The watchers are waiting for some hitch to occur somewhere in the system. Then they scramble into action, like worker ants in a nest, rushing to shore up a crumbling wall or foundation, keeping the edifice upright and sound.

And as they watch, they are watched. Television cameras scan their every move. And behind them stand senior watchers, the safety net, making sure there are no mistakes, no lapses of attention. They could be monitoring an *Apollo* moon shot. Total commitment. The essence of EDS.

ROSS PEROT DOESN'T own EDS anymore. He sold it to General Motors in 1984 for $2.5 billion in a merger that was supposed to revolutionize the American auto industry. Perot's entrepreneurial flair wedded with GM's financial resources would put the Japanese to rout. *Newsweek* featured the story on its cover: GM REINVENTS THE WHEEL. *Business Week* touted ROSS PEROT'S CRUSADE as a "one-man campaign to make GM competitive again." Corporate raider T. Boone Pickens called it "the best acquisition GM has made in my lifetime."

On its face, it did indeed look like an ideal combination. In that first blush of euphoria, Perot and GM chairman Roger Smith dreamed of transforming the way America does business. They talked of a second Industrial Revolution. Neither man put much stock in the hazy notion that the country was becoming a "service economy." As they saw it, the United States of the twenty-first century would still have to produce goods, ranging from cars and computers to dishwashers and vacuum cleaners. But Smith and Perot agreed on something else: Competition from abroad was getting tougher. U.S. companies, if they were to stay on top, couldn't keep using the same old manufacturing techniques conceived at the beginning of the century. Better systems had to be found, and computers were the key.

That's why GM was so keen on EDS. It wanted Perot's computer commandos to charge into GM, take the hundreds of IBM mainframes scattered in dozens of auto plants around the country and pull them together into an efficient, integrated system. When a new car rolled off an assembly line in Pontiac, Michigan, the nearest Firestone plant would know to send over a new set of tires. There would be dramatic savings in costs; parts would be available on time and in precisely the quantities needed.

It was less clear what EDS would get out of the deal. One attraction, certainly, was the business. With GM under contract, the company's revenues quadrupled to $4.4 billion within two years; its work force nearly tripled. It was set to enter the 1990s as a titan of the electronics and telecommunications industry, nearly on a par with mighty IBM. But for Perot personally, the incentive was far less tangible. He clearly didn't need the money. In giving up control of the company he built, he got something he prized even more highly: a fresh challenge, a new sense of purpose.

That might sound a bit hokey, but, as Perot puts it, "What do you do when you think you've done it all, and then somebody shows up and asks, 'How would you like to build the Panama Canal, the Eiffel Tower and the Empire State Building and, if you've got any time left over, a couple of pyramids as well?' You do it."

And why not? GM was a new world to conquer. Here was a new chase, a fresh start, an unclimbed mountain. There was a dash of idealism and a patriotic call to arms. As Perot put it to David Remnick, a reporter for the *Washington Post*, "Former GM chairman Charlie Wilson had always said, 'What's good for General Motors is good for America.' So, what better thing to do with EDS than try to help make the best cars in the world? It was a mission."

Perhaps predictably, given that grand but hazy goal, the mission was a fizzle. Perot once described himself as the grain of sand that irritates the oyster to make a pearl. At GM, Perot produced only inflammation. Anger and frustration, on both sides, soon dispelled the initial good feelings. "Revitalizing GM," Perot complained less than a year into the partnership, "is like teaching an elephant to tap dance. You find the sensitive spots and you keep poking."

The trouble with that strategy is that GM's brass didn't like being poked, especially in public. In the niched-away, cloistered world of the automakers, where everyone belongs to the same churches, sends their children to the same schools and lives in the same neighborhoods around Cranbrook or Bloomfield Hills, Perot was a parvenu. He didn't join the club. Worse, he wasn't an insider—a cardinal sin at GM.

Perot was aghast at how slow GM was to change with the times, to streamline its operations to compete against Japan. He was openly critical of the company's tendency to try to solve problems by throwing money at them. He accused GM management of being more concerned with "perks" and bonuses than with performance. And when his criticisms on the inside weren't listened to, he grew more strident. He went public, just as he did at Texarkana Junior College and Annapolis. He bypassed Smith and other top GM executives and took his suggestions for improving the company to the board of directors. He talked to reporters. He visited plants and dealerships around the country and spoke to the people he believed to be most important to GM's future: the assembly-line workers who actually built the cars. In short, he did what he had done all his life. He stirred things up, tried to do the right thing, as he saw it.

And after a time, GM got tired of Ross Perot. Just weeks before the GM board was to vote on a hefty bonus for its top management (in a year when profit margins were slumping and layoffs were imminent), Perot was kicked out. In an extraordinary move, the GM board voted to pay him $740 million for his 11 million shares—twice their market value—in return for a written promise to curb his tongue. Perot would retain his title as "founder of EDS," but he'd have no further say in GM. The payment was widely described as "hush money," but if so, that would have been a fatuous hope on GM's part. Ross Perot has never been good at keeping quiet.

The GM episode is revealing on several levels. For one thing, it points up the sharp differences between entrepreneurs and managers. George Gilder, in *The Spirit of Enterprise*, writes that entrepreneurs, like artists or scientists, live to create new markets and ways of seeing the world. "They are limited only by the compass of their imagination. They bring new things into the world in a process that they themselves control." Managers, by contrast, do just that: "manage." They maintain what has been set in motion and what they've come to control. They can be every bit as talented, enterprising and even creative as the entrepreneur. They can improve and run what an entrepreneur has built, often better than he would himself. Witness John Sculley's contribution to Apple Computer. But on the whole they lack the entrepreneur's quick reflexes and adaptive abilities. And they seldom possess the creative hunger to start something from scratch or radically reshape an existing order.

Ross Perot and Roger Smith, archetypes of the two breeds, might thus have been destined to split. "Ross Perot in GM was like a rhinoceros in a crockery shop," says Kirby Warren, a business professor at Columbia University. "Smith is the typical bureaucratic manager. He knew that GM needed to change, but he wanted to move slowly and carefully. Perot wanted to move immediately and dramatically. He wanted to completely rebuild GM."

The exceptional quality here is that sense of urgency, the preference for decisive action. People like Perot are natural fighters. They have to keep pushing. "They feel they are living on the edge, that their success will not last," says Harvard psychoanalyst Manfred de Vries. That's certainly true of Perot. Remember the slogans about life on the "razor's edge," the admonitions that one is "never more on trial than in a moment of excessive good fortune." Nothing is ever good enough, or as good as it might be if only we tried a little harder, worked a little longer, built a slightly better team.

In Perot's case, another compulsion was at work as well: a moral one. We've seen it before: the need to speak out, to do the right thing. "Entrepreneurs have an overriding concern to be heard and recognized, to be seen as heroes," says de Vries. In this sense, the debacle at GM gave Perot a broader focus. It became a symbol of the decline of industrial America, a case study of a national crisis of leadership. And so the task of changing GM from within became, for Perot, the game of prodding it to change from without.

As Perot sees it, somebody had to go out and sound the alarm, and it might as well have been him. It's all part of the empire builder's compulsion to *take responsibility*.

"I'm in control here," declared an imperious Alexander Haig the day Ronald Reagan was shot. He was wrong, perhaps fortunately for the nation, but his mind-set makes for a useful comparison. Like Haig, Ross Perot is always stepping in, making waves, trying to get things moving, even if it's not really his business or his area of expertise.

If that makes him seem part zealot, part petulant voice in the wilderness, part prophet, he doesn't mind. "I don't care what other people think of me," he says, as long it gets them to focus on the issues. "I'm in a unique position," he says. "I've got the freedom, the independence and the platform to communicate. I'm in a position to call attention to the problem."

Let's define the problem.

For Perot, the truly *big* problem is the loss of national resolve, symbolized by America's slumping industrial competitiveness. GM is thus only part of a bigger crisis. "Detroit is just one industry. All our big corporations are adrift," says Perot. "We've lost the steel industry and the electronics industry as well. We've got a huge trade gap and a two-trillion-dollar budget deficit. If we don't get our economic house in order, if we don't get our biggest companies back on their toes, the competition—Japan, West Germany and Asia—is going to tear our heads off."

Listening to Perot talk, another Rockwellian image springs to mind, this time the old army recruiting poster: UNCLE SAM WANTS YOU! The trumpet has sounded, and somewhere, deep inside, I feel as though I'm supposed to spring out of my comfortably upholstered chair in Perot's office, run down the hall and enlist in the nearest "Save America" crusade. It's too bad that sounds a little snide, because Perot's *right*. It's obvious that the country is stumbling. But how does a nation get back on its feet? How do you translate grand theories into the day-to-day operations of a company?

The answer, says Perot, is leadership.

"You see, the one thing I've always stressed at EDS is that the product is key. To stay in business and make money, you've got to have the best product and the best service. And how do you do that? The only way to be the best is to work through other people. It all gets down to leadership, how you deal with your people and how well you treat them."

Ross has said all this before, with a bow to Mao, Attila and his own Texarkana upbringing. Do unto others as you would have them do unto you. Treat your workers with dignity and respect. Create a working environment where people feel needed and feel that their work is worthwhile. Where there's mission and vision, excellence follows.

"All I ever wanted at General Motors was to build better cars, the best in the world," Perot once told *Newsweek*. "GM spends $3.6 billion a year on research and development, more than any other automaker in the world, and they're not first or best in anything. It used to drive me crazy. And the funny thing is that they could have changed without spending more money. All they had to do was capture the full potential of the people in the organization."

And how to do that? Perot spelled it all out in a *Fortune* magazine article: "How I Would Turn GM Around." His message was to create a more egalitarian, team-oriented corporate climate.

"Starting today," he wrote, "GM's relationship with the United Auto Workers will be a team relationship, not an adversarial one."

"Starting today, in order to build the finest cars in the world, GM will listen to its customers, listen to dealers who sell cars, listen to the men and women who assemble cars in its factories. From now on, the customer will be king!"

And so on.

Perot wasn't saying anything publicly that he hadn't said at GM. Trouble was, GM's managers and directors had never been prepared to do anything about it.

In fact, GM's brass was thunderstruck at Perot's temerity. Consider his suggestions for saving money. The practice of rewarding managers with hefty bonuses while laying off assembly-line workers in a bad year was offensive enough to Perot. Worse was the day-by-day frittering away of shareholders' money. His solution: among others, to cut perks at every level. Close the subsidized executive dining room (gasp!), where top GM execs ate vastly more opulently (and inexpensively) than the poor prols who ran the assembly line and paid full value for their lunch in the company cafeteria. Cut out limousines. Lease the teak-lined boardroom that took up an entire floor of GM's New York headquarters and was used only one afternoon a month. Do away with the heated garage where top excutives kept their cars while other workers trudged through the snow in the company parking lot.

These might seem like piddling moves, Perot explains, but they're important as symbols. "What does it say when you give executives privileges far beyond the guy on the assembly line?" he asks. "It says, 'We're not in this together.' It says, 'I am special; you are ordinary.' " How can you get people to pull together in such an inherently adversarial climate?

The painting "The Spirit of '76," with its ragtag band of marchers, seems to catch Perot's attention—though I had a sneaking suspicion that that was just part of the performance. "You know, the whole episode reminds me of Valley Forge," where Washington's troops, camped for the winter, were short of food and warm clothing. Had Washington fed his officers better than his troops, Perot says, the Continental Army might have dispersed, ending the Revolution.

But that, he adds, is just what's going on at GM and all over the country.

Given Perot's convictions, I wonder fleetingly if it wouldn't have been more honorable, and effective, to have stayed on and worked harder to change GM from within. I also wonder how realistic Perot is being. GM, one of the biggest companies in America, is no EDS that will respond immediately to its founder's directives. It employs some eight hundred thousand people; millions more work for its suppliers. It's fine to say, then, that "starting today" GM's service problem must be solved "immediately." Nothing's going to happen "immediately" at GM or any other large factory in America, or almost anywhere else in the world, for that matter. Perot's call to arms sounds strident, unrealistic, autocratic—not to mention a shade naïve. Surely not even Perot believes that, "starting today," the autoworkers' union and GM management are going to forge an amicable partnership.

There's also some question whether Perot's "family" principles really apply in practice. It was interesting to read some of the letters to the editor that followed Perot's *Fortune* article. One former EDSer wrote that "not even Perot's EDS does what he says GM should do. Bureaucracy exists at EDS just as it does at GM. Perhaps Perot should have gotten out of his office and talked to the little people." Another writer noted one of the ironies in Perot's prescription for GM. "For all his talk of 'teamwork' and 'unity' in the workplace," the man said, "the 'troops' in EDS have the reputation of being the most overworked and undercompensated professionals in the data-processing industry."

Surely the problems surrounding GM are more complex than can be described in a few gung-ho sayings. And while Perot boasts that EDSers receive their rewards while still sweating from their labor, the evidence suggests the picture is more ambiguous. According to one employee, it's not uncommon for EDS staff to put in sixty- to eighty-hour weeks without getting an annual raise. The company requires its people to pay for a sizable portion of their relocation and training expenses; what's more, the portion paid by the company is rolled into a promissory note. If an employee leaves the company before three years are up, he gets whacked with the debt. It's apparently not uncommon for EDS managers to take advantage of this system to deny their people raises and bonuses—the better to meet their own profit objectives and enhance their "performance." Burnout and employee dissatisfaction, not surprisingly, run as high at EDS as anywhere. An employee who expressed some of these reservations to *Fortune* did so anonymously. The reason: If he were identified, he said, he'd be fired.

Does this give the lie to Ross Perot? Not really; it merely underscores the obvious: Things are more complicated than can be reduced to slogans. And yet we *need* the slogans. We need their simplicity and their clarity, the punchy sense of mission and esprit they can provide.

When given the choice between simplicity and complexity, great leaders invariably opt for simplicity. Men like Perot are energizers. They offer direction and inspiration. Their message becomes fuzzier with amplification; the more magnified the vision, the dimmer it is. Perot can't promise that EDS would be a model corporation, free of the bureaucracy that he rails against at GM. He can only offer the possibility of it, and then only at the margin and for perhaps a brief time. An exceptional entrepreneurial success, perhaps, can stay exceptional for only so long. In the meantime, Perot can only continue to do what he's always done. Be himself. Play the maverick. Push for change.

GM clearly would never have listened; Perot is too much of a firebrand, too outspoken and too intent on fast results. He would have drowned. GM proved too big even for Ross Perot, and perhaps EDS is, too. Maybe GM's buyout came along at the right time. Perhaps it's the moment for Ross Perot to move along.

I asked Perot, if he had to do it over again, whether he would speak out in the same way, and so lose once again the company he built from scratch.

"You bet," he says. "And I wouldn't have to take a Gallup poll to decide. You've got to stand by your principles. You've got to do what's right. If you want to get to the core of Ross Perot, that's the core."

CHAPTER FIVE

THE SPIRITUALIST

◆

WASHINGTON HAS a lot of days like this: so gray and wet that the granite and marble government buildings blend into the pavement and slide soundlessly into reflecting pools.

It's February and cold. The few people on the streets late this Saturday night are just that—on the streets, homeless. The rain has driven them off the steam grates where they usually take refuge and into the shelter of the subways and the national monuments: the Lincoln Memorial, Constitution Hall, the Smithsonian. And this is where James Rouse finds them.

For two, maybe three hours, he and his wife make the rounds. They bring coffee, sandwiches and conversation, the last a special gift for people without television or much companionship. But this is no mission of mercy; professional social workers are out in force, bringing their own supplies of sustenance. Rouse, in a sense, is there on business. For the founder and chairman of the Rouse Company, the country's biggest and richest privately held real estate development company, has embarked on a quest. He has set up the Enterprise Foundation to house the homeless and transform America's run-down inner-city slums into comfortable, affordable homes for the poor.

That's why Rouse is on the streets of Washington. Like a chief executive walking the factory floor, he's getting to know the system and its product. He is ever alert. He wants to meet the people he hopes to help. When he returns to his headquarters in Columbia, Maryland—the celebrated "new town" of seventy thousand people he raised out of farmland two decades ago—it's with a renewed sense of mission. The urban poor constitute the fastest-growing social class in America, Rouse says, and he wants to stop the trend. He approaches the task with evangelistic fervor. There is no profit in housing the poor, but like a father with a crippled child Rouse doesn't care: He wants him to get better. He will do everything he can to make it happen. America *can* eliminate poverty, perhaps by the year 2000.

LOVE. IF YOU had to say what drives James Rouse, seventy-four, that would be it. Love like a father's love, who expects the best, forgives the worst, accepts the flaws and offers guidance and structure.

"Love" is a family word and a word of God, and Rouse is a family man guided by his God. To hear him and his staff at the Enterprise Foundation tell it, we are all one big family and we had better wake up to our familial obligations and take care of our brothers and sisters. Not just in the usual sense—gifts to the church, donations to United Way, dollars to the street people. But an all-out effort to rid American cities of slums and get people off the grates.

It seems almost too good to be true, this bald-headed, grandfatherly tycoon wandering around in the rain. It doesn't fit our image of the successful businessman, let alone a businessman as hugely successful as James Rouse. But then, there are many sides to James Wilson Rouse, this self-made yet selfless mogul who has personally reshaped the way we Americans live.

Rouse, after all, built Columbia and invented the shopping mall as an alternative to unsightly suburban sprawl. He coined the term "urban renewal" and spearheaded the drive to revitalize the nation's inner cities after the race riots of the 1960s. *Time* magazine once heralded him on its cover as America's "Master Builder," a visionary entrepreneur who created Boston's Faneuil Hall, Baltimore's Harborplace, New York's South Street Seaport—the "festival marketplaces" that brought fun and vitality to urban renovation.

You have only to walk through Harborplace to appreciate the scale of Rouse's success. Fifteen years ago, the city's waterfront was a 250-acre moonscape of broken wharfs and abandoned warehouses, the crime-infested ground zero of a modern-day Dresden. Now, *Time* describes it almost lyrically: "From early morning until well past midnight, natives and tourists by the thousands turn Baltimore's Inner Harbor into a continuous celebration: milling on the promenades, perching on the bulkheads, dangling feet in the drink, flirting on the benches, lounging in the outdoor cafes, ogling, jogging, strolling, munching, sipping, savoring the sounds and sweet air."

What a cavalcade. What an adventure! To follow Rouse around one of his creations is to step into his particular vision of heaven. He shakes hands with the proprietors of foodstalls, sniffs the flowers, beams at tourists, peeks into antique shops. Soon you discover that some of this man's success lies in his ability to be rejuvenated by his work. It happens at every stage of a project: The conception stage, where "feasibility" is ignored and imaginations run wild. The planning stage, where flourishes are not sacrificed to economics. The construction stage, where Rouse springs about the building site with all the enthusiastic vigor of Santa giving instructions to his elves. And then, finally, during the opening ceremonies, when the unending festival of his marketplace begins.

Small surprise that Harborplace is the linchpin of Baltimore's renaissance. It created thousands of jobs. It draws more visitors than Disneyland. It triggered a rebirth of the city's entire downtown. Most important, it lives up to Rouse's criterion of the city as "a warm and human place, with diversity of choice, full of festival and delight."

Rouse has always displayed an extraordinary ability, as *Time*'s enchanted editors put it, to "blend showmanship and rock-solid business sense into a magnetizing force in our cities." He's worked his wizardry not with government assistance but through a hard-headed drive for profit. Along the way, he made himself and those around him wealthy. He gathered an empire of loyalists united by his philosophy of service, quality and vision. Rouse was one of the first to combine what used to be antithetical goals—respect for the environment and real estate development—and to do it with style and human understanding.

Like Ross Perot, Rouse has grown both as a legend and as a sort of national patriarch. Once obsessed with creating the perfect environment for nurturing healthy, average Americans—building Columbia as a "perfect city" for middle-income families—he has now refocused his concerns. Helping the poor and the homeless won't enlarge his fortune. But Rouse, a man who never used money to "keep score," as the cliché goes, couldn't care less.

"This is by all odds the most important work I've ever undertaken," Rouse says of his six-year-old Enterprise Foundation. So far, the foundation has raised more than $250 million for low-income housing projects in twenty-seven major cities. That's not enough to solve the problem; there are roughly eleven million substandard housing units in America, and Enterprise has fixed up only a few thousand. But raw numbers aren't the point. The goal is to become a catalyst for change. The foundation gives grants and low-interest loans to community groups for specific renovation projects. Rents must be kept low, so that families won't be priced out of their homes after the work is complete. It offers technical and business advice to urban renovators, and for some projects helps secure favorable bank financing by offering to guarantee the developer's borrowings. Most important, "Rouseketeers," as cynics sometimes call the dedicated bunch, are urban evangelists and grass-roots organizers. They prod neighborhood and church groups to organize and throw themselves into projects sponsored by the foundation. They have lobbied Congress to provide tax breaks and other incentives for companies contributing to the cause. They back hundreds of neighborhood outreach programs and sponsor community groups in cities where the foundation operates.

All these activities are coordinated in Columbia. Here, information is gathered and stored. Here, grand schemes for urban renewal are drawn and conceived. For the first time, grass-roots organizations in cities across the nation have someplace to go for help. Momentum for change is building. To test the effectiveness of its programs—and set an example for the nation—the foundation has targeted Chattanooga, Tennessee, as a model city. The goal: to wipe out the city's slums within ten years, without displacing the residents.

There's something quintessentially American about that dream. Perhaps it's the jaunty boldness. Remember the heyday of "American ingenuity," those glorious times when the merely difficult could be done tomorrow; the impossible would take a little longer?

Rouse and the Enterprise Foundation epitomize that "can do" ethic. They're picking up the ambitious and as yet unrealized theme of the Great Society: social equality through equal opportunity. But Enterprise people don't believe it's all up to the government. They believe that private initiative, with some government financing, can crack the problem. They are off and running. And Rouse, the force behind them, has pledged to devote his life to the effort—and to do it with love.

IS ROUSE NAÏVE? It's almost impossible not to think so. There's a story about how *60 Minutes* canceled a sequence on Rouse after Harry Reasoner visited him at home, found a stuffed bear in a bathroom and decided he was just too good—too *uncontroversial*—to be true.

Tales of Rouse's otherworldliness are legion. Preoccupied, he's been known to walk into doors and stick his finger, instead of a key, into the ignition of his car. In the late 1960s, when his firm faltered in an ambitious expansion plan, Rouse personally guaranteed the Rouse Company's debts, at the very real risk of personal ruin. Courageous but, some say, foolhardy. The view from the trenches, where the foundation's real work is done, can be especially ambivalent. One city planner, left to work out the details of an extensive inner-city rehabilitation program after Rouse swooped in for a morale-boosting speech, voiced a common complaint: "I love him, but he doesn't always know what we are doing. Now that the grand scheme is in place, he talks as if the project were done. But the big job is still ahead of us."

Skeptics have questioned the value of his big projects, the festival marketplaces. Some say they are no more than community fun houses that add little to a city's economy. Others point to a string of failed projects; in Richmond, Toledo and Flint. Still others blame him for what they call the "boutiquing" of America. "Every old-town area of the country feels the same these days," says John MacArthur, publisher of *Harper's* magazine. "Whether it's New York's South Street Seaport or San Francisco's Ghirardelli Square, they all have the same generic look. They all have river walks, ye olde arcades, cute little restaurants and retail outlets with names like the Smuggler's Table and Fisherman's Wharf." Rather than encouraging diversity, he concludes, Rouse and his ilk promote a "horrible uniformity."

If so, it's the uniformity of success: flattery by imitation. Rouse, in any case, is anything but naïve. Those who know him well speak not only of his evangelistic zeal but of his hardheaded realism. "To suggest that he's naïve is completely wrongheaded," says David Maxwell, chairman of the board of the Federal National Mortgage Association (Fannie Mae) in Washington. "To accomplish anything great, you have to reach. Jim Rouse reaches far, and he may occasionally overextend himself. But when he says the whole city of Chattanooga is going to have fit housing in ten years, there's fire in his eyes and fire in his belly. He combines the skills of a mortgage banker with a visionary's passion. If anyone can get the job done, he will. The country needs more people like him."

Certainly few Americans have had the impact Rouse has. "What Baron Haussmann (the eighteenth-century city planner) was to Paris, Rouse has been to the United States," Henry Reuss, former chairman of the House Banking, Finance and Urban Affairs Committee, once told *Baltimore* magazine. "For the breadth and scope of his influence on the nation, I think Rouse is unexcelled."

"Rouse is the epitome of the great leader," says John Gardner, head of Common Cause and a former secretary of health, education and welfare. "He's an evangelist in the lay sense. He feels very deeply about what he is doing, about the country, about the seriousness of the problem he's tackling. Most important, he has the most uncommon gift of being able to inspire people to pursue, enthusiastically, the goals that he and they share."

My own impression, as a banker and a management consultant before becoming a journalist, is that the Enterprise Foundation is one of the most creative—and savviest—so-called charitable organizations ever. Rouse has gathered together a band of sharp, young, unapologetically idealistic but experienced executives who know Wall Street as well as skid row. And while most pro bono outfits rise or fall on the ebb and flow of charitable contributions, the Enterprise Foundation has worked out a self-perpetuating scheme of financing.

It's an ingenious concept. The Rouse Company made its reputation building innovative marketplaces in down-and-out urban centers. Generally they thrived, attracting lots of visitors, reviving downtowns and making pots of money for both the cities and the developers. Rouse is putting that same principle to use today, but with a twist. As a subsidiary of the Enterprise Foundation, he's set up the Enterprise Development Company, a for-profit, tax-paying real estate group modeled after the Rouse Company, to build malls and downtown "festival" projects in dozens of cities across the nation.

The aim is to make profits—big profits that will be used for a novel purpose. Once the development company is firmly established, Rouse says, it will channel money into the not-for-profit Enterprise Foundation. The foundation will, in turn, re-lend the money to neighborhood groups to renovate homes and build low-income housing. He figures the development arm of the Enterprise group will eventually funnel between $20 million and $30 million into the foundation every year. "I wanted," he says, "to build a development company that would make a *gigantic* fortune—not for the rich, but for the poor."

Rouse, in a moment of flippancy, thought of naming the foundation the Robin Hood Trust. The idea is apt: Take from the rich, give to the poor; though in this case, "taking" is earning, and "giving" is a calibrated mechanism for kicking the poor a rung or two up the socioeconomic ladder.

As Rouse sees it, good housing is the ticket to opportunity and the means to self-improvement. Like most self-made men, he disdains the dole. He wants to help people help themselves. And how to do that better than to give people a fresh start, to eliminate the *dis* in *disadvantage?*

Rouse is trying to make the American dream live for the bottom stratum of society. The starting point in any good and productive life, he believes, is the peace and security that comes from having a safe, clean home of your own to return to after a hard day's work. With the house comes a sense of dignity and well-being. With that comes the desire for more—more money, more respect, more education. In a word, progress. The essence of the American dream.

NANCY ALLISON HAS been Rouse's secretary for twenty-eight years. She's a model of efficiency, juggling phone calls and appointments and sending a steady stream of work to her two assistants. James Rouse is a busy man, she readily concedes. But ask her to describe her boss, and she'll nod her head toward the immense sheet of glass that sheathes Rouse's office and makes a mockery of the word *private*. Like Ross Perot, James Rouse doesn't close himself off, and he's not into the trappings of power.

I'm sitting in that office now. One wall is covered with photos: Robert Kennedy, Lyndon Johnson, Robert McNamara—people who sought Rouse's advice on housing programs and fashioned enduring relationships. Beyond a broad expanse of windows, spreading outward from the office tower that is Rouse's headquarters, is the parklike setting of Columbia: woods, footpaths winding along narrow roads, lakes and hills and the houses all hidden in trees. Flashing outside his door like a beacon for an all-night hot-dog stand is a red-and-blue neon tugboat, the cheery logo of the Enterprise Development Company. The tugboat came from one of the company's first projects—Waterside, in Norfolk, Virginia—and it's emblematic. The development group is the financial tugboat for the foundation, and the foundation is the tugboat for pulling the poor out of poverty.

I've come to find out more about this remarkable septuagenarian, and why he's taken on his crusade. In his signature tweeds, Rouse hardly cuts the image of the real estate mogul. He looks more like an amiable college professor, short and a little plump, or the generous proprietor of a candy store, wanting—and able—to please. He bounds from behind his desk, runs his hand over the top of his head, as if to brush his few sparse hairs out of his eyes, and shuffles piles of papers to make room for the two of us at a circular conference table. This is not to be an audience with the prince.

Rouse goes out of his way to make you comfortable. Yet he wastes little time getting to his point.

As Rouse sees it, America treats the poor shamefully. We profess to be a caring people and an open society, yet we insulate ourselves from the hardships of others. We believe our own myth, that America is a beacon unto nations, and that our laws guarantee freedom and equal opportunity. We have a welfare system that cushions the poor and the unemployed (and, arguably, perpetuates a permanent underclass). Yet we have few programs designed to change the equation of want. We don't try to *improve* the lives of the poor, or create opportunities for social advancement so that the poor can hope one day to not be poor.

That's the critical failing, says Rouse. The Enterprise Foundation grows out of his belief that the United States has fallen behind every advanced nation—even the Soviet Union—in meeting the "human needs" of its poorest citizens. "The free enterprise system—our system—just doesn't do the job," he says. "But it can. It can."

Rouse makes a persuasive case. "How many people in this country live in poverty?" he asks. He brushes aside any quibbles about definition. "Roughly thirty-six million. That's twelve percent of the population, and the number's growing by about a million a year. We act as if we don't see it, or as if the problem weren't growing. But poverty is changing our society."

He's armed with lethal statistics. "Of young black men seeking work in America, forty-eight percent are unemployed. A young black man graduating from high school has about an even choice between work or a life on the hustle. He must live, either way, so what's it going to be? Alcohol, drugs and crime, or a legitimate job? Given the barriers, you might ask whether he has a choice."

If the problem were confined to the inner cities, it might be more easily overlooked. But it's not confined, and cannot be ignored. Trendy magazines write about America as the newest "Third World" country; some U.S. slums rival the worst of Calcutta. CBS not long ago aired a controversial documentary on the near-total breakdown of the black family. *The New York Times* reports that the City of New York, the country's biggest urban landlord, has over the years accumulated a stock of run-down apartment buildings housing nearly forty thousand people—a population roughly the size of Pasadena, California. The city had hoped to stem the tide of urban decay by seizing the buildings from delinquent landlords. Instead, *The Times* reported, most of the tenants of these buildings were actually *worse* off under the city's management. Living conditions nosedived as overworked, underfinanced and simply negligent municipal housing authorities stopped inspecting and maintaining their buildings, even while spending an astronomical $280 million in 1987 to house homeless families in expensive but substandard mid-Manhattan hotels. Presidential candidates nibble at the edges of these problems, trying to find a vision that might galvanize the country and get them elected. But none succeed. Meanwhile, the problems of poverty, crime and social disaffection keep getting worse, like a cancer gnawing at the nation's innards.

"Think about it," says Rouse. "Why is it that we have become the most violent nation in the world? Private police in the United States now outnumber public police. We have more people in jail, per capita, than any country in Western civilization. Think of that. Think of this judgment on our society."

Rouse is a traveler. Wherever he goes—Tokyo or Calcutta, Denver or Detroit—he says, "Take me to see the worst." Like the realist painters, he sees the details of the landscapes he visits. He wants to know what he is up against. He wants to see the ugly; it keeps him focused on creating beauty. He shakes his head, as if shaking off frustration. "We are unique in this world." While millions of poor people live in squalor, abandoned by society, Americans are "anesthetized," says Rouse. "The conditions we see in the United States don't exist in any other industrialized free society. Not in Western Europe, not in Japan. There's no worse than the South Bronx or, say, parts of Brooklyn or Harlem."

Rouse's hand is on his forehead, scratching, digging at the world's ills. He has said this a thousand times, in speeches at Rotary

Clubs across the country, in testimony to Congress, in interviews with journalists.

I mumble something about the Great Society and unmanageable problems. Rouse cuts in, his outrage sparked, "It can't be unmanageable!" Why? "Because it's so well managed in other countries." He rubs his head and continues. "The thing that is of transcendent importance is that the national heart, soul and spirit is not troubled about the condition of the poor. Not troubled because the wealthy and the powerful don't know the lives of the poor. They drive through the bad part of town on the way to the airport, but it's a glassy-eyed look. They've seen it too much on the news, in the newspapers. The only thing, the *only* thing that has awakened the mentality of America is the homeless. There is something about seeing a man sleeping on a grate, or reading about a mother and child slowly dying on the streets, that has a different emotional appeal than reading about the poor."

Rouse pauses to let the images sink in, then says, "But something can be done. We are the richest country in the world, with the greatest problem-solving capabilities in the history of man. There are answers, a whole lot of answers."

He is a forceful evangelist. Even before he cites the gloomy statistics he knows by heart, I know something about the world he wants to change. I've listened, sympathetic yet impotent, to my child's South American sitter tell harrowing tales of her life in the Brooklyn apartment building she cannot afford to leave: nightly robberies, shootings and drug deals. My own neighborhood, a fringe encampment in Harlem, is getting too expensive for lower-income blacks and Hispanics (but certainly no safer for the self-styled "pioneers" who have ventured in). As Rouse goes on, I see myself grabbing for the *New York Times* real estate section each Sunday morning. I scan for signs that prices in my neighborhood are going up. With gentrification under way, could my bit of square footage be worth a little more?

To Rouse, such thoughts are almost obscene. Gentrification—the process of changing a neighborhood from lower-middle class to upper-middle class, mostly through renovations that pave the way for rent increases that in turn prompt landlords to sell off their units as co-ops and condos—forces poor people out of their homes and puts growing numbers of the marginally housed out on the streets. While the ranks of the poor swelled from 25 million in 1975 to 36 million in 1986, demolition and gentrification have whittled down the housing supply. What's more, says Rouse, the bulk of the houses available to lower-income or poor families used to be provided by the "trickle down" effect. "New housing was built, people moved up as they grew older and more prosperous, and their old houses became available for people at the bottom of the income scale."

Needless to say, housing no longer trickles down very far. With demand rising and supply falling, prices have soared. The median U.S. home cost roughly $150,000 in 1988, and rents (for those who can't afford to buy) have risen apace. And that's just an *average* price. What is a poor family, or even middle-income family, to do in a city like New York, where a cramped one-bedroom apartment in a decent part of Manhattan costs $220,000? People like me, with salaries good enough to dream of buying but not good enough to buy our dreams, find "bargain" neighborhoods. We scout the outskirts of established neighborhoods, buy "handyman" specials and hope that others like us will follow. In a word, we gentrify—and so the cycle repeats itself.

But why does James Rouse care what I do, or about the people at the receiving end of that vicious cycle? After all, Rouse is no Pollyanna, wringing his hands over sick children and wounded animals. He's a captain of industry, a real estate megamogul whose festival marketplaces and downtown projects paved the way for much of the gentrification he now worries about. Is Rouse having an old-age angst attack, trying to curry favor in the hereafter (like a Rockefeller or a Carnegie) with a sudden burst of philanthropy?

Hardly. Rouse's friends say there's no paradox here, no struggle between conflicting sides of a divided personality. As early as 1947, Rouse and a couple friends rehabilitated a slum area near Johns Hopkins in Baltimore. A few years later, Rouse crisscrossed the country as a member of the World Federalists, dedicated (before the Korean War broke out) to promoting world peace through disarmament. As a member of Dwight Eisenhower's task force on housing programs, he helped draft America's basic blueprint for urban renewal. Along the way, he wrote an optimistic treatise called *No Slums in 10 Years*, a prescription for aggressive social action that clearly shows up in his thinking today. When Rouse created Columbia, he did it as an outspoken supporter of integration. He hired and housed lots of minorities. He hoped his city, built during the worst of the 1960s race riots, would be a model of friendly coexistence, as it largely turned out to be. And in 1973, the year the first families—low-income and wealthy, black and white—moved into Columbia, Rouse happened to help a Washington, D.C., church group buy and rehabilitate a couple of run-down buildings in a project named Jubilee.

For Rouse, Jubilee was a turning point. It became the seed of the Enterprise Foundation. Rouse's experience in the inner cities over the years convinced him that there were solutions to poverty in America. Many have said that, but the thing about Rouse is that, believing there were solutions, he felt obliged to act. "We can't just stand wringing our hands at this dreadful condition at the root of our society," he says. So now James Rouse the empire builder, the brilliant financier, fund-raiser and developer, is out to change the world. He wants to do everywhere what Jubilee Housing is doing in Washington.

WASHINGTON IS A small city built on grandiose plans. Its grid of numbered and lettered streets are crisscrossed on the diagonal by boulevards named for the states of the union. So that when logic says you're at Twentieth Street and N, you're really at Massachusetts Avenue and New Hampshire, also known as Dupont Circle, and the hub of Washington's trendiest set.

Gentrification has swept the area and is no longer even a relevant term. Two decades ago Dupont Circle was Washington's Haight-Ashbury, the drugs, sex and rock-and-roll capital of the Capital. But the old brownstones, then more than a little seedy, have been renovated, co-oped and condoed by the same people who would live on New York's Upper West Side, Boston's Back Bay or San Francisco's Pacific Heights.

Dupont Circle may be a microcosm of the forces that have helped create America's low-income housing crisis, but for Rouse it's also something vastly more personal. Nearby, almost out of place amid the embassies and consulates lining Massachusetts Avenue, stands the Church of the Savior. This is Rouse's church. The congregation is small and unconventional: a mere 140 members, ministered to by a courtly, Old Guard, silver-haired son of the South named Gordon Cosby, a renegade intellectual who believes in the idea of mission. This tiny group of parishioners who call the big, awkward brownstone their headquarters decided during the worst of Washington's hard times to do something about the terrible living conditions of the city's poor. They founded Jubilee Housing.

If great enterprises start small, it can be said that Cosby and his flock of concerned Christians were the inspiration, even the model, of Rouse's Enterprise Foundation. "If I had to look back at the most powerful influences in my life," says Rouse, "Gordon would be there. Partly because of his values and the precepts by which he lives, but also because he started this thing called Jubilee, which in turn started me."

This "thing called Jubilee" was Rouse's introduction to grassroots low-income housing. The name springs from the biblical solution to the problems of wealth and poverty. Every fifty years, during the year of Jubilee, the people would cancel their debts. Farmland was to be returned to the families who had originally owned it; IOUs would be wiped out. Life could begin afresh. The socially solid congregation of the Church of the Savior contemplated nothing so radical, of course. But they did believe they could help the poor to a fresh start by providing them with decent homes.

So it was that Jubilee Housing was born. It began modestly enough, buying and fixing up two, then three, now nine apartment buildings housing some 350 low-income families. For all its diminutive scale, the project is arguably one of the most innovative urban renovation projects in the country. It's a wholly private, nongovernmental initiative. Its success owes as much to the sweat equity of the tenants as to the generosity of outside benefactors. Most important, it's a model of forward thinking. Jubilee has its own job center to help people moving into the projects find work, pay the rent and, ideally, save enough money to step up the socioeconomic ladder. It set up a day-care center so that mothers heading single-parent families could work. There's even a low-cost "cooperative" health clinic and a "compassion committee," where people fallen on hard times can get a little help.

None of this has worked ideally, or even always as intended. But it has worked, and it has done so without losing money or depending on charity. Rouse couldn't help but notice. After all, he had told the founders of Jubilee that what they wanted to do was impossible. "I told them there was nothing they could do for the poor," Rouse recalls. "I was a very discouraging counselor. I said, 'You're too little. You don't have the resources, the staff or the organization.' The wisdom of the day was that you needed a big program, backed by the federal government or at least the city."

Happily the people at Church of the Savior didn't listen. They went ahead with Jubilee, and in 1973 bought their first two apartment buildings—the Mozart and the Ritz. When no bank would finance the deal, they asked Rouse to put up the money. He did, $200,000, against "my most considered better judgment," as he puts it today. "I went to see the buildings. They were a disgrace. The mailboxes, the doors, the pipes had been ripped out. The elevators didn't work and the halls were filled with garbage. I gagged when I walked in the doors."

Today, he considers it the best investment he ever made. In defiance of conventional wisdom, Jubilee made a go of projects that not even Rouse would take on. It proved, he says, that there are answers to the problem of poverty. "A whole lot of answers."

HOW ROUSE CAME to join the Church of the Savior, and why he got involved in Jubilee Housing, is key to understanding the man. The values they represent run like a current through his career, carrying him along and channeling his thinking on everything from Columbia to the basic concepts behind the festival marketplace.

The Church of the Savior entered Rouse's life one spring day in 1963—the day he picked up the telephone and called Gordon Cosby, out of the blue. "Jim had just read *Call to Commitment*, a book written by a member of our congregation," says Cosby. "It touched something in him, so he called up and invited my wife and me to his house. We didn't talk about anything in particular. He's the sort of man who just wants to get to know you, which is a lot more than 'What can you do for me?' "

The book, in fact, was a biography of Cosby. It told of his call to the ministry and commitment to a faith that was impressed upon him early. His father was a Baptist, his mother a Presbyterian, and they hit on a novel way of handling the ensuing religious tangle. "I get the first," said his father. "You can have the rest."

So Cosby was a Baptist. By the time he was fifteen, he had met his future wife (the daughter of a Baptist pastor) and was preaching several times a week to a black congregation in Virginia. After a whirlwind education at Hampden-Sydney College, he married and, in 1942, joined the army and saw action in Normandy and the Battle of the Bulge. "A lot happened to me there," Cosby says. "I saw too many men die, most of them unprepared for what they were up against." One incident affected him especially. During the height of the D-Day fighting, a frightened soldier came by Cosby's tent. It was the morning before a major assault on German lines, and the boy believed he was going to die. "Don't give me any stuff about philosophy or theology," he said. "Just talk to me about God." Later that day, Cosby learned that the soldier had indeed been killed. That experience crystallized the deep unease Cosby then felt about a church that, as he puts it, "wasn't doing its job, that concerned itself less with genuine faith than with something that America settles for as religion."

Cosby's dream, formed during the war, was to start a church in Washington. He saw it as a nondenominational, interracial parish concerned with "understanding faith." And in 1947, following that dream, Cosby founded the Church of the Savior. By the 1950s, it had grown big enough to move into its current headquarters on Massachusetts Avenue. "Understanding faith," in time, came to mean more than passing the offering plate and holding occasional bake sales to raise money for this or that cause. It came to mean "making the church real" by making a difference in people's daily lives. It meant, ultimately, taking up a cause like Jubilee.

ROUSE AT THIS point had not entered the picture. During the 1960s, as the Church of the Savior explored the spiritual frontiers, he was buying up farmland in Howard County, Maryland, halfway between Washington and Baltimore. It was to be the site of Columbia, his bold experiment in urban living.

Perhaps Rouse's obsession with creating a "perfect city" was a way of re-creating the world of his youth. Rouse loves Maryland; it has always been his home. He grew up as the youngest of six children in Easton, a small town on the eastern shore of Chesapeake Bay. It was, Rouse once said, "big living in a small-town way." Easton is famous for horse farms and lush countryside, and by all appearances his family lived a prosperous, happy life in a rambling Victorian house a stone's throw from the water. Rouse remembers a boyhood of canoeing, swimming and oystering. Most of all, he remembers that big white house filled with life and laughter.

All that was cut short when Rouse was sixteen. First his mother died of a stroke, then his father nine months later of cancer. The bank foreclosed on the house, the family split up. That was 1930, at the start of the Great Depression. After living for a time with a sister in Hawaii, Rouse came back east and went to the University of Virginia on a scholarship, but left after a year to study law at the University of Maryland at night. He parked cars and worked as a legal clerk at the Federal Housing Authority to pay tuition. Four years later, in 1937, Rouse graduated from law school. Soon, he and a friend founded the firm that was to eventually become the Rouse Company. But at the beginning, he was a mortgage banker, not a developer. That gave him an ironic and sobering power: to take away other people's homes, as his had been taken from him.

Rouse, an immensely thoughtful and almost reticent man, doesn't talk much about that phase of his life. He moved on toward development, but with a twist. Rouse has never failed to maximize the profit on a project, but he prefers to do it by making people happy, perhaps as happy as he was in Easton, by giving them hopes that approach an ideal rather than settle for the merely acceptable.

Which, of course, is what he set out to do in Columbia. By 1963, Rouse had bought up fourteen thousand acres of rolling Maryland countryside, a property almost the size of Manhattan. He saw Columbia as a social experiment. It would be America's first successful "new town." It would be the future home of one hundred thousand people of all incomes, races, religious denominations and lifestyles. Like Cosby and his church, Rouse cared about the big questions. What is the optimum size for a city? A village? A neighborhood? A school? How do you build a better city?

Rouse tackled the job in the same way that he invented the suburban shopping mall. He looked at what had already been done and tried to do it better. "First I went to Sweden and England," Rouse says. "They were doing pioneer work in urban living. I thought we would find something that would be useful in thinking about our city—say, in the realm of education, psychology or sociology. But I didn't. Their projects were all developed by the usual 'experts'—architects, engineers, bureaucrats, finance people." None seemed to have thought hard about what the people who would live there would like. "It was a real shock."

Rouse may privately have welcomed the setback. It was liberating. It meant that Columbia could be his own. He would be exploring new territory. To get the innovative thinking he wanted, Rouse called together his own panel of experts—fourteen leading authorities in fields ranging from education, public health and psychiatry to communication, law and urban planning. Over the course of four months, they met every two weeks for two days and a night, struggling with the core questions of the optimum city life.

The results initially fell far short of Rouse's expectations. He didn't want his experts to think about what was feasible. He wanted them to "think biggest," to "consider the optimums." What was the best of all possible school systems, the best health system? Should you put a church on every street corner, or can man and God relate on turf shared by several religious groups? What do you do about police, unemployment, child care and libraries? What are the sources of victory, joy, happiness and light? What causes depression, worry and failure, and what can be done about it? You would think people would rejoice at such an open-ended inquiry. Instead, Rouse says, "It was hell. I couldn't get them started. They only saw the obstacles."

To help guide the discussion, Rouse gave his experts a copy of a talk he planned to give at the University of California at Berkeley. It was called "The Purpose of a City," and in it Rouse argued that the "highest purpose of a city was expressed in the biblical injunction: 'Love the Lord thy God with all thy heart, and with all thy soul, and with all thy mind . . . and . . . love thy neighbor as thyself.' "

There's that word again. Love. It was to be what Rouse calls his "North Star" in planning Columbia. "Think of what that would do," he says, energized by the idea even now. "It would direct our thinking about the city in such a different way. We would have to be concerned with creativity and the best possible development of people. This would be a city of tolerance and compassion, without prejudice."

Rouse's colleagues were not convinced. The morning before the first of the panel's meetings, two of his most trusted advisers arrived to talk strategy. "Whatever you do, don't talk about love," they told him. "These are very sophisticated people. They're academics; experts in their field."

"Okay," Rouse replied. "I promise not to embarrass you."

But that night's session was a disaster. One after the other, Rouse's experts told him that his plans for Columbia would never work. "It was a real lesson in the vested negatives by which we all live," he says. And Rouse told them so. " 'I'm going to be a very rude host,' I said, 'but this is the worst night I've ever had. You've all been called in to think about a new city, you've all accepted, you're all being paid, and all you can say is that it's foolish.' "

The group turned in for the night, but the next day was no better. Rouse told his wife, "I feel as if I'm walking through mud. There's no morale in this at all."

The stalemate went on for two days. Finally, about eleven o'clock on a Saturday morning, it broke. Chester Ratkin, a sociologist then at Penn and now at Columbia, by nature a thoughtful and quiet man, leaned across the conference table and addressed his colleagues. "You know," he said, "we are missing the whole point of this. We are being asked to think about how you nourish *love*."

Rouse delights in this story. It was his vindication. Finally somebody had used the "L" word, and no one sneered. "The whole mood changed. From then on, it was the most exciting group meeting. Straight through, every day."

At this point, it's probably time to say the obvious: James Rouse the empire builder is James Rouse the spiritualist. He attacks the same problems as the clergy, but differently. Like Cosby, who seeks to make the church "real," Rouse wants to infuse the real with spiritual value and happiness. He seems almost to be taking a leaf from Aristotle: "The goal of the city is to make men happy and safe." And how to make a perfect world? Imagine the physical relationships that would make it up. Put together a team of "experts on life" that would, as Rouse exhorted them, systematically "think about the optimums."

Soon the ideas began to flow. Excitement about Columbia built. What had earlier seemed impossible or frivolous now seemed achievable and reasonable, even inspired. Rouse's "experts on life," as he called them, bought into his credo, the slogan that he has plastered all over the offices of the Rouse Company and the Enterprise Foundation: "Feasibility will compromise you soon enough."

They talked about the basic problem of a city: full of life and intensity, but too big and too impersonal. The solution: Divide Columbia into a series of "villages," clustered around a "downtown" of shops, cinemas and offices. They wanted to avoid the too-often-bland uniformity of the suburbs. There would be row houses, apartment buildings and detached houses for low-, middle- and high-income families. There would be Cape Cods, Colonials and modernist glass boxes. Communities would be linked by minibus routes (ten cents a ride), and there would have to be a terrific library. (Columbia now has the largest lending library in the state). A third of the city would be open space: woods, bridle paths, golf courses, tennis courts, community swimming pools. Someone thought that the Washington Symphony might make Columbia its summer home. (It did.) They planned for a hospital (linked to Johns Hopkins, one of the best medical centers in the world), created a model educational system (Columbia's schools boast one of the highest college-admission rates in the country), took steps to open a college (there are now three) and a music conservatory. They debated whether Columbia could afford to set aside fifty acres for a wildlife preserve. (They decided it could.) They even concerned themselves with where the children's playgrounds should be located. (The best places, they sensibly concluded, would be where the sun shone longest, so that they would be free of snow at the earliest possible moment.)

This style of thinking captures the essence of James Rouse. When you look at the optimums instead of the possible, when you consider the human instead of the functional or the convenient, it's easier to nourish love.

PERHAPS THAT'S WHY Rouse picked up the telephone that spring day in 1963 and called Gordon Cosby. He, too, was part of Rouse's plans, though the developer at this point probably had little inkling of the effect the minister would have on his life.

Not long after that initial meeting, Rouse asked Cosby for help on Columbia. He wanted him to work with a task force that was investigating the religious life of the new town. Rouse was looking for ideas that bucked the standard "church on every corner." He believed we shouldn't have a church for every faith, Cosby says. Rouse thought that would be divisive, that the church ought to foster community feeling and inclusiveness, not the exclusiveness that often accompanies ecumenical distinctions. "If you were trying to build a city where it's easier for people to love one another, what would you do?" Rouse kept asking.

Cosby's answer was interfaith centers jointly owned by Catholics, Jews and Protestants. Each religion retained its values and traditions, but shared office space and programs. That wasn't an entirely new idea, of course, but at the time it was still novel. "More important," says Rouse, "it raised the level of tolerance for differences throughout Columbia." In very fundamental ways, Rouse's approach to Columbia has helped change the way its inhabitants think about one another. He used real estate, architecture and urban planning to attack prejudice and fear.

Rouse's relationship with Cosby grew. He and his wife started going to the Church of the Savior's School for Christian Living. Under Cosby's ministration, prospective members of the church had to study as long as two years before joining the congregation. Cosby himself taught the course, in which he tried to express the ideas he had been struggling with all his life. The textbook was called *The Recovery of Life's Meaning.* For Rouse, already a profoundly religious man, it became something of a second Bible. Its message was powerful—and difficult.

"It asserted a very simple Christian theology, a strategy for living," says Rouse. "It said that all people are born to be co-creators with God. That they are His instruments for working His will on earth. It's a very simple concept. But demanding."

Demanding, because buying into that theology compels you to *act.* To become *responsible* for carrying out God's will on earth. And Rouse bought into the creed. It helped give him purpose, meaning and definition in life, not only out of obedience to God, but also to himself. For if you mean to live a good life, and define a good life as living consistently with a moral code that includes love and helping your fellow man, then you are committed to making that belief a part of your daily work.

That goes a long way in explaining why Rouse has been able to accomplish so much. He is literally acting with God on his side—a source of enormous self-confidence. What's more, he believes himself lucky. Unlike Oral Roberts and his evangelist ilk, who see themselves as God's anointed on earth (singled out to spread His will, to, in effect, *be* God on earth), Rouse thinks of himself as just *being there*—to help God out, be His hands and feet, so to speak, His co-creator. For unlike Christ, whose kingdom was not of this earth, Rouse has carved out an empire that more than a few secular empire builders might envy. Through the Enterprise Foundation, he has set out to adopt the poor and the homeless so that, with luck, they can have a little more happiness on earth and maybe a little more faith in the ephemeral kingdom.

Rouse doesn't talk about this responsibility. It's his own. Nor does he preach (though he became an elder at the Church of the Savior and, later, a lay minister). He simply carries out the task: co-creation as an act of love.

ROUSE THE SPIRITUALIST, Rouse the businessman. Are they such different roles? Like Steven Jobs and Ross Perot, Rouse has been able to combine philosophic conviction with tremendous organizational and motivational ability. That gives him the strength to carry out his particular vision of the world.

"Profit is not the legitimate purpose of business," he likes to say. "The legitimate purpose of business is to provide a service needed by society. If you do that very well and efficiently, you earn a profit, perhaps an enormous profit. But if you forget that, and approach business as profit instead of as service, you get lost in the manipulation of markets, hype and all sorts of different things that distract you from your primary goal—again, offering a service that is needed and yearned for by society."

And the festival marketplaces, his Faneuil Hall? Were they a "service"?

Rouse thinks so. "For a good many years, people didn't really like their cities." Rouse is talking about the flight to the suburbs, the burned-out hulks many cities became after the riots of the 1960s. "They didn't want them to be empty or all chopped up. They wanted them full of life: neighborhoods, a sense of community, free association, diversity. A baseball game is closer to people's basic yearnings than the suburb. At the stadium, people come and go and have a good time together."

In the early 1950s, prompted by that sort of thinking, Rouse and a handful of radical young businessmen established the Greater Baltimore Committee to stop the deterioration of the city's downtown. They won a reluctant Baltimore's backing to tear down and rebuild twenty-two blocks in the city's heart. The lively Charles

Center, with its offices, apartments, shops and theaters, lifted the city's expectations of what it could be. Before long, infected with Rouse's enthusiasm, the city fathers plunged into an ambitious plan to connect Charles Center to Baltimore's waterfront. Harborplace was born. Today, downtown Baltimore is bustling with gleaming new hotels, shops, office buildings and renovated brownstones. Talking about that dramatic transformation, Rouse quotes Daniel Burnham, the once-radical urban planner who redesigned Chicago's waterfront more than a century ago: "Make no little plans. They have no magic to stir men's blood and probably will not be realized."

Today, few other cities in America have experienced the sort of rebirth that Rouse's adopted hometown has. Why? "Because people who once believed nothing could happen in Baltimore now believe anything can happen," says Rouse. And this, of course, is the driving principle behind everything Rouse does.

"Not many things that are alive," says Rouse, "were an overnight brainstorm." Certainly the concept of the festival marketplace was not. The idea emerged gradually from Rouse's fascination with the Farmer's Market in Los Angeles. "It started in the middle of the Depression," he says. "The farmers would pull in and sell their produce off the tailgates of their trucks. Gradually people made stalls, then came cafés where you could buy something to eat, then came other kinds of stores. It evolved into a gathering place where people could meet and talk with their neighbors. It became a place of pleasure, even delight. It was the genesis of the festival marketplace."

Not all of Rouse's attempts to recreate the Farmer's Market worked out. His first effort, Plymouth Meeting, built in Philadelphia in the sixties, was a bust. "It was just stores," Rouse explains. No one came, and no one bought. "It wasn't lively enough. It didn't delight."

Rouse was not about to make the same mistakes in Toronto in 1972. Sherway Gardens was a huge success from the very first day and still is. "The highest sales per square foot of any mall anywhere," Rouse boasts. To avoid a repeat of the Plymouth fiasco, Rouse and his planners offered almost an excess of activity. The center is filled with stores, stalls and specialized retailers selling everything from gourmet cheese and ice cream to designer furniture and Swiss-made bread-slicers. These days, people are used to finding such variety in close quarters. But in 1972, it seemed a radical recipe for disorder. Only Rouse's close attention to every detail brought the project off.

Boston's Faneuil Hall established Rouse's reputation once and for all. A jewel of the urban renaissance, it became a model for all festival marketplaces to come. The hall itself, along with neighboring Quincy Market, was a rickety old brick and timber shed, the size of a football field, that traced its history to the days of merchant ships and whalers. It once marked the center of Boston's waterfront, bustling with fishmongers, cheese and fruit vendors and ships' chandlers.

Like its progeny-to-be, South Street Seaport, Faneuil Hall had a heritage too rich for the wrecker's ball. But it was a white elephant; no one knew what to do with it. The city held a competition and selected a winning plan. But coming up with a feasible design was far simpler than raising the money to finance it. Few banks wanted any part of what was then a highly experimental—and risky—inner-city venture. The plan foundered for a couple of years, and then Boston called in Rouse. "Everybody else had the sense to know it wouldn't work," he says. "I went in on a hunch. I thought it was a natural way of bringing life to the city, and that it would naturally be appealing."

In fact, Rouse refused to do a feasibility study. He knew the experts would say it was unworkable. "And they would have been right," he says. "By all conventional rules, that project couldn't be done. But we did it, and it was an enormous success." Like Harborplace in Baltimore, Faneuil Hall was a magnet for Boston's downtown. It helped spark a whole inner-city revival. Today, it's full of strollers, shoppers, people just passing by on their way to someplace else. Faneuil Hall has helped make the waterfront a place people seek out, rather than avoid. A chamber of commerce dream. Rouse calls this the excitement of "chaotic variety." And going back to Rouse's notion that man is God's spiritual co-creator, he considers the responsibility to make America's cities fit places to live to be the "number one priority of our civilization." Without the cities, he says, there would *be* no civilization.

Obviously Rouse is less interested in a building itself than in how the building is used. He's anything but an architect's developer; he seldom builds with beauty or striking effect foremost in his mind. "We place too much emphasis on the role of the architect as an artist, and not enough on his role as a social servant," says Rouse. If Columbia looks a bit like the manicured subdivisions that dot the suburbs of America, well, that's all right. Rouse and his seventy thousand neighbors know the difference. "It's a real city and a wonderful place to live," he says.

That difference has something to do with details. Rouse is obsessed by them. For instance, he vetoed individual mailboxes in Columbia in favor of "gang mailboxes." "Like the old community well," he says. Rouse planted over half a million trees and reserved thousands of acres of parks and playgrounds. He made sure the town library was at Columbia's center, so that it would be a convenient meeting place. The aim in each case was the same: to bring people together and re-create the satisfactions and security of traditional small-town life. At Columbia, every kid can walk or ride his bike to school. Columbia's central library apparently has the highest circulation, per book, of any central library in the country. And Columbia has become a national sensation in soccer, competing in the final rounds of just about every major high school tournament in the country. "It's the Columbia neighborhood system," a coach explains. "These kids all know each other."

Lots of well-established, affluent small towns in America can make that boast. But what distinguishes Columbia, and what makes Rouse proudest, is its sense of racial and class harmony. The risky social experiment has more or less worked. Columbia draws strength from diversity; more important, it seems to value diversity for its own sake. Recently a Chinese delegation from Peking arrived for an inspection. Rouse wanted to invite some Chinese-Americans from Columbia, and in issuing the invitations found that over the last six years more than two hundred Chinese families had settled in Columbia. Some of the high schools were even offering courses in Mandarin. "I think the Chinese, the East Indians and the Koreans are here partly because of the black-white relationships," says Rouse. "There are more interracial marriages in Columbia than anywhere else in the world, I expect. On one level, that's unimportant; on another, it's remarkable. It's almost as if people become part of the spirit of what Columbia is, and they are applauded for it."

It's important to realize that while Columbia preceded Rouse's downtown marketplaces by a decade, they are similar. If Columbia investigated the optimal suburban way of life, the inner-city festival marketplaces acknowledged the decay of the city, brought on in part by white flight to the suburbs, and sought ways to stop it. But all of Rouse's projects share a theme. They were built not just to make a profit, but to provide social value. They were, moreover, an expression of Rouse's belief that you improve your own life by improving the lives of others.

In that light, it was quite natural for Rouse to call Gordon Cosby out of the blue one day and join the Church of the Savior. It was an equally fluid, graceful shift to turn his energies from housing typical Americans to housing those who would give anything to become typical Americans. The Enterprise Foundation, in a sense, is Rouse at his truest.

THE CHURCH OF the Savior may have launched Jubilee Housing, but the war against poverty is not being waged in Dupont Circle. That battlefield lies a mile or so to the north, in a neighborhood called Adams Morgan.

In the 1950s and 1960s, Adams Morgan was one of Washington's best areas: affluent, solidly white, a sort of uptown Georgetown. That changed with the race riots, and the neighborhood became home to many of the poorest people in the city. If you walk up Connecticut Avenue, you can see the path of change. At the Hilton, where Connecticut branches into Columbia Road, the boutiques and bistros of Dupont Circle abruptly give way to a more Latin theme: Puerto Rican record stores, Caribbean restaurants, corner bodegas where you can buy plantains or play the numbers. It's a lively place, and an increasingly attractive one for outsiders.

Washington's gentrifiers are at work here, too. Old houses are being spruced up; apartment buildings are being turned into condos.

Where Columbia Road crests the hill at Eighteenth Street, just before it dives into some of Washington's worst slums, there's a renovated brownstone, painted red, with a Christian bakery in the basement. This is Jubilee Housing. It hums with the spirit of urban renewal. James Rouse likes it here. He and his wife, Patty, are on Jubilee's board, and they drop by regularly. "We feel refreshed there," says Rouse. "No one walks around telling you what wonderful Christians they are. They never make anyone feel uncomfortable. They just go about their work, joyous in the faith."

I was curious about Jubilee, not just as an interesting social experiment, but as a way of gauging the Enterprise Foundation. I thought I might find something that would persuade me, as I wanted to be persuaded, that the foundation could achieve its goals. That, at least on a small scale, it could emancipate the poor from poverty.

It's been almost fifteen years since Rouse walked into the Ritz, the first of Jubilee's rehab ventures, and gagged at the stench. A lot has happened. The building, like the others Jubilee has bought, is beautifully, even elegantly maintained. It has problems. Tenants sometimes don't pay the rent, then skip just before eviction; kids scrawl graffiti in the hallways. But for the most part the rents get paid and the graffiti gets cleaned up. The apartments themselves are neat and clean and in good repair. There's plenty of heat and hot water; the atmosphere is of security rather than despair. Contrast that with most low-income projects elsewhere. The difference is astonishing.

Rouse touts Jubilee as the inspiration for his Enterprise Foundation and an engine of social progress. But progress at Jubilee, I found, is more ambiguous than clean, well-lighted apartments.

ROSA HATFIELD AND Jubilee Housing have grown up together. She manages the company's nine buildings—a smooth and flexible operation, thanks to her. She collects rents, works with tenant committees and passes problems of cash flow and angry temperaments to the support groups that Rouse and the Church of the Savior have organized around Jubilee. She likes her job and the $16,800 she takes home in yearly pay. She takes care of her four children, all of whom work and some of whom are bound for college.

Flash back to 1973, when Jubilee bought the Ritz. Hatfield scooted into an apartment just days before the building was sold. Figuring rents would skyrocket when the new owners took over, she just hoped to hang on until something else came up. This was a familiar story for her. Black, unmarried and on welfare, she was turned down almost everywhere she went. "It just seemed there was no hope for a woman on welfare getting decent housing," she says. And the Ritz was hardly decent. The front door was missing. The broken elevators were used as garbage dumps. Rats and roaches were everywhere. But, she says, "it was a place to stay." She paid $160 for her two small bedrooms, two thirds of her monthly $241 welfare check.

That's a real success story, on the face of it. Considering the obstacles, Hatfield's step up the socioeconomic ladder is no less impressive than a suburban high school student going on to Harvard. And Rosa is not alone. Among the more than 350 families under Jubilee's wing, there are dozens of similar stories. Unwed teenage mothers are able to finish school and find jobs because of the day-care Jubilee provides. Health improves because of the better living conditions. And then there are the children: having a decent place to live makes life easier. They seem happier and, when older, less prone to the frustration and violence that is a constant of life in the ghetto.

Yet there's an ambiguous undercurrent in the upbeat statistics, and it isn't difficult to see why. Imagine. A group of white Christian do-gooders comes into a tenement, works hard to clean the place up, starts all these social programs—child care, physical hygiene, nutrition. But how many tenants help? "Only one," says Rosa Hatfield. Herself, and she participated only reluctantly, coaxed out of her apartment by a social worker who fed her children in a common room in the basement, helped them with schoolwork and encouraged them to play games.

You can look at Jubilee's effort in two ways. To outsiders, it looks like a model of community action: the concerned, caring, committed liberal ethic at its best. But to the insiders—the Ritz's mostly black tenants—the Church of the Savior crusaders were unwanted white interlopers, or worse. The tough ones, mostly young men, laughed at them. The shyer tenants, including Hatfield, mistrusted them and kept away. All accepted Jubilee's favors without thanks. "I was scared," Hatfield explains simply. "I didn't like white people. I didn't trust them. I didn't want to have anything to do with them. I'm from the South, and in the South whites weren't supposed to care how blacks lived."

That's changed, for Hatfield at least. Today, she sounds born again. Surly suspicion turned to repentance, cleansing and now salvation. She talks about the old days in a detached, methodical voice. She's found the path and she's not straying far. It's taken her fifteen years to get where she is. She's a proud, successful example of what Jubilee is all about.

Even so, the irony remains. "Jubilee did everything. They asked nothing of the tenants," says Hatfield, and I can't get that out of my mind. Again the scene: all these church people bustling about, and the tenants not lifting a hand to help themselves be helped. Indeed, when Rosa Hatfield began working with Jubilee—first helping take care of the children, then minding the books of the Ritz, ultimately managing its buildings—she was persecuted. She was an "Auntie Tom," a sellout to the whites. After vandals put sugar in the gas tank of her car and painted obscenities on her front door, she moved out—even as she continued to work for Jubilee.

But that was long ago, and many of those resentments and problems have faded. Today, Jubilee manages its buildings jointly with the tenants. Each building has a board of elected representatives. They share in the decision making, write the house rules, set the tone of their buildings—as any co-op board in New York would do, with the same mixture of dedication and apathy. There's a more balanced racial mix in the buildings; relations are not without tension, but they work smoothly nonetheless. And Jubilee's health and employee programs are clearly making a big difference in people's daily lives. Yet these gains are so much a product of individual initiative and attention. They are the work of a small, committed group focusing on just a few buildings. The question is whether Jubilee's hard-won but limited success can be replicated on the scale envisioned by the Enterprise Foundation. How many Jubilee Housing Corporations would have to be formed to undertake the work Rouse contemplates?

Rouse is well aware of the problems. He's not inclined to gloss over them or minimize the hurdles. He's not naïve. In fact, he's so conscious of the difficulties that he seems almost surprised that I would raise them, as if I'd expect anything different. Rouse isn't looking for gratitude. He's concerned only about long-term results.

"What else can you do?" he asks. You can either stand on the sidelines and wring your hands, or you can try to do something, even if the effort isn't fully appreciated or fails to get immediate results. That's the choice, he says. Which really is no choice at all.

Rouse is back on the theme that opened our talk. "More can be done about poverty than we're doing. The truth is that big problems respond to little solutions. What we have to do is take the problem apart, deal with it in pieces, and put it back together with a new awareness. The mission is not to support the poor, but to make the poor unpoor."

His biggest hope is the city of Chattanooga, Tennessee, which has given itself a mandate: to get rid of all substandard housing in ten years. The Enterprise Foundation has been asked to come up with the program. The cost has been estimated, the money has been raised, the plans have been laid. If Chattanooga can do it, says Rouse, other cities will follow.

CHAPTER SIX

POWER

◆

CHATTANOOGA, TENNESSEE. My flight seems only to have just left Atlanta, yet we've already begun our descent. It's late fall. The foothills and mountain ridges of the Great Smoky Mountains are ablaze with autumn golds, reds and greens. Without warning, the Tennessee River slashes through the mountains, then doubles back to embrace a pocket of civilization that must be Chattanooga.

This is still a labor town, long dependent on its river for commerce and prosperity. Factories account for an unusually large share of its jobs. Like many urban centers in the nation's rust belt, Chattanooga has been hard hit by changing times and new technologies. Unemployment is on the rise. So are crime and poverty. But none of this is visible from the plane or, later that night, from the mountains above the city where I'm staying with friends.

What mountains! It's easy to imagine Union troops climbing their steep flanks as Confederate guns fired upon them from Lookout Mountain. Its sister, Signal Mountain, gave the warning: "They're coming, they're coming. The Yankees are coming." Now, the Civil War cannons hold permanent ground, cemented to their stations, memorials always. The scenic, flat-topped cliffs are home to lawyers, doctors and architects, white urban professionals with prestigious jobs and old Chattanooga money. Here on the mountains you're surrounded by the spectacular splashes of color I saw from the air. In the evening, with a cocktail in hand, you look out over a sea of twinkling lights that hides the seedy streets, the run-down commercial strips, the low-slung rows of shanties. From the mountains, Chattanooga looks clean and harmonious. It's hard to see the blight.

James Rouse sees the blight. In the spring of his seventh decade, he has inspired Chattanooga to give itself a mandate: to rid the city of all substandard housing—in effect, to banish the heaviest burden of poverty—within ten years. It will cost some $200 million to rehabilitate some thirteen thousand inner-city homes. Success will require a broad partnership between banks and government agencies, foundations and religious institutions, low-income neighborhood groups and wealthy individuals and corporations. The plan, developed by the Enterprise Foundation, rests on the premise that people can work their way out of poverty, if given the right kind of help. "It is a philosophy not of 'doing for the poor,' " the *Chattanooga Times* wrote, "but of working with low-income people to build their capacity to help themselves."

This is powerful talk. The city's commitment has opened Chattanooga to raw winds that scrape across newly exposed wounds. Terrible schools, and not enough money. A dying downtown. Racial tensions. Logic would say, "Don't try. The commitment can't be made good." But Rouse does not preach logic. He preaches power. He tells Chattanooga's business and civic leaders that they can do it if they want to. And before they are fully aware of the problems, they are committed. They are energized by Rouse's evangelism. They come to see their city through his eyes. Sure, we have problems, but we can overcome them. Sure, we have houses so rotten that rats would rather live outdoors, but we will fix them. After a flurry of newspaper articles and initial meetings, of course, the enthusiasm wanes. The vision begins to strike people as unrealistic. The core of committed community leaders grows smaller as support fades away. Rouse comes to be seen as a Pollyanna who swoops into town with a thick report and a fine speech. It would be different, people begin to say, if he were the guy who had to actually go out and do the work.

Rouse has seen all this before. It's the natural cycle of any ambitious project, the more so when the challenge is something that has never been done before. This is where he is at his best. Rouse gets behind his people. When morale sinks, he encourages. When momentum stalls, he's out there pushing, pulling and persuading. He tells his people that the work has only just begun, and that it's doable. He shifts their focus from the enormity of the problem to the grandeur of the solution. He stirs things up, acts as a catalyst for events that would otherwise not happen. He goads, cajoles and, when necessary, bullies people to do their best and keep the project on track. He does whatever it takes to get the job done. His strength and his commitment renew people's belief in themselves and the goal. Working through others. It is the essence of leadership, and the essence of power.

IT IS ALMOST alien to think of this kindly man with his rumpled tweeds and balding head as a wielder of power. But Jim Rouse is. At one time he thought about going into politics. "I didn't, because I thought I could get more done independently if I really gave my life to it," he says. "But no doubt about it. I was very conscious of the importance of being successful in business and the power that it brought—the unreasonable power that it brought. A successful businessman who joins the board of an organization or nonprofit social group wields an influence out of all reason. The typical high school principal is more important in the community than the big corporate executive. The local minister is, too. Yet while they are enormously respected, they are not respected in terms of what people want to get done." It's the businessman, Rouse says, who holds that power.

Power means different things to different people. Political scientists think of it as the ability to influence others, to work the system so as to get things done the way you want them done. Pop culturists apply that personally. "All life is a game of power," writes Michael Korda in his best-selling book *Power!* "The object of the game is to know what you want and get it."

Fair enough, I suppose. Power certainly involves the ability to control our day-to-day lives. The more power we have, the easier and often more fulfilling life can be. Doors open to you. People can be more easily persuaded—or forced—to do things your way. There is social prestige, and personal and professional rewards. Still, there is power and there is power. For Korda, power is a game where your gain is inevitably someone else's loss. To play this "power game," he writes, you need to know the rules. You need to know where the "lines of power" converge in the office—literally. You need to know how to "play" a cocktail party and exploit the trappings of power. As in, "Phone me in the limo."

It's impossible to imagine James Rouse charting power lines at the office. He and the others in this book see power very differently. It's a force for change and creation, rather than a prize in a corpocratic struggle. "Power is opportunity," says Rouse. "It's a means of realizing your responsibilities in life." In Rouse's case, that purpose is not to control the universe, but to change it. He understands why "magic" and "power" were in ancient times synonymous. With power, you can make wonderful things happen—miracles, even, like building an ideal city or ridding America of urban decay. But like all successful magic, there's a secret to it. The key to power gathering is power giving, a concept that for the most part is alien to the zero-sum power game described by Michael Korda. "Power," says Rosabeth Kantor in *The Change Masters*, "is not a matter of domination of others—winning over them and cutting them out—or of monopolization of resources, but rather of coalition building to persuade others to contribute what they can to an innovation."

In this sense, genuine power is essentially deflective in nature. James Rouse—or for that matter any of the people in this book—did not become powerful through himself, but through others. Empire builders magnify not themselves but the goals that their associates and followers devote themselves to.

"What do I really like?" says Steven Jobs. "I like building neat things with really great people."

"What gets me excited? Building things, the thrill of getting people together and figuring out how to reach a common goal," says Robert Swanson.

"Effective leaders have a natural ability to reach out to others," says Ross Perot. "They ask people's help and give them responsibility."

Ted Turner is almost openly contemptuous of people who talk about power as if it were a tangible commodity. "People have asked me for years what it's like to be so powerful," he says. "I say, 'Well, you show me the power.' If I didn't get the common cold, if my kids got straight A's in school, if my wife didn't spend half her time raising hell with me, I'd feel powerful. Ronald Reagan can't even get a clean air bill through Congress. Where's his power? As far as I'm concerned, there is no power. Power is a myth, an absolute myth. The only power in this world is the power of persuasion, to get other people to go along with you a little bit of the time. And in the end, that's their decision, not yours."

The unanimity on this point, almost down to the phrasing, is revealing. Executives who run the country's biggest companies instinctively embrace the lesson that Mikhail Gorbachev is struggling to put across in the Soviet Union: that the most efficient way to wield power is to democratize it. To be sure, it is possible for a single man, operating on his own, to build an empire. Donald Trump proves the point. It would be a mistake to say he has *created* an empire. More accurately, he has gathered a huge stash of an already existing commodity—money. In contrast, those who create a product or develop a concept that changes the way people live seldom do so on their own. Theirs is a group effort, a product of teamwork, evangelizing and consensus building. Their favorite word in discussing their success is *we*, meaning the team. The empire builder clearly sees himself as first among equals and will brook no challenge. But he also considers his firm to be "family." As often as not, he attributes his success to his lieutenants.

This is not modesty, false or genuine, but realism. The most successful chief executives—the empire builders, if you will—assign themselves a dual role. First, to set the company's direction—to lay out the general vision and keep the company on track. Second, and vastly more important, to *empower* others to help the venture on its way.

That's almost become a cliché, but the notion of empowerment is more subtle than it appears. It goes without saying that superior leaders "empower" followers by delegating responsibility and decentralizing decision making. But empowerment is more than participatory management. If it weren't, any top executive could build an empire. So what makes the empire builder special?

One answer is the intrinsic power of the empire builder's ideas.

Charles Garfield, a management consultant in California, has made a study of the psychology of empowerment. By way of example, he tells how in the late sixties he was assigned to the Grumman Aerospace team that was building the *Apollo 11* mission's lunar module—the first manned craft to land on the moon. "Something extraordinary happened as the work got under way," he writes in his book *Peak Performers*. "Thousands of ordinary people who had been competent workers—project managers, secretaries, technicians—suddenly became superachievers, doing the best work of their lives." Within eighteen months, Garfield's section improved its performance rating from the lower 50 percent of the company to the top 15 percent. "Want to know why we're doing so well?" a Grumman manager once asked him. "He pointed to the pale moon barely visible in the eastern sky," Garfield writes. " 'People have been dreaming of going there for thousands of years, and *we're* going to do it.' "

That may be a little too inspirational for a skeptic's comfort, but its truth is undeniable. People who shoot for the moon, and go about it methodically, often command the best efforts of others. A noble goal, shared, is an incredible source of power. A strong current of idealism was at work at Apple; those who worked with Steve Jobs were revolutionaries, buying into a dream and out to change the world. Genentech attracted some of the nation's top young scientists for much the same reason. Robert Swanson convinced them that, working together, they could usher in a "biotech revolution" in medicine. Empire builders, ultimately, are seducers. They tap into others' dreams, their deepest needs for recognition, reward or great accomplishment, and they channel those energies into their own goals.

It's not just the drawing force of a goal or an idea that empowers. Perhaps even more important is the thought process behind it, the way an idea is realized. Great entrepreneurs think differently from the rest of us—not always more creatively, but certainly more assertively and with greater freedom. Morton Lefkoe, a communications consultant in Westport, Connecticut, says that exceptional leaders are masters at what he calls "context creation." When confronted with a problem that seems to defy solution, they change the context in which the problem exists. Lefkoe uses a puzzle to illustrate his point. Try, for example, to connect the circles below using no more than four straight lines, without lifting your pen from the page.

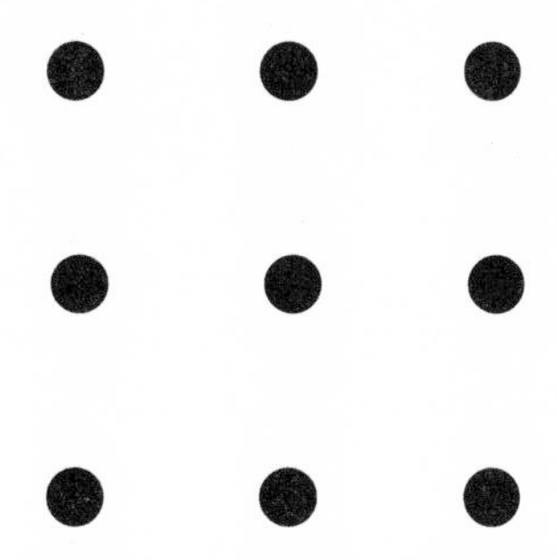

The solution depends on your definition of the problem. Most people consciously or subconsciously assume they are not permitted to go outside the box. But why not? It's just an arbitrary (albeit symbolic) box. The solution is not all that difficult, once one ignores the artificial "boundaries."

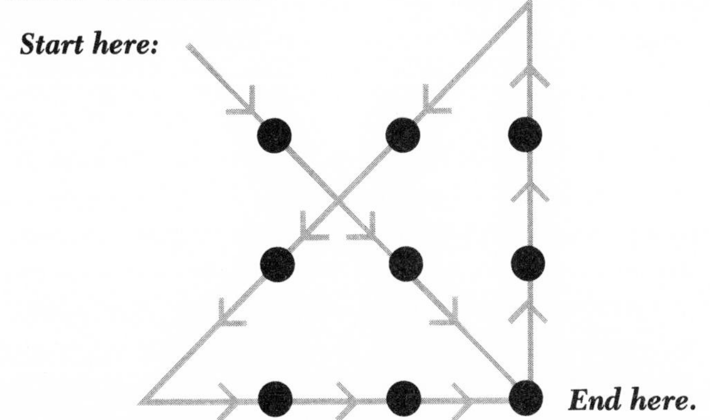

Lefkoe argues that this is more than a casual exercise. It hints at a person's outlook on the world, his sense of personal and intellectual limits. According to the people around him, Steve Jobs's greatest strength is his ability to think freely, to break down assumed or conventional boundaries. You see that in Rouse as well. Remember the panel of experts he assembled to help plan Columbia—the panel that trashed his ideas as unworkable and foolish?

All the team could see at first were the obstacles to the enterprise; it was, as Rouse put it, a triumph of "vested negatives," a case study in how difficult it is to force oneself into a new way of looking at the world.

Rouse changed that by changing the definition of the problem. Rather than asking the experts to solve the daunting issues of urban life, he urged them to consider a different question altogether. How do you create an environment where "love"—fellow feeling and a genuine sense of community—can flourish? It was a bit like turning around a telescope and peering through the opposite end; it changes your perspective. When Rouse's urban experts accepted that the only way to avoid the pitfalls of the past was to think about old problems in new ways, there was a meeting of minds. People got excited. They plunged into the concept and, over the ensuing months, hammered out ambitious, no less idealistic plans of their own. Columbia was born, and worked.

Not long ago, I read a commencement address that Rouse gave at Johns Hopkins in 1985. He called it "Think Biggest," and it's something of a how-to manual on the psychology of empowerment. "The beginning point in any enterprise," he said, "is to discuss the best that ought to be." Think of what's best, then tailor your solution accordingly.

This is a way of thinking that begins not by attacking the problem, but by working backward from the solution. By focusing on the ideal solution rather than the immediate problem, you bring power and effectiveness to an enterprise. In Rouse's words, you "raise up images of what might be—should be—and evoke action that might not otherwise occur. Such images are often dismissed as visionary and impractical, but that is a state of mind that discounts change and keeps us chained to the present. In fact, images of the best that ought to be are reasonable and desirable human aspirations. When held up and articulated, they give meaning, strength and direction. They are empowering to those who keep them in their hearts and minds."

This is the way of thinking that produced Columbia, Rouse says, and the principle now being tested in Chattanooga.

* * *

CHATTANOOGA'S TEN-YEAR PROGRAM to make all its housing fit and livable could mark a watershed in the way Americans think about their cities. Just about every metropolis in the nation is scarred by slums and run-down neighborhoods, where the tenements and dilapidated housing kill off hope and ambition and faith in human potential. In the face of problems so pervasive, and the failure of government programs to find a solution, it's all too tempting to simply accept poverty and poor housing as one of those problems that we all just have to live with, just another inescapable aspect of the human condition. But does it have to be that way?

Rouse suggests that it doesn't, and Chattanooga will prove him right or wrong. The idea is to create a grass-roots, citywide support system, built around a fledgling community-action group called Chattanooga Neighborhoods, Inc. Backed by public and private sources, CNI offers financial assistance to people fixing up their homes. It's not a giveaway program. Low-income people will be eligible for small weatherization grants, but other improvements will be financed through subsidized low-interest loans. All but the lowest-income homeowners will be asked to invest some of their own money, as well as build up "sweat equity" by working on the rehabilitation themselves. Funds for the program are supposed to come from a variety of sources, ranging from federal, state and local grants to tax abatements for private investors.

But the Enterprise Foundation's plans for Chattanooga require more than money. They call for a degree of community involvement unusual—if not unique—in America today. As Rouse sees it, success depends on building psychological momentum for change. Financial assistance must be backed by public encouragement and public pressure. And how to build that momentum? For one thing, the CNI has started setting up neighborhood associations that, partly through peer pressure, will prod whole neighborhoods to spruce up their homes and streets. There will be block parties, door-to-door canvassing, tax breaks for home rehabers. So-called "targeting" committees will get after people who let their houses deteriorate. Church groups, civic associations, schools and community outreach groups are getting involved. Private realtors are being called upon to provide training and subsidized assistance to homeowners. At the same time, the city is getting tougher on landlords. Along with the "carrot" of financial incentives, there is the stick of stiffer enforcement and tougher legal action on housing code violations.

This is much more than real estate development. Rouse is talking about basic political changes—changes in the way people lead their lives, changes in the way *things have always been done*. The core of Rouse's plan is an effort to shift responsibility for the city's poverty from the poor themselves to the community at large and, in doing so, to spark a joint effort to fix a problem that no one else in the country has been able to solve. It's obviously a form of evangelism, as much an appeal to the heart as to the head. It is a call to set aside skepticism and rationality. And why? Because the cause is just. Because in life people arguably bear some responsibility for others. Because, as Ross Perot might put it, *it's the right thing to do*.

Can it work? That depends on whom you talk to. The *Chattanooga Times* calls Rouse's plan a "grand mission," a goal that can only be reached by "working together." A city official, smitten by Rouse's rhetoric and his vision of what might be, likens the housing initiative to the building of a great cathedral in medieval Europe, a triumph of faith over pragmatism. If the so-called "realists" had held sway in the fifteenth century, he argues, Chartres and Notre Dame would in all probability never have been built.

Yet there are also those whose optimism about Rouse's dreams has been tempered by involvement. One of them is Bob Corker, an energetic young Chattanoogan who ironically was the driving force in bringing Rouse to Chattanooga in the first place.

On face of it, Corker would be a natural disciple. A decade ago, when he was twenty-five, he started a real estate development company that, by Chattanooga standards, is *big*. It pulls in some $80 million a year. Corker's rich. Were he particularly acquisitive, he could buy anything he wanted—the biggest house in Chattanooga, a sports car or two, weekend vacations in New York, Paris or the Caribbean. All this would be possible, that is, if Corker wanted it. But he doesn't. Not your typical yuppie entrepreneur, he's looking for something different out of life. He's a man in search of a mission.

"Listen," he says in a fast staccato, talking about his work and his involvement with James Rouse. "My life has been a fairy tale in many ways. By thirty, I was very successful. Not by Donald Trump's standards, perhaps, but certainly by mine. Then, suddenly, I found myself walking around wondering what it was all about. I was working sixteen hours a day. But I had this empty feeling."

Then Corker took a vacation in Haiti. Dismayed by the poverty and poor living conditions, he returned to Chattanooga wondering what he could do to help the poor of his own hometown. He went down to Americus, Georgia, where Habitat for Humanity is running some progressive programs to alleviate poverty. He liked what he saw but, as a businessman, didn't think Habitat's programs had the staying power to really change things. Then one day he heard that Rouse was in Chattanooga giving a speech. He went, listened and was inspired. "It was a very moving talk," he says. "I was especially interested in the fact that he had this nonprofit organization that supposedly was funding itself through the profits of a development company." Corker was about to go see Rouse when a friend suggested something more ambitious. "Why don't you be an ambassador for Chattanooga?" he said. Why not persuade Rouse to take on Chattanooga as a client, a sort of test case for eliminating substandard housing in a medium-sized U.S. city?

And so the Enterprise Foundation came to Chattanooga. Corker and his friend anted up twenty-five thousand dollars apiece to fund the foundation's study. They agreed to serve on a city steering committee and help mobilize support. During the first year and a half of the project, Corker figures he put seven hundred hours into the effort. That's the equivalent of holding a part-time job, and Corker had his company to run. It was representative of the commitment he and a handful of other community leaders were putting into the venture. But after a time, doubts began to arise.

For instance? I asked.

"Well," Corker said, "the whole idea, the goal. Now, I'm a very optimistic person, very positive. But the goal—alleviating poverty in ten years—that bothered me. In the kind of work I'm in, you tell someone you're going to do something, you do it. No commas."

The trouble was that as the project progressed, Corker became increasingly skeptical that the goal was realistic, that the project could be delivered, no commas. "Rouse's assumption was that neighborhood groups would pull together. But that doesn't happen here, because unlike Baltimore, we don't have any neighborhood groups," Corker explained. He was even more skeptical about another premise of the Rouse plan—the very basic assumption that the city was behind it. "Rouse keeps saying that, but it's a bunch of crap. About fifteen people in Chattanooga are behind the plan. That doesn't mean the whole city won't be," but right now, he says, "there's a huge amount of apathy."

Corker is also troubled by Rouse's theatrics. "Rouse's way of doing things is headlines, newspaper and TV," he says. "The project raised all these expectations. People wanted to find out about it. Think of the headlines: CHATTANOOGA TO DO AWAY WITH SUBSTANDARD HOUSING." For Corker, this was a source of enormous anxiety, not least because he suddenly came to realize that it wasn't the Enterprise Foundation that was supposed to solve the city's housing problems under the plan, but Chattanooga itself. "Maybe I was naïve, but I thought Rouse was going to come down here and, with our help, do away with substandard housing. As the clock kept ticking away, I finally realized that I had it all wrong. The Enterprise people weren't going to make it happen. They were just supplying the plan, the vision. *We* were the ones who were supposed to do everything," from arranging the financing to marshaling community support. That revelation, Corker says, "was absolutely mind-boggling."

CORKER'S EXPERIENCE IS not rare. Rouse raises expectations very high, and it's hard to sustain them. Corker is still involved in the Chattanooga project, and he has no intention of giving up or dropping out. But he feels his energy and commitment are slipping. He's discouraged. "This thing has created so much anxiety. Am I going to be doing this for forty years?" he asks. "I just got married. I'm tired. My zest for life is disappearing. My company is growing. I'd like to take a little break."

Burnout. You see this so often, talking to people who get swept up by the likes of Jim Rouse. This is the view from the trenches, the vantage point of the foot soldiers in an empire builder's crusade. And whether the empire builder is Rouse, Steve Jobs, Robert Swanson or someone else, the stories are always the same. It's not that these followers are weak, or wavering, or lacking in faith or loyalty. To the contrary. It's just that they're human, and that very few people possess the almost superhuman single-mindedness, energy and passion of a Rouse. The odd thing about the empire builder is that he so often seems to invert the basic laws that govern the rest of us. By expending energy, he creates energy. His passion feeds upon itself. The empire builder himself rarely burns out. He consumes those around him.

Bart Harvey, deputy chairman of the Enterprise Foundation and Rouse's right-hand man, has not burned out. Perhaps that's because he's a conduit for Rouse's passion. He helps channel his boss's energies; he's not a tool that Rouse uses directly, to eventually wear out. His own psyche remains intact.

Harvey is a good example of the talent Rouse attracts. He doesn't have to tell you that he's from a wealthy family, that his father heads a prominent investment bank, that he went to Harvard, twice—once for a B.A. in English literature, then again, after a trip around the world, for an MBA. He has the zest, good looks, assurance and expensively tailored clothes of a waspy Wall Street whiz kid. Which is precisely what he was six years ago, before he met Rouse. Young at thirty-five and energetic, Harvey walked out of a mid-six-figure investment banking job with Dean Witter in New York to take on a fifty-thousand-dollar-a-year job with Rouse. Why? Like Corker, he was impressed. "Impressed with Jubilee Housing, impressed with the notion that that program could be duplicated on a larger scale around the country," impressed with Rouse's "rare mix" of talent.

Harvey, like Corker, was another one of these talented young men looking for a purpose in life. They flock to people of Rouse's stripe, partly to be ennobled, partly for the cachet, partly for the ultimate promise of riches, power and social prestige that flows from the association. And Rouse promised all of that. He was different from anyone whom Harvey had ever met. "You always feel he has his eye out," Harvey says, "for what's best for others, not himself. He focuses on what matters, *what really matters*. For me, that's the hooker."

Harvey has only a few minutes to talk, but he wants to get it across that Enterprise is no slowpoke charity shop; nor are Rouse and his people dewy-eyed idealists. He's juggling phone calls from senators, dealing with bankers in New York on intricate loan packages, consulting with the Enterprise Foundation's field managers in several dozen projects around the country. "Rouse is extraordinary," he says between calls. "He's at once a visionary and a pragmatist. Some people may say he's naïve, foolish or whatever. But when it comes time to implement a plan, he knows *exactly* what he has to do to get things done. No one works harder. No one thinks harder about the details. Nobody follows up the way he does."

You hear that refrain again and again, too. People like Rouse will do whatever it takes to get a job done—literally almost anything. Perhaps Corker didn't understand that, didn't quite see what Rouse is up to in Chattanooga. The goal was not, strictly speaking, to alleviate poverty. It was not to come up with a plan. The goal was to make things happen, to get things started, to prod, push and pull the city to change the way it sees itself and thinks about its problems. The plan itself was merely the *excuse*. The plan itself, as an architect or engineer might interpret it, wasn't even supposed to *work*.

"If you want to change the image of the city," Rouse once said, "Don't change the image. Change the city." For the Enterprise Foundation's work to begin in Chattanooga, Rouse had to persuade the town—or more precisely, a small group of community activists within the town—that it could attempt the impossible and succeed. There's that old Chinese proverb, "A trip of a thousand miles starts with a single step." Rouse's main goal is to get Chattanooga to take that first step.

For once the trip begins, it's hard to turn back. Once people are committed, momentum builds. In Chattanooga, as elsewhere, momentum meant creating a *cause* and building support. That in turn meant theater—television, newspaper headlines, public excitement, fine speeches and newspaper editorials. Only then would there be any meaningful community participation. Chattanooga may not be able to solve its housing problems in ten years. In fact, it almost certainly will not. But unlike just about every other city in the country, Chattanooga has been *empowered* to try.

It all gets back to power. David McClelland, head of McBer & Company in Boston and author of *Power: The Inner Experience*, says all people need it, even if they don't recognize the need. He divides power into four ascending stages. The first, "oral" power, is the power of a child who seeks control over an environment on which he is more or less totally dependent. The second, the "anal" stage, is marked by increasing self-mastery and independence. The third, a "phallic" phase, distinguishes people who seek mastery over others. By controlling power and its trappings—rising to top management posts, owning fancy cars, buying expensive jewelry for one's wife—they rise in their own and others' esteem.

The fourth stage, says McClelland, is characterized by "non-manipulative power-sharing." Instead of bearing out Freud's maxim that man is by nature a wolf out to devour and destroy others, this is the power of "Messianism." "People at Stage 4," McClelland writes, "satisfy their need for power by joining organizations in which they subordinate personal goals to a higher authority. They say, in effect, 'Not my will be done, but thine.' Great religious and political leaders from Jesus Christ to Abraham Lincoln to Malcolm X have felt they were instruments of a power beyond the self. Their goal was to act for others on behalf of this higher authority. This may not be good for me, they say, but it is good for others." B. F. Skinner, the noted behaviorist, put it another way in *Beyond Freedom and Dignity*: "Yield to a higher authority, serve it, and you will be happy."

Not for nothing has Rouse the spiritualist been called the "Messianic Master Builder." Not for nothing did he give a talk last year called "The Leader as Servant." We bear a responsibility for life, he says, not just to ourselves and family, but to society. And if, as Rouse sees it, you strongly believe in something, if you have faith, you should try to write those tenets as large in life as possible.

Which is where Chattanooga comes in. Rouse believes with evangelical certainty that his work is a kind of "demonstration" the country needs. He wants to prove that we can "make the poor unpoor," that what once might have been impossible has now become possible. "Times change," he says. "History moves forward. The time has come for a big, bold image of the American city as the best it might be for all its people."

If Chattanooga becomes that image, Rouse believes, others will follow. It would become an example, a beacon, a shining city on the hill. Another of those "right" things to do.

CHAPTER SEVEN

THE BUILDER

◆

SILICON VALLEY lies only an hour's drive south of San Francisco, but it might as well be a hundred. This is not the California of the Pacific Northwest, with its rugged coastlines, fog and harsh westerly winds. Here the sun shines unstintingly and a dry, recuperative wind blows down from the Santa Cruz Mountains, hot and fragrant with the smell of eucalyptus.

The Valley is a wedge-shaped finger of land, a scarf on the tail of San Francisco's kite, bounded loosely by Palo Alto to the north and San Jose to the south and braced by a pair of highways to the east and west.

Route 101, the easterly road, brushes the cusp of San Francisco Bay as it runs southward through land that must once have been beautiful. Now it's the Strip, an unending stretch of used-car lots and fast-food outlets that are the crude artifacts of America's peculiar brand of progress. Architect Robert Venturi wrote a book called *Las Vegas* in which he glorified the fried-chicken shack shaped like a chicken and the hot-dog stand lodged within a giant hot dog. But to those who live in the Valley, 101 is not romantic. It goes on for forty miles, six lanes wide with a stripe down the middle. Along it, slipped in between a thousand Midas Mufflers, McDonald's and Mister Donuts, are Menlo Park, Sunnyvale, Cupertino and Los Gatos. Here the computer was born, here genetic engineering became a reality. Route 101 is the Conestoga Trail of the postindustrial age.

The symbolism is tempting. One hundred and fifty years ago, restless easterners looking for a better life loaded their belongings and their dreams into giant wooden wagons and headed west. Their goal was the same: survival followed by hard work rewarded by prosperity in the golden land.

Driving the Strip one May, my windows shut and the air-conditioning on high, it was hard to miss the point. There are visions and there are visions. I said good-bye to the Taco Bells and K marts, and made for the highway to the west. Route 280, as clear as its twin is blemished, sweeps high through the foothills of the Santa Cruz Mountains. You can't see far when your vision is blocked.

ROBERT A. SWANSON leans back in his chair, casual yet expansive. It's a device he uses to put journalists at their ease, like a thoughtful host offering a cup of tea to start the circulation and the conversation. Swanson has grown accustomed to celebrity. In his early forties, he is a wunderkind of American industry, the president and founder of giant Genentech, Inc., America's premier biotechnology firm. He is the maker of miracle drugs that are changing our lives and notions of what medicine and science can accomplish. He is the father of modern bioengineering.

We're in his office at the company's headquarters in South San Francisco. The city's fathers, in better days, carved its name in giant block letters in a marble cliff overlooking the town. Motorists driving north along the Strip can see it from miles away, a beacon of sorts: SOUTH SAN FRANCISCO. But that was long ago, and a beacon of prosperity it is not. Today, it's a gritty industrial backwater, its factories and machine shops in permanent decline. The contrast to Genentech is stark: the old and the new, the phoenix and the dinosaur. Everything about Genentech sparkles. Flags snap at their mastheads. Beds of flowers burst with color along the driveways. Genentech's sleek white two-story buildings, trimmed like racing yachts with a thin blue stripe three-quarters up their sides, gleam in the bright California sunshine.

It's easy to talk with Swanson. A relaxed, easy smile blows out his cheeks like little pink balloons. Journalists describe him as "short," "chunky," "chipmunk-cheeked." His high school English teacher nicknamed him "Chipmunk," in fact, because of his "cute, charming, irresistible" smile. Another childhood friend remembers him as "Beaver," not just for the sixties TV series, but again for the physical resemblance. As in eager beaver, bursting with energy, industry and ideas.

But today, Swanson calmly listens. Now and then he takes a call, laughs, suggests how to fix this or that problem, whom to contact, when to meet. The low-key, casual style fosters the illusion that Genentech, at this moment at least, runs itself. There's no rush of responsibilities, no barrage of telephone calls, no secretaries interrupting with urgent messages. Genentech feels more like a think tank or university research lab than a modern multinational corporation. It's a place where people work quietly, intensely, free from distraction. It's a world waiting patiently for someone to look up from his laboratory workbench, gaze triumphantly around the room and shout, "Eureka!"

Which is more or less just what's happening. At Genentech, Swanson has for perhaps the first time melded the worlds of pure science and business. Before anyone else, he saw that the fledgling science of gene-splicing, born in 1973, could yield immediate commercial benefits. His scientists are the new "gene doctors," the magicians who are tinkering with the body's basic genetic blueprint in hopes of finding cures to some of mankind's oldest and most intractable diseases. And he's the man who sees to it that the system runs smoothly, that at the moment of discovery the world hears and profits.

Swanson has done his job well. The small venture he began in 1975 vaulted into the ranks of America's *Fortune* 500 companies faster than any start-up in history. Genentech's scientists have been second to none in getting human cells to clone useful genes and antigens and turning them into useful products. If the list of the company's successes reads like a history of the bioengineering revolution, that's because it is. The team Swanson brought together has scored almost all of the infant industry's major scientific coups. In 1978, Genentech cloned human insulin, an "artificial" drug now widely used to combat diabetes. In 1981, it duplicated gamma interferon, a promising tumor-fighting substance that is revolutionizing the way we treat cancer. In 1984, it created a blood-clotting factor that for the first time allowed hemophiliacs to live relatively normal lives, and in 1985 it began marketing Protropin, the world's first human growth serum. Roughly a quarter of a million American kids who might otherwise not grow taller than five feet can now expect to reach a normal height.

Call them "designer genes." Bioengineering is a powerful technology that will change society to the core. Primitive bioengineering has already developed disease-resistant, high-yield strains of rice and wheat that have alleviated famine in many parts of India and Southeast Asia. Modern human biotechnology will change the way we live, even how long we live. By the year 2050, some experts predict, scientists will have isolated the gene that makes men age—and perhaps have found a way to prolong our lives to 125 years or more.

Big dreams. But Robert Swanson merely shrugs. Not a speculative dreamer, he has his sights fixed on the more immediate horizon. "What is possible today?" he asks. He ticks off possibilities that his own scientists are working on: cures for arthritis, cancer, AIDS. New ways to help people cope with pain or depression. Prenatal remedies for certain genetic birth defects. "There's just an enormous amount to do," he says. "We're making headway. Things are beginning to snowball because of the enormous research and investment going on. What's happening is similar to the explosion of drugs that came out after World War II. Like penicillin. New drugs come in groups, which generates whole new ideas and makes things happen. It's exciting. It's very exciting for me and for Genentech, because it will change people's lives."

Swanson is buoyant and confident. Listening to him ticking off miracles, it seems that nothing could upset his happy optimism or halt Genentech's rise. "We're constantly expanding," he says, gesturing out the window, tracing an arc of progress as he points out a new lab, a new warehouse, the company's "old" headquarters. When a neighboring firm moves or goes out of business, Genentech takes over the space. The firm's white-coated technicians, ID cards on the fly around their necks, dash between buildings, running a construction-site gauntlet between the dump trucks and bulldozers of the builders and the Porsches and BMWs of Genentech's researchers and executives. "The place where they're digging is the expansion on the expansion," Swanson says. He's joking, but it's true.

It's the fall of 1987. Swanson, in fact, is at this moment on the verge of his greatest triumph. After a bruising battle with the Food and Drug Administration—a battle that temporarily drove down the company's stock prices by half—Genentech has won formal approval to begin selling its first true blockbuster: Activase, otherwise known as "tissue plasminogen activator," or t-PA. It's an anti–heart attack drug that in test cases around the country proved astonishingly effective in dissolving arterial blood clots and saving lives. Swanson thinks Activase could cut the fatalities from heart attacks in half. Victims of even the most serious coronaries will be able to lead normal, productive lives. All his energies are focused on getting this new product to market. It's impossible to overstate its importance, he says. It may just be the closest thing we've had to a wonder drug since the invention of penicillin.

Swanson flips on the intercom and asks his secretary to get me a video of a TV documentary that CBS filmed at Detroit Hospital, one of the clinics where Activase has been used experimentally to treat patients. "It's amazing to see," he says. People carted into the hospital crippled with pain and their lives in jeopardy are up and walking about within a few hours; even some of the most serious cases leave the hospital within days, suffering little or no permanent damage to their hearts. These lucky few who received the drug in Genentech's test program would call it a miracle. Many of them should be dead, and they know it. "My own heart was thumping as I watched this," Swanson says of the video. "Do you know that one person dies of a heart attack in the United States every ten minutes? One every ten minutes!"

It doesn't have to be that way. Activase, properly used, can stop America's number one killer in its tracks. It would be difficult to overemphasize the potentially huge contribution Genentech's new drug could make to society. On the other hand, it would be easy to underestimate Bob Swanson.

* * *

A COMMANDING PRESENCE he's not. Short, balding and prone to pudginess, this genial, thoughtful, fundamentally shy man hardly cuts the image of the driven empire builder. There's none of the charismatic passion of Steve Jobs, the swashbuckling bravado of Ross Perot or Ted Turner. Next to them, Swanson seems pale, boring even, a technocrat among Technicolor heroes. But then, how are empire builders supposed to look?

Swanson is deceptive, a confirmation of contrarian clichés. Behind that quiet exterior lurks a will of steel. His still waters run deep. Judging from outward appearances, he could easily be thought of as a corporate cog in pinstripes and wing tips who by happy accident and a winning grin fell into a great entrepreneurial venture. It would be tempting to think of his rise as the quirky triumph of Mr. Nice Guy, as if Beaver Cleaver had grown up to somehow, *somehow* finish first in the race to fame and riches.

And that would be wrong. Swanson is formidable. He's the archetypal entrepreneur, a genuine pioneer. Of all the men in this book, only he deliberately and explicitly set out from the beginning to build an industrial empire. Not from the time he found that his new venture would survive and prosper, mind you, but from the very first moment. The goal, Swanson said from day one, more than a decade ago, was to "build Genentech into a one-billion-dollar pharmaceutical company by 1990."

A billion-dollar company by 1990. It's not merely the ambitiousness of that goal that's impressive, or even Swanson's ability to persuade people that it was reasonable. The striking thing is that Swanson will do it, and that in all probability he'll do it *ahead of schedule*. Since 1976, Genentech has grown to take its place among the giants of the industry: Merck, Eli Lilly and Du Pont. Now, with t-PA on the market, it stands a good chance of becoming the fastest-growing company in the country. Genentech expects to sell some $650 million of the new drug in 1989. That may be overly optimistic, but since 1988 was also a successful year, even a partial success will propel Genentech past the $1 billion sales mark—leaving its rivals far behind.

* * *

THE BUILDER

IF GENENTECH IS SPECIAL, it is so because of Bob Swanson. He is the builder, the company's moral architect. His drive, fascination with science, flair in finance and strategic planning created the company and pushes it forward. But who is Robert Swanson? What drives him, what made him what he is today?

The answers from his colleagues, friends, teachers, even an old girlfriend, were disconcertingly similar:

"Boy, that's a tough question," said Robert Byrnes, formerly Genentech's number two man. "I'm not sure I ever felt I really knew Bob."

Tom Kiley, a lawyer who worked with Swanson for twelve years, says, "I've known him longer than his wife has." But what really makes him tick? "I don't know, I just don't know. He smiles a lot, he dresses up in funny costumes at company parties, he spends incredible hours talking out problems and working with people. But after all those years, all that effort, do you ever see the real Bob? Do you ever feel you're getting the whole story? I guess I've never felt that you were."

Another senior Genentech officer put it flatly: "Bob's just kind of a cold fish." Then he backpedaled. "That's not quite right. He's just not, well, not very *emotive*."

Swanson is unquestionably one of *the* most private people I've ever met. I got an inkling of that on the flight from New York to San Francisco. I spent most of the trip leafing through newspaper clips, mulling over questions I wanted to ask. The batch of articles must have been two inches thick, amounting to tens of thousands of words, yet there were no more than half a dozen sentences of anything remotely personal. Swanson's private life was a blank slate.

Even his publicity photos implied a certain elusiveness. From a glossy reprint of a *Business Week* cover story provided by Genentech's energetic public relations people, Swanson grins into the camera. His pink cheeks glow like a besotted priest's and his hair, carefully trimmed around a bald spot, looks for all the world like a tonsure. This monk of Silicon Valley is in his monastery, the labs where the sacred biotechnology revolution is taking place. He leans against a crate of test tubes, a high priest in the ritualistic white coat of science. Behind him, a clutch of technicians confer. He might be one of them, the medical researcher, the microbe hunter, were it not for the red tie. It's stop-sign red: bright, luxuriant, rich. A power tie. A badge of success and, under the circumstances, a warning. "I am not what I seem," it says. "I don't just serve my God. I play God."

There were other signs, other rituals. After my first interview, as Swanson walked me to the door, I asked casually if his public relations people could arrange a quick tour of the company sometime during the coming week. No, Swanson said, everyone was too busy. Then I asked if I could chat briefly with some of his associates—say, David Goeddel, Genentech's chief scientist. "Nope," came the reply. They're too busy, too. Finally I asked if I could come to that Friday's "hoho," an end-of-the-week bash the company periodically throws to break tension and keep spirits high.

These hohos have become legend in the Valley. Whenever Genentech scores a breakthrough or introduces a new product, it throws a big jamboree. Swanson and Genentech president Kirk Raab show up dressed as bumblebees or surfers in frilly blond wigs. Fireworks light up the sky, sometimes with such intensity that aircraft have to be diverted at nearby San Francisco International Airport. Bands play into the night. It sounded like fun, and a good way to see the personal side of the company. But no, the hoho was also off-limits. "It's just for family," Swanson explained succinctly.

The monastery is cloistered. No outsiders allowed.

Secrecy runs deep in the man. He's so intensely private that he removes snapshots of his wife and children from his desk before receiving unfamiliar visitors. Of course I called Goeddel and others, in spite of Swanson's prohibition. "Sure," Goeddel said. "I'd be glad to talk with you . . . as long as you clear it with Bob's office." Then I phoned a former Genentecher, now head of a Silicon Valley electronics firm. He'd also be happy to talk—as long as Swanson gave him the okay. "I talked with a reporter a few years ago," the man recalled, "and Bob got so mad that I promised never to do it again." But, heh, call back if you get "permission."

And so it went. Back in New York, stonewalled, I asked a *Newsweek* stringer, Nadine Josephs, for help. A woman noted for her ability to extract colorful anecdotes about reclusive personalities, she was, better yet, friends with friends of Swanson. Anticipating pay dirt, I settled back to await Nadine's report. After several days of digging, she called. The result: zippo, at least at first. Her friends, Swanson's friends, all called in to check with "Bob." And shortly thereafter I talked again with Swanson. He was very upset, "kind of angry," to learn that I was checking into his personal life. He was worried about his family's security—a not uncommon, or unreasonable, fear. Men as wealthy and prominent as Swanson are vulnerable to threats of kidnapping, extortion and needless intrusions.

Still, there was another dimension. For a man who is so outgoing at the office, so open to others, why do his closest associates consider him so closed, so inaccessible beyond the normal bounds of work? I asked him about it.

A long pause. "Work is work, and family is family," Swanson said finally. These two worlds should not overlap. "It's a matter of respect for the privacy of others." Another long pause, then an analogy. "To me, it's like baseball. You work together as a team, you practice as a team, you play the game. Then, people go home to their own houses."

ROBERT A. SWANSON was born in Brooklyn, New York, on November 29, 1947. His father was an electrical maintenance foreman at Eastern Airlines, his mother a homemaker. When their son was still young, they moved to Miami Springs, Florida, a friendly working-class neighborhood bordering the airport and buffered by a canal and railroad tracks. Some might say it was the wrong side of the tracks.

Swanson's grade school teachers remember him as eager, alert, hardworking and, said one, "dedicated to his parents." He was an only child. Or, as Swanson prefers to put it, "a first child." Perhaps that's an important distinction. An "only child," on some obscure plane, might half think of himself as a vaguely unwanted child, or one who caused his parents such trouble or anxiety that they didn't want another. But perhaps a "first child," as Swanson's parents encouraged him to think of himself, would have no such doubts.

Whatever the case, Swanson's was a typical boyhood. He loved to go fishing. He caught butterflies and put them in jars. He was on the high school tennis team. He worked hard at his studies and, in 1965, graduated tenth in his class of twelve hundred at Hialeah High School. He was president of the National Honor Society, a member of the Key Club (an honor society sponsored by the local Kiwanis for, as one former classmate describes it, "Ivy League–type kids") and the German Club. Eric Richey, a classmate who now teaches at Hialeah, remembers Swanson as "a standout, a striking-looking guy, really friendly, yet reserved."

His high school English teacher describes him as "an irresistible, charming, diffident kid, thoroughly involved in everything he did. He was an active listener, gentle, very well liked." Especially by the girls, it seems. Hialeah's Class of '65 yearbook lists him as a "Shipmate with Anchor," a sort of teenybopper sorority sweetheart. Swanson himself was not so frivolous. He signed his yearbook picture that year in characteristically goal-oriented fashion: "MIT Class of '69."

Getting into MIT was literally a lifetime ambition, not only his own. No one in Swanson's family had ever finished college. His acceptance by perhaps the most prestigious technical college in the land was thus the fulfillment of a family destiny. "I was part of a continuum," Swanson says. "Each generation was supposed to do better than the next. That was what my family was all about." It was a classic immigrant drive to excel, but it was also more than that. Swanson's family took a gamble in sending him off to Massachusetts. "We only had enough money for my first year," he says. "If I didn't get a scholarship after that, it was back to a state school. That was another of my family's attitudes. We said, 'Let's go for it.' "

That says a lot. Dropping out of an expensive school like MIT for lack of money would be no humiliation. Lots of bright kids have had to do it. But the Swansons would not have seen it that way; for them, it would have been a humiliating defeat. One thing Swanson remembers from his earliest days is how his parents emphasized the importance of setting high goals and standards. "Particularly my mother," he says. "She always said, 'Shoot for the best. Nothing but the best.' That's since become a key part of my whole attitude: Set high goals and work your fanny off to achieve them." If he did well academically in high school, it was due as much to hard work as to intellectual quickness. And he always had focus; he did what he liked and was good at, and he always went after things with energy.

Setting goals was a family affair. That's partly how he got to MIT. As a boy, Swanson was caught up in the excitement of *Sputnik* and the space race. One day he told his mother that he'd like to be a scientist, maybe a chemist. Instead of saying, "That's nice, dear," the family began planning. "We all sat down and we thought about it. We made the decision together. The question for us was, 'Okay, what's the best school for that?' We picked out MIT and strove for it."

Swanson's parents taught him not only to aspire to be the best, they showed him *how* to be the best. Any hurdle could be overcome with patience. It was all a matter of step-by-step planning and thorough preparation. Nothing must be left to chance. Take his first haircut. "My parents were big on explaining to me what kind of things would be happening to me, and why," Swanson says. "Before I went to get my first haircut, they put a sheet around my neck and made clipping noises around my head, just so I'd know what to expect at the barber." They also taught him the importance, and satisfaction, of teamwork—at least his father did.

Arthur John Swanson, a cigar-chomping union man, was very different from his wife. Swanson's mom, says a high school classmate, was "just a face, very reserved." She rarely invited other children over to the house. If she was the main goal-setter in his life, she was also the source of his reserve. Swanson's father, by contrast, was an outgoing, all-around-popular guy. He coached his son's Little League team. "Bob's father was a real motivator," recalls Eric Richey. "He'd charge you up and stress teamwork. And he wasn't overly protective of Bob."

Perhaps Swanson's father realized that being an only child was a burden. His son needed to mix more with other kids. So he pushed him into team sports, which young Bob came to love even if he didn't naturally excel at them. He learned the importance of teamwork and watched closely as his father, the model communicator, tried to get his boys to perform to the max. "I think my dad was a great coach," Swanson tells me. "He had the patience to be there and spend the time. He always had a very positive outlook. He got along well with everybody in his interactions. He was able to help kids accomplish their goal, which was to win the ball game."

"Interactions." "Helping the kids accomplish their goal." Swanson's choice of words is so formal. I mean, this is Little League we're talking about. How goal-oriented, how *serious* can you get?

Swanson draws lessons of life from games. "One of the things that came out of Little League," he says, laughing but not joking, "was an understanding about myself. If you were five runs down at the bottom of the eighth inning, most kids would say, 'Oh my God, it's over.' My approach was always, 'We're only five runs down. We've gotten that many runs before. We can DO it!" The emphasis, very audibly, is Swanson's. Is it any coincidence, today, that Swanson defines his role at Genentech as "cheerleader, coach and quarterback"?

There was another echo here. This could very well be Steven Jobs speaking. "My job," he told me before I ever met Swanson, "is to take a slightly longer focal point on things we have to do, so that when things get difficult or fuzzy, I can keep everybody on track."

This isn't to say that a comparison with Jobs somehow validates Swanson. To the contrary, Swanson is that rare entrepreneur who still heads the company he started, who has built a major corporation from the ground up. If anything, his management methods validate those of Jobs. But like Jobs, Swanson epitomizes the businessman as visionary, the leader who generates an idea, gives it concrete definition and marshals the forces to make it real. Perhaps the most critical element in that process is building a team that buys into the dream. For Swanson, that's a matter of bridging the traditional gulf between science and business.

Swanson, too, is a seducer. Remember work as "fun" and "management by values"? Remember Jobs at NeXT, "building from the heart" and emphasizing the "top line" over the "bottom line"? Swanson promises these things in much the same way. "This is a science-driven company," he tells his researchers time and time again. "The logic of good science is good business. Don't worry about money. Anything you need, you've got."

He's selling a dream that, for a scientist, is as seductive as you can get: Do your work, do it your way, don't worry about constraints of time or money. If Genentech's rise is a tale of vision and inventiveness, that's largely the reason. Other companies would sooner or later have cashed in on the new advances in biotechnology. But Swanson did it first, ahead by as much as a decade. The social benefits of that acceleration are beyond estimation. Imagine how many people might needlessly die if t-PA were to come on the market in 1998 rather than 1988.

And the reason Genentech was first, pulling the rest of the industry along? Because, Genentechers say, the company is built from the heart. Because it's built on superior "values."

I'M NOW BEING introduced to those values, even if I don't realize it at first.

We're sitting in Swanson's office, denuded of personal touches—Spartan furniture, a few abstract oil paintings, a bare desk.

Swanson is looking sheepish. He has spun around in his chair and grabbed a glossy brochure off the top of a well-stocked pile. "It's one of the things I use, well, that we use, as a working thing around here. It's really a statement of philosophy, uh, of what we believe in. And, uh, we try to live it because it, uh, deals with the goals that make this place an enjoyable place to work."

The "it" is Genentech's corporate credo—as Swanson says, a statement of the company's goals and the kind of working environment it aims to create. But why is Swanson so tongue-tied?

Because, I suspect, he's embarrassed. The credo sounds as though it's been lifted from Tom Peters's best-selling management bible, *In Search of Excellence: Lessons from America's Best-Run Companies*. That's the book that made the "credo" one of the trendiest buzz-concepts around, and the parallel isn't lost on Swanson. So there we sit, side by side, both a little embarrassed, as the nation's chief bioengineer earnestly ticks off the Commandments of Success and Happiness, Genentech-style. The Moses of post-industrial management.

What's on the list? First, "Profitable Growth: The Ultimate Measure of Success." Why profits? Swanson asks. "Well, it's a measure of the health of a business. It's understanding who your customers are and what their needs are, so that you can design a product that they will buy and pay you more than you can make it for." And why growth? "Well, you have to have certain economies of scale to be competitive. And growth provides opportunities for personal development. It's the only way people can grow to the limits of their ability and their desire. If a company isn't growing, how do you get ahead? You wait for your boss to die."

And so it goes, from "Profitable Growth" to "Exceptional People: Genentech's Greatest Asset." Swanson is also big on "Scientific Leadership: An Uncompromising Commitment to Excellence." Ditto for "Open Communications: The Key to Teamwork and Achievement" and "Informal Environment: An Enjoyable Place to Work." He personally welcomes each new Genentech employee to the company—and lays on with his mission statement. "They're pretty simple concepts," Swanson says, smiling as he reads from the (conveniently) billfold-size blue-and-yellow brochure. "But most people, their eyes get a little wide. They haven't thought about these things in this way before."

My eyes, too, are a little wide. Not with revelation, but more with that glassy stare into middle distance that says, I can't believe what I'm hearing.

It's early in our interview, and I haven't yet realized how central this is to Swanson's management style. A dozen escalating impressions flash across my mind. Bemusement. (So, even top CEOs have their little tics.) Rising incredulity. (He's *serious*.) Dismay. (*This* is a lion of industry, this smiling, pontificating pussycat?) Panic as the clock ticks away. (Help! What's happening to my interview?)

By this time, Swanson has warmed to his theme. He's talking

energetically about the importance of hiring exceptional people, how hard it is to find them and keep standards high. It's not competence or even sheer brilliance that's so hard to get. It's people who share the same values. Suddenly Swanson has left his mission statement behind and is getting into what really makes Genentech—and himself—tick. He uses words like "freedom," "latitude," "openness" and "initiative." Swanson machine-guns the point with half a dozen maxims:

"You have to be free to make mistakes. If you're not making mistakes, you're not pushing yourself hard enough."

"People must be encouraged to take risks, to experiment. That's the only way to get everybody fired up and onto a solution."

"We don't have much of a hierarchy at Genentech. It's ideas that count, and ideas are rarely associated with a title. What's important is to have people who say, 'Hey, this is a great idea. Let's do it.' That's what freedom is all about. That's what's key to Genentech."

It all comes back to *values*, Swanson says, giving his brochure a decisive snap. They shape an organization and distinguish run-of-the-mill enterprises from great ones. "It affects the whole atmosphere. If you're working with people who are motivated the same way you are, work is fun." If it's not, you might as well be doing something else.

These are clichés, to be sure, but it would be a mistake to discount them. "It's not bull, it's not public relations hype," says Genentech chairman Thomas Perkins, a founding partner of Kleiner & Perkins, Silicon Valley's premier venture capital firm. "From the very beginning, the emphasis on values was part of Genentech's business strategy."

That strategy had very little to do with idealism, and everything to do with common sense. To succeed, Genentech early on had to attract the best young scientists around. "We asked ourselves what it would take to do that," says Perkins, and the answer was to offer them something they couldn't get anywhere else: freedom—the freedom to do work they would normally do at a university, if only they could get the funding and the university's backing. And here Genentech had an edge. Very few universities could afford to underwrite sophisticated bioengineering research; it takes lots of money, lots of equipment, lots of staff. What's more, institutions that could undertake the work were often hobbled by what Swanson calls the "feudal hierarchy" of the university research system. "When a young scientist discovers something, the senior guy in the lab gets the credit," he says in disgust. That stifles independence and creativity.

Swanson took a different approach. He understood that he couldn't simply recreate the conditions of a research lab and call it a business. He had to convince scientists, whose rewards were usually only those of status within their own cloistered scientific community, that Genentech could offer the prestige and flexibility of a university as well as the financial rewards of business. Beyond that, he had to convince them that the power of the marketplace and the laws of supply and demand could be just as inspirational as the gods of pure science.

So Swanson set out to gather into the Genentech community an elite inner core of talent. "We have to have the best. Only the best," Swanson said so often that it became something of a mantra. For without the best, given the state of the science at the time, Genentech could not expect the dramatic breakthroughs it needed to have even the slightest chance of succeeding. Swanson was in this sense an architect. He knew that without a strong foundation, built on an inspired design, his unorthodox edifice wouldn't stand. And he knew that you couldn't cut corners on the cost of materials.

First, Genentech promised to fund its scientists' research, eliminating the need to compete for public and private grants, while at the same time offering all the attractions of academia: independence, flexible hours, association with other experts in the field. Swanson in particular recognized that traditional pharmaceutical companies actually hindered their scientists' work. Fearing that publication would jeopardize their patent rights, they kept researchers from writing articles or otherwise publicizing their findings. Genentech, by contrast, guaranteed the right to publish—simultaneously protecting itself by pursuing an unusually aggressive patents strategy of filing applications almost before its researchers' work was done. More important, it gave credit where credit was due. "At Genentech," Swanson says, "the people who make the discoveries get the credit." No more "chief researcher" grabbing the glory.

Today, that credit amounts to more than applause. Genentech pioneered the use of what has since come to be known as "junior stock," shares sold to employees at a significant discount but that cannot be traded until the firm attains certain sales goals. Stock options are offered to nearly all employees (their use is most limited at the *top*, in stark contrast to the general practice of giving options only to senior executives), and so-called "R&D partnerships" let scientists take a stake in the profits of products they develop. None of this may seem especially unusual today, but at the time, Genentech's management innovations were truly revolutionary. If profit sharing and stock options are now routine in the Valley, it's partly because of Genentech.

A distinctive corporate culture emerged: an emphasis on reciprocity and collegiality, an absence of hierarchy, a climate where people are judged by the quality of their work and ideas, and where teamwork and flexibility are at a premium. In short, all the good things in Swanson's mission statement. Genentech's scientists, accustomed to the cutthroat competitiveness of university labs, found the atmosphere exhilarating. And the esprit has endured. As organizations grow, they often lose touch with the basic values on which they were founded. Genentech has expanded from a few dozen employees to more than two thousand, but Swanson has worked hard to preserve its specialness.

"Bob is a very patient, deliberate man," says chairman Perkins. "He possesses in abundance a characteristic that all exceptional business leaders must have. That's a love of their organizations. They are willing to put in endless hours of training, of communicating the corporate ideal and the corporate ethic. Companies like Genentech are characterized by a distinctive *way of thinking*. It says, 'This is the way that *we* do things.' "

Creating such a culture involves much more than defining and refining, ad nauseum, the company's goals. "It's deeper than that. It's a whole philosophy," says Perkins. "Bob spends an enormous amount of time thinking about basic questions: How do we do things at Genentech? What kind of people are we? What does this imply for how we treat our people and our customers? What do we do when a customer has a problem? What's our role in society? On what philosophical basis do we resolve conflicts?

"I've been in the venture capital business for four decades," he continues, "and the longer I'm in it, the better I understand the importance of this. The president who doesn't have the time or the focus to develop a corporate philosophy and then instill it at every level of his organization will never have employees who will walk through fire for him. That doesn't mean his company won't be large or successful; it might well be. But it won't have that specialness, that extra something that distinguishes a truly great company from a merely good one."

It certainly won't be the kind of company to develop a product that changes the world.

EVERY REMARKABLE AGE is defined by a relatively small time and place: Athens of ancient Greece, Florence of the Renaissance, Paris between the two world wars. Civilization flourishes, changes direction.

In 1975, Silicon Valley was such a place. It was home to an exuberant explosion of discovery, innovation and money-making, a second Industrial Revolution. The Age of Aquarius was over; the Gilded Eighties were yet to come. The youth rebellion, the generation gap, the Vietnam-era ferment on the campuses had gone the way of love beads and long hair. A new band of rebels was coming into its own, kids around thirty who had bucked the nonconformist pressures of the times and gone into business, finance or venture capital. At Harvard University's commencement exercises that June, graduating MBAs were booed, as always since the sixties. But it was the last hurrah of a dying zeitgeist. Henceforth they would be celebrated.

The year also marked the beginning of a startling entrepreneurial wave. In 1975, some 325,000 new companies were incorporated in America. In 1976, the figure was 375,000; in 1978, 478,000; in 1982, 566,000; in 1986, 702,000. Silicon Valley had reinvented entrepreneurship. "Entrepreneurs" were once vaguely grubby people who started nondescript businesses in garages. The electronics revolution changed all that. Steve Jobs became a folk hero. The excitement was not just in computers and electronics. In 1975, Silicon Valley was poised for a second great leap: this one into the mysterious world of biotechnology. Robert Swanson knew next to nothing about the field. Yet he would come to dominate it within a few short years. He would build a personal empire and, along the way, create a new industry.

To appreciate the significance of his achievement, it helps to meet a man and his two cats. The man, Herbert Boyer, a burly, casual bull of a man given to poker and pretty girls, is a world-class biochemist at the University of California in San Francisco. As for the cats, Watson and Crick, if you know something about their namesakes, you'll know something about biotechnology.

James Watson, an American researcher, and Francis Crick, a rambunctious Brit, are the Lewis and Clark of modern biology. In 1953, they unscrambled the structure of DNA—the famed "double helix" that is the genetic building block of life. As they described it, an organism's genes are like long, twisted ladders, whose "rungs," measuring about ten molecules wide, determine the human genetic code. Differences in race, features, hair coloring, even intelligence and physical ability, are nothing more than kinks in these long nucleotide chains.

It's impossible to overstate the importance of that discovery. It set in motion a chain reaction of scientific inquiry that worked one of the greatest conceptual revolutions in history, no less important than the notion that the sun, rather than the earth, is the center of the solar system. Scientists learned to "sequence" DNA, to determine where a particular trait can be found in the genetic code. They found that certain "restrictive enzymes," bodily proteins, can act like scissors to "snip" a strand of DNA at precise and predictable points. Finally, in 1973, came the most dramatic advance of all. Two maverick biochemists, Boyer and his colleague Stanley Cohen, worked the miracle of life itself. They cut strands of DNA from two separate organisms, stuck them together and "tricked" the new gene into reproducing. They created the world's first clone, a bit of life that never existed before. Cohen and Boyer dubbed their technique "recombinant DNA." The new science of gene-splicing was born.

In retrospect, you might have expected society to be grateful. Not so. This was still the heyday of Earth shoes and the ecology movement. Fears that new life-forms might escape the lab and pollute the gene pool touched off extraordinary controversy. In the public mind, genetic engineering seemed more likely to produce monsters than miracles. Countless articles sounded warnings on the mutant theme. Some featured unsettling photographs of deformed children and animals and warned that genetic engineering could cause such tragedies to multiply. Others made the same point less stridently: In a cartoon in *The New Yorker*, a half-man, half-fish applies for a job as a lifeguard. "What are your qualifications?" asks the functionary reading the fish-man's application.

The battle grew so heated that for a time it threatened to impede further research. Debates over the potential dangers embroiled universities. Congress proposed to regulate the work. The National Institutes of Health issued safety guidelines. Environmental groups, many motivated by a sixties-style antitechnology ethic, mobilized to ban experimentation altogether. Getting personal, the radical *Berkeley Barb* listed Boyer in its 1975 Halloween issue as one of the "10 Biggest Bogeymen" in the San Franscisco area.

Enter Robert Swanson. Boyer, at this point, was at his wit's end. He was tired of being tarred as the father of the "gene bomb." His lab was short of money. Research was stalling out. He couldn't afford the equipment he needed or get the people he wanted. Then came a telephone call from someone he had never heard of. The soft-spoken, almost reticent voice on the other end of the line asked for a little time to talk and mumbled something about how there "might be some money involved." Boyer blinked, thought twice and offered Robert Swanson fifteen minutes late on a Friday afternoon.

* * *

THE BUILDER

IT'S IMPORTANT TO understand how Swanson came to make that phone call.

When he arrived at MIT in 1965, he exhibited all the traits that had made him successful at Hialeah High School. He studied hard. He methodically set goals by identifying very deliberately what he liked and wanted to do, and then just as deliberately set out the steps for getting there. Though not a brilliant student, Swanson completed the course work for his chemistry degree in just three years, then petitioned the college to admit him to the Sloan School of Management as a senior. Why abandon science for graduate study in business, his academic adviser asked? "I told him I loved science and ideas," Swanson says today, "but it was a little too 'thing'-oriented. I enjoyed working with people."

As in high school, he was again the team player and, in time, a team leader. He was eager to prove himself—academically, since his freshman grades put him in the lower third of his class, and socially. He joined the Sigma Chi fraternity. Fred Middleton, a former fraternity brother and a vice-president of Genentech, remembers him as "one of the guys, fun-loving, always laughing at others' jokes." He played on a water polo team, signed up for intramural hockey and, inevitably, was once again christened "Chipmunk." He ran for lots of school and fraternity offices, but ended up in the one that suited him best: social chairman. "It was," Middleton notes, "much the same role that he now plays at Genentech."

At Sloan, Swanson took the only course offered in entrepreneurship. It was all about venture capital and the mechanics of starting a company and raising money. "It *really* excited me," he says, emphasizing *really* with an almost boyish enthusiasm. "It involved the whole process of developing a new product. How do you take an idea and make it concrete? How do you put together the right team of people? Here was a whole new complexity. As a venture capitalist, out on your own, you not only have to find a new idea. You also have to build a whole company."

Immediately upon graduating in 1970, Swanson joined Citibank in New York, one of the few companies willing to hire a trainee in venture capital. Three years later, he was sent to San Francisco to open the bank's venture capital arm on the West Coast. He enjoyed the work and did well. The bank recognized his talent, and before long his bosses started talking about sending him to the Far East. It's time to move up in the company, they said. It's a great opportunity and a great promotion.

Swanson was flattered. He was, after all, just twenty-five years old. At an age when many of his peers were completing the bank's training program, he had vaulted into middle management. He sat on the board of directors of several California companies. He reported directly to some of the bank's most senior officers. And now he had been slated for an important post in Asia. Trouble was, Swanson didn't want to go. "It was a tough choice," he recalls. "I decided this venture capital stuff was fun. I wanted to keep doing it. But I also felt a driving need to be out on my own. So I told Citibank that I wasn't really a banker. And I left."

It would have been so easy to stay, to rise within the bank hierarchy and go on collecting those fat paychecks. Instead, Swanson took an offer from a client he had done some work for at Citibank—Kleiner & Perkins, the most important venture capital firm in the San Francisco area. It was a peculiar offer; it was essentially to sit around and think.

In those days, getting a job at Kleiner & Perkins was a little like winning a Rhodes scholarship. It meant you were *anointed*, a member of a very small and very special elite. Thomas Perkins and Eugene Kleiner were legend in Silicon Valley. If an entrepreneur can be likened to a pioneer setting out on the Conestoga Trail, Perkins and Kleiner would be Mississippi riverboat gamblers. For more than two decades, they have scoured the narrow confines of the Valley, searching for high-tech ventures they can bankroll and guide through its changeable business currents. In a game where more players go bust than strike it rich, they triumphed. The roster of their successful start-ups includes some of the brightest names in high tech: Lotus, Tandem, Compaq Computers, Sun Microsystems. They seemed to have an unerring eye for the right opportunity, for discovering and backing farsighted people who saw a business or a trend in the making. In Robert Swanson, they saw something very special.

Aura is important, a mixture of what you sense and what you know. I remember the embarrassment I felt after drinks one night with an ambassador and his wife in Tunisia. At one point we were joined by a fourth, whose name I never caught. Only later did I discover the man was a renowned diplomat, a globe-trotting international troubleshooter. If I'd recognized who he was, I would now be better able to describe him, his way of laughing and pulling at an ear as he tells a story about a camping trip in the Sahara. But would I have been able to sense his worth without the help of a public résumé?

I doubt it, and so I was curious about what Tom Perkins had seen. I had come to Swanson armed with clips and a knowledge of his business; I *knew* he was an empire builder. But Perkins, in 1975, only sensed Swanson's potential. And then when he was still just this *kid*.

"Bob came to our attention when he was with Citibank," says Perkins. "We had invested in a venture that Citibank was also backing, and it was a very, very troubled company. Things went wrong right from the beginning. It was a situation where most directors panic and run around like chickens with their heads cut off. Bob didn't. He kept his cool and worked to resolve the problem. Even though it was ultimately a disaster, Kleiner and I were impressed. Everybody looks good when things are going well; it's only when there's trouble that the men get separated from the boys."

And so Perkins called up and offered to take Swanson on as a partner. "Join us," he said. "Take some time. Do some thinking."

Do some thinking? Incredibly, Perkins meant it literally. He was determined that nothing should cloud his protégé's point of view. He wanted it as fresh and clear and limitless as the vistas along Route 280. So he gave Swanson the start he needed: freedom, time and a place to think. He *incubated* Swanson in much the same way that Swanson's scientists would later incubate the embryos and man-made proteins of the giant bioengineering firm he would come to found and head. In return, Swanson had to produce. He had to scour the Valley for opportunities. His ideas had to be good, and they had to make money. Lots of money.

Unfortunately the ideas, at least as Perkins appears to have seen them, weren't so good. And Swanson didn't make his bosses a whole lot of money. Basic philosophic differences began to crop up. Kleiner and Perkins hired Swanson as a general venture capital partner; he was more interested in starting a company and managing it himself. Swanson wasn't sure he liked the idea of helping get a venture off the ground and then letting someone else run it and gather all the glory. Ultimately there was a parting of the ways.

At least that's one way of putting it. Others describe the separation more brutally. "The truth," says one close associate, "is that Kleiner & Perkins let him go. Bob was out on the street." Fired. Kaput. "They decided that he did not have the makings of a venture capital partner."

It isn't clear just why, but there's not much doubt about the result. Being fired is a wrenching experience for anyone. For Swanson, it must have been devastating. "I remember Bob telling me that it was one of the worst times of his life," says Robert Byrnes. "He was unemployed. He didn't know what to do."

In fact, though, Swanson did know what to do. He started over. What other choice was there? In retrospect, it's interesting how calmly Swanson dealt with his change in status from boy wonder—ahead of his peers professionally with a high-visibility job—to unemployed. On the surface, here was a man used to accolades and success facing his first big rejection. Before, everything had gone his way: high school honors, MIT scholarship, Citibank. But in reality Swanson's accomplishments had not come easily. "Bob always had to work very, very hard for his successes, and at the same time he is very, very proud," says one friend. "At one level, then, I think he has always felt he had to prove that he was unique, that while he might have been no better than average intellectually and physically, he could still be a standout. With energy and stubborn persistence and vision, he could be 'the best.' "

Another source also talks of this hidden dimension to Swanson's drive to suceed. Deep down, he says, "Bob is still proving himself.

He has this attitude: By God, I'll show them." And why? For one thing, "Bob is short [about 5′ 6″]. I think that from an early stage his response to diminutive stature was to prove himself and his abilities."

Others who at one point or another knew Swanson well say much the same. There was nothing negative, nothing aggressively or unwholesomely competitive about Swanson. But the desire was always there to be better than people thought he was. Classmates from Hialeah High remember that he was not a natural athlete, that he worked hard to carry his own weight and made up for any shortfalls in ability with hard work and enthusiasm. One enviously recalls how Swanson got A's in physical education, even though he was barely good enough to make the tennis team. Swanson did well scholastically in high school, but a college roommate remembers that Swanson got C's and D's his freshman year at MIT—notwithstanding the fact that he got the scholarship he so desperately needed.

In short, the case could be made that Swanson is a proud man driven to excel by his awareness of his shortcomings. But while pride might make it difficult to accept reverses, Swanson's resilience is remarkable. Rather than harboring a dark need to show the world, he is more a man who enjoys thrusting himself out of what management guru David Silver calls the "comfort zone." "Accomplishment is like sailing a boat," says Swanson. The best part is tacking against the wind. "The most exciting thing is to overcome resistance. That's what really gets me excited." Faced with the option of sending out his résumé to another venture capital firm or tacking into that wind, Swanson picked what most would consider the high-risk road. Starting a new company, in an almost nonexistent field, was to be the "liberation" that Jobs found at NeXT. It was going to be "fun."

"The degree of uncertainty in life goes up whenever you make a change or major decision." Swanson's looking back on that decision in a nighttime telephone conversation. "Yet doing these things, putting yourself in these positions, is a necessary part of growing. If you don't put yourself at risk, or throw yourself in situations where it's not clear how you're going to come out, then you can't grow. If you're too comfortable, you're not striving. After all, a good challenge is a lot of fun."

On the other hand, there are challenges and there are challenges. It's one thing to bet on yourself after careful deliberation. It's another to plunge into something recklessly. "I never really thought of Bob as a risk-taker, to be perfectly honest," says Swanson's college chum Fred Middleton. "He thinks things through and knows how he'll get over the bridge to the other side, with a pretty thorough plan. In fact, Bob's only a calculated gambler."

As anyone knows who makes a living betting on chance, calculated gambles are the only ones worth taking.

After he was bounced, albeit gently, out of Kleiner & Perkins, Swanson's "calculated gamble" turned out brilliantly. During his year at the firm, he had become interested in the infant science of gene-splicing. He sensed there was an opportunity there, perhaps a great opportunity, the sort that industrial empires are based on. And so he threw himself into the subject. Like Steve Jobs, banished to corporate Siberia at Apple, depressed and looking for direction, Swanson began to read. He relied on his chemistry background to bone up on the new technology. He made lists. He talked to people and immersed himself totally. "The more I heard about this new technology, the more excited I got," he says. "I knew, I was completely convinced, that this was going to be great."

Why? For one thing, Swanson was astonished at the sheer fecundity of the process. It seemed to him very much like a biological perpetual motion machine. Once you bioengineer a gene to produce a particular trait—something that might be developed into a useful drug—it multiplies automatically. A genetically altered bacterium, for instance, begins to reproduce almost immediately; within twenty-four hours the original organism, once the sole member of its species, subdivides into some 20 million bacteria, all busily manufacturing whatever end product it has been scientifically programmed to produce.

What's more, Swanson was struck at how slowly researchers were moving to exploit Boyer and Cohen's discovery. It was as if an atomic bomb had exploded, and everyone witnessing the event had applauded and then gone home, not realizing that the "fireworks" had forever changed the world. Even Boyer's lab saw the technique merely as a way of obtaining test samples of substances that occur naturally in only the minutest quantities.

Swanson, by contrast, thought that recombinant DNA would be the key to whole new industries. Out on the street, wondering how to make ends meet, he decided that he might as well go for the ultimate. He could establish the first major new pharmaceutical company in thirty years, using the new gene-splicing technique to duplicate the body's proteins, hormones and enzymes. Along the way, he thought he could advance science a quantumfold.

The dream was ambitious in proportion, perhaps, to the depths from which it came. For someone like Swanson, tenacious by nature and driven to prove himself, being fired would have been a powerful motivator. "Bob always wanted to build a business," says lawyer Tom Kiley, who worked with Swanson for twelve years. The experience at Kleiner & Perkins served to vastly increase his "grit level." Another associate described Swanson's down-and-out period as a rite of passage: "Out of the ashes came a Genentech. Certainly most of the start-ups I know about were begun out of necessity—people out of work."

As he poked around the Valley, talking to scientists, finding out what was going on in the field, Swanson found himself pretty much alone. As it happened, Kleiner & Perkins had several years earlier invested in a fledgling enterprise named Cetus, a future competitor of Genentech's and the first of the Valley's biotech start-ups. It had lost money from the beginning. Swanson went to see the Cetus people and, essentially, offered his services. Instead of merely researching the new gene-splicing technology, he suggested, why not turn it into a business? Why not use it to create new products, develop commercial applications *now*? His inquiries, he told Cetus, turned up no inherent reason why it couldn't be done.

The people at Cetus saw it differently. "They kept saying that biotechnology just wasn't a commercially viable industry yet," says Swanson. "They said I was being too optimistic, that things would move pretty slowly." He got the same message nearly everywhere in the Valley. It might be ten years, he was told, before you could even *think* of marketing the first bioengineered drug. Swanson thought that was ridiculous. "Maybe this is where my stubbornness comes in," he says, "but no one who said that what I wanted to do was impossible ever had a good reason why. What was the problem? I wondered. Is there some technical hurdle that has to be overcome? There was never a good answer."

SO IT WAS that Swanson called Herbert Boyer. He showed up at the appointed hour, a serious figure in a navy blue suit, pressed to a knife-edge crease. Boyer, jeans-clad and wild-haired, listened casually as Swanson posed the question that everyone else had dismissed: "Can this technology be developed now?"

"Sure," Boyer said.

Swanson was stunned. He wondered briefly whether Boyer was joking. After all the searching, all the angst, he couldn't believe he had found someone who shared his optimism. "Boy, was I glad to talk to him," Swanson recalls, still full of zest over the lucky encounter. The fifteen-minute meeting spilled over into several hours of brainstorming as they repaired to a local bar for a pitcher or two of beer. By the end of the evening, they had an agreement and a rough business plan, mapped out on napkins. Each would put up five hundred dollars to form a partnership to exploit recombinant DNA technology. Swanson proposed a name: HerbBob Enterprises. Boyer winced. Several months later, in April 1976, they incorporated Genentech, Inc., Boyer's abbreviation of "genetic engineering technology." Boyer, the scientist, set up Genentech's labs as an independent consultant. Swanson, the venture capitalist, would handle the marketing and the money and build up the company.

The rest of the story is well known. How Genentech's team of scientists created the first biotech drug—somatostatin, the artificial insulin that has helped so many diabetics. How the company has since engineered a slew of miracle medicines ranging from Protropin, the growth serum, to its anti–heart attack drug, t-PA. How Genentech's success changed the whole financial character of the venture capital industry.

THE BUILDER

Success never comes overnight, but the date when Genentech burst into the public eye can be pinpointed with absolute precision: October 14, 1980, 7:00 A.M., Pacific Standard Time.

The sun had risen over San Francisco Bay, flashing on the sailboat-white buildings of the pristine Genentech compound. In New York at that hour, excitement was building on Wall Street. It was 10:00 A.M. At exactly that moment, Genentech went public in the single most widely anticipated stock offering in history.

The response was overwhelming, unbelievable even. It was as if the fledgling biotech industry had suddenly become a billionaires' crapshoot, and everyone was elbowing his way into the action. Within one minute, at precisely 10:01 A.M., all Genentech's shares had been sold. Within the span of six breaths, within twenty blinks of the eye, Tom Perkins, who had put up $100,000 to back Swanson's venture, reaped $350 million on his four-year-old investment. And the carnival wasn't over. Genentech's investment bankers sat glued to their phones for the rest of the day. In a trading frenzy, the company's newly minted shares climbed beyond the initial $35 offering price to $50, then $65 and finally $88. It wasn't enough for investors to double their money overnight; they did it over the lunch hour. Swanson himself did even better. He made nearly half a billion dollars. At thirty-two, he was the One-Minute Megamillionaire. What a vindication of his vision! What a resounding defeat for the naysayers he encountered on his way.

How Swanson handled that triumph is revealing. The week of the stock sale, as the millions rolled in, he skipped town on his honeymoon. When he returned, newly rich and famous, he splurged and bought his bride a new car. A Volkswagen.

There's a moral in that frugality. His wife's Volkswagen is an expression of Swanson's deep financial conservatism. "Bob abhors ostentation," says Tom Kiley. "He is very conscious of the favorable reputation Genentech enjoys with its investors. That means no squandering of money that could be put to otherwise productive use—no company cars, no company jets, no extravagant perks." Top execs have to find their own places in the company parking lot, just as any secretary does, and Swanson held out to the end when Genentech's execs decided it was time to replace their battered gray steel office desks with something more upscale.

Careful husbandry is bred in the bone. Swanson has seen first-hand how cherished goals can slip away for lack of money. A venture capitalist before starting Genentech, he saw young companies squander their start-up capital—and go under. Growing up, he saw his family's dreams dashed. Swanson's parents, their brothers and sisters, all attended college, but not one of them was able to finish. "Something always happened," says Swanson. "The money ran out. The war. Something."

For Swanson, gains are never more than tenuously won. Ross Perot posts a slogan in his office: A MAN IS NEVER MORE ON TRIAL THAN IN A MOMENT OF EXCESSIVE GOOD FORTUNE. Swanson echoes the sentiment. "The danger comes once you feel you've arrived," he says. "When you feel that way, you're on the verge of not being very good at what you do." That basic insecurity, that sense that nothing is ever irrevocably yours, is one of Swanson's greatest assets, so valued that he deliberately cultivates it. Like others in this book, Swanson is a control freak, the more absolute the better. The determination not to let up, not to neglect the tiniest details, to persevere in the face of fickle circumstance, are all part of the mind-set. It's key to his drive and ambition. It's the force behind Genentech, architected into the very core of its value system.

VALUES CAN DISTINGUISH a company. But they're no substitute for business judgment and management ability.

Swanson is a rarity in Silicon Valley. He's an entrepreneur who has also proved he can manage. Usually ventures such as his follow an undeviating script. A visionary entrepreneur starts a new company. He has a brilliant idea, finds the right people and gets the technology off the ground. But soon he fades from the scene, even as his company continues to prosper. Perhaps he was a poor manager, prompting his financial backers to shunt him aside in favor of someone more experienced, someone brought in from the outside. Or perhaps a larger company simply buys him out and afterward reshuffles the staff. Whatever the case, it's rare in the Valley to see the founder of a company still at its helm after five years. Swanson has been at the helm of Genentech for more than ten.

The reason, says Thomas Perkins, is Swanson's ability to grow with the company. He's not merely a visionary, even though he's almost universally credited as being the first to see the commercial possibilities of biotechnology. There's more to vision than seeing; Swanson couples that with a commensurate ability to manage his company's progress. He has the tenacity to stick with his judgments, even in the face of conflicting advice.

"In the early days of biotechnology," says Tom Kiley, "people said that the place to start was with animal health care products or the production of artificial fuels like ethanol." The perception was that the technology had no immediate human applications, partly because it was so new, and partly because of regulatory hurdles on human testing imposed by the Food and Drug Administration. "Bob correctly perceived that this was wrong," Kiley says. "He believed that by producing pharmaceuticals, you could have a product that would sell for thousands of dollars a gram rather than for pennies a pound. In other words, high value, low volume. And he was totally convinced, rightly as it turned out, that the market was there."

Kiley identifies other areas where Swanson stuck by his own notions of what Genentech ought to be.

From the beginning, he insisted on building a fully integrated company. Many advisers argued against it. They said Genentech should be primarily a research firm, making discoveries and licensing them to such giants as Eli Lilly, as it did with artificial insulin. Swanson said no. He saw that the biggest profits lay in marketing drugs, not inventing them. If Genentech built an organization from the ground up, from the lab to the drugstore counter, then it would be able to compete with the major pharmaceutical companies and retain its independence. It could generate enough cash to fund the research that it cared about, not merely the research that the giants were willing to underwrite, and it could afford to find and hire the best people in the field—the people Genentech would need if it was going to remain at the forefront of the industry, as Swanson was determined to do.

In addition, Swanson insisted that Genentech target products that were unique or in critically short supply. An example was insulin, a product that occurs in nature in only the minutest quantities. There had to be a ready market, not supplied by another drug maker, and there could be no entrenched competition. Because Genentech could not hope to duplicate the massive distribution networks of the largest pharmaceutical companies, it deliberately narrowed its market. It would produce only drugs that could be used by hospital-based specialists, easily reached by the small but elite sales force that Swanson was even then assembling.

For Swanson, nothing was more important in building Genentech than its people. Again and again you hear the refrain, "Hire only the best." Create the best possible working conditions, so that the best people will come and do their best work. Swanson's insistence on "the best" created an embarrassment of riches. In its infancy, says Kiley, Genentech had too many people, most of them overqualified for their jobs as they found them. Swanson's first hire was a young partner at one of San Francisco's top law firms; he would ultimately help Genentech rewrite patent law as it applied to biotech products, but initially (since Genentech as yet had no products to patent) he had very little work. Genentech's twelfth employee was the former chief financial officer of Chase Manhattan Bank, and his number two man was a top executive of one of the country's largest health care companies, American Critical Care. He put together a marketing team—before Genentech had anything to market—so that Genentech would have seasoned management in place as it grew larger and more complex. "He could see down the road that he would need all that extra horsepower," says Kiley. "He saw that these people's jobs would quickly grow and demand the full range of their talents."

Hiring the best also meant getting people's best efforts. That, in turn, was a matter of teamwork and corporate culture. Swanson and Boyer from the beginning shared a common vision of that. "I was very lucky to find him," Swanson says. "He was not only a leader in his field, but he held philosophies and basic values very similar to mine." Just as other leading entrepreneurs stamp their companies with their personal imprint (Steve Jobs at Macintosh, for instance, insisted that every Mac computer bear the autograph of its makers), so did Swanson. Hence Genentech's emphasis on scientific freedom, informality and ingrained egalitarianism. Hence the profit sharing, the stock options and the R&D partnerships. "Everyone in the company is a shareholder," says Swanson. "If you are an owner, you act differently. You are interested in the whole company, not just your little part of it."

LOYALTY IS IMPORTANT. Friendships with Swanson dissolve once people leave the company. "He sees it as something of a betrayal," says Robert Byrnes, who left Genentech four years ago. But while you're on the inside, that loyalty is golden.

"Bob was always especially loyal to the scientists," says Byrnes. He likes to hang out in the labs; he cares about the science and has never forgotten that Genentech is only as good as the products its researchers invent. He therefore backs them to the hilt. "I remember a discussion about a couple of our scientists," says Byrnes. They were good people, tops in their field. But people on the business side were complaining that they were going too slowly, that they were not carrying their weight. "Bob listened politely, disagreed and backed the scientists up," Byrnes recalls. "After a year or two, they ended up doing some very significant things for Genentech."

Tom Perkins sees that loyalty as well. "People feel they can trust Bob to do the right thing, that he's not going to manipulate them or scheme and contrive. When the going gets tough and you're under pressure, a lot of people will cut corners. Bob won't. So people trust him."

Trust. We're back to values, for trust, too, is built. What if Swanson had given in and fired those scientists? What message would that have sent? It would have meant that Genentech does not in fact place science first, that after a point good science is *not* good business. It would have been a signal to other researchers that they'd better not spend too much time trying to get things right, better not push for the ultimate. Be sensible, the signal would say. Play it safe and shoot for what's attainable, before the company's higher-ups get impatient and pull the plug. That would go against everything Swanson stands for. After all, how do you set high goals and standards, as his parents taught him to do, as he coaches his employees to do, without taking risks?

Perhaps one reason Swanson still heads Genentech is that he so tenaciously stuck to his original vision of the company. "I don't think Bob will ever give up Genentech," says Fred Middleton. "He'll hang on to what he created. Bob was looking for an opportunity to excel, and the company's success is enormously fulfilling for him. He's the emperor of the place."

And yet he hardly acts the emperor, which may be yet another reason for his staying power.

Roberto Crea, an Italian researcher who headed Genentech's laboratories until 1978, roomed with Swanson during Genentech's first years. It was a lifestyle totally without pretension. Arriving in San Francisco, Crea entered the apartment and found Swanson sleeping on a mattress on the floor, his bike tucked under a Ping-Pong table in the living room and a no-frills black-and-white television perched precariously on a steamer trunk. Even after Genentech went public, making Swanson rich, the newly minted mogul continued to drive a battered Datsun.

Crea's point in telling these stories is that Swanson today is little different than he was then, at least in his fundamental view of the world. At work, there's the same openness and democratic approach. "He was always ready to talk to anyone, the lab technician or the dishwasher," says Crea. A former high school classmate was struck by that as well. Swanson attended his tenth reunion and told one classmate how he was starting a company, and how he hoped it would succeed. Five years later, he was back at another reunion—this time as one of the most powerful businessmen in America. What did he talk about? Not his company, but how thrilled he was to be associated with Boyer, who had won the Nobel Prize. About Genentech, he happily said that it had worked out. His only boasting, it seemed, was to allow that he did *not* have a private parking space in the Genentech parking lot.

If power corrupts, it generally does so through arrogance. And Swanson, however big of ego, seems too down-to-earth, even naïve, to be susceptible. People who know him well say he'll continue to grow at Genentech not because he loves the position and the influence, but mainly because he loves the science. He's like the humanist king who commissioned Titian to paint his portrait. When the master dropped a brush, the sovereign stooped to pick it up. So, too, for Swanson. He may rule his kingdom, but science reigns. "He's built one of the best scientific capabilities in the world at Genentech," says one Genentecher, "and that's his chief satisfaction."

Perhaps. Swanson may like science, but he likes building his company more. I remember listening to Steve Jobs telling an interviewer what drives him. "You see something out there and you know you have to do it," he said. "It's like helping something to be born. It's not a push, it's a pull. It's a target in the distance, and I'm running toward it. And I think that everybody at NeXT feels that way. They're great people; the best I've ever worked with. We all share the same goals. We all see this thing out there, and we're all running toward it as fast as we can."

I asked the same of Swanson: What makes him run?

"You know," he said, "we talked about overcoming resistance. I don't think anybody consciously seeks out problems, but it's fair to say that we, well, we're seeking thrills. The thrill of getting a group of people working together on a common goal.

"It's like a chess game, open to lots of players. You're all thinking the same way and sitting around together, and everybody's kibitzing and trying to decide on the best move. And you're all moving in the same direction, working for the same thing.

"That's fun. That's what really gets me excited. Working with people to build things. Creating something that wasn't there. Yes. To me, that's exciting. That's the most exciting thing of all."

CHAPTER EIGHT

GLORY

◆

IT WAS an eerie case of *déjà vu*. The day I was supposed to interview Steven Jobs, he kept me in a holding pattern for nearly a week. Now it was happening again.

Twenty-four hours before our scheduled meeting, Ted "the Mouth of the South" Turner called up to cancel. He was writing a memoir, and he had to be uncharacteristically circumspect. Talking to me, or to any journalist, "would be dilutive of my autobiography," he said, struggling to get his mouth around *dilutive*, evidently his publisher's term, so that it came out "di-di-lu-u-tive," a sort of stutter on top of a drawl that made it almost impossible to understand what Turner was talking about.

That wasn't all. Turner was mad. "Pissed to the eyeballs," one of his assistants said later. That morning, *Newsweek* hit the stands with a scathing article about Turner's favorite subject—himself.

Nine months earlier, in the summer of 1986, Turner had bought MGM, the famed Hollywood movie studio. But the deal wasn't working out. He borrowed virtually all the money he needed to finance the acquisition—a whopping $1.5 billion—and the crippling debt now threatened to bring down Turner Broadcasting System, the cable television empire that Turner had built from scratch to become the nation's fourth major network. TBS needed a bailout, and just then it had gotten it. A consortium of cable TV companies allied with Kirk Kerkorian, the California movie mogul who sold MGM to Turner in the first place, injected $550 million into the company. In exchange, that is, for a pound (or maybe fifty pounds) of Turner's flesh. Turner had to reduce his personal share of TBS stock from 87 percent to 51 percent—barely enough to ensure his continued control.

It was a painful loss of face. And *Newsweek* rubbed it in. In a story headlined THE COMEUPPANCE OF "CAPTAIN OUTRAGEOUS," the magazine reported that Turner was the laughingstock of Hollywood, the "pigeon" in a "sensational score" by Kirk Kerkorian. He hadn't merely paid a steep price for MGM, it seemed. "He took a bath," said one respected Hollywood analyst. "He came to town fully clothed and he left in a barrel." Coming on top of his improbable and ultimately unsuccessful bid for CBS in the spring of 1985, Turner's vaunted "nothing is impossible" attitude was looking a little thin. All things considered, *Newsweek* concluded, it appeared that the wind had finally left Ted Turner's sails. For good.

Which explains why Turner was so mad. Red-eyed, ass-kicking, top-popping mad. Nobody from *Newsweek* was going to walk in his door that day, or any day soon. An aide quickly got on the phone to New York to deliver a brief message: "Don't bother."

At least, that's how it was supposed to be. In fact, the message never arrived. I was already en route to Atlanta and, entirely unsuspecting, walked into the buzz saw of Turner's wrath. He didn't waste any time chewing me up. "Comeuppance, my ass. You show me comeuppance."

Turner complained that he'd been savaged. Those Hollywood types had it all wrong; they were resentful of his success. Most of them wouldn't recognize a good deal if it hit them between the eyes. "Why, I've got nine Oscars!" he said, waving his arm toward his outer office where, indeed, nine golden Oscars for Best Picture (from *Singin' in the Rain* to *Gone With the Wind*) stood in a glittering row. They were eloquent testimony to the film rights Turner had acquired with MGM—films that could now only be shown with Ted Turner's permission and, presumably, only on the cable network owned by Turner.

The tirade went on. I waited to be called "numbnuts." Or "stupid." Or any of the other blistering epithets that Turner has been known to so volubly bestow on those who earn his displeasure. But they never came. Turner kept his anger in check. He clearly wanted to talk. The subject that we were to discuss, after all, was, well . . . The Subject. Dear to Ted Turner's heart. Dearer even than himself and his wounded vanity.

And so Turner turned gracious. He showed me "his" Oscars. "Count 'em," he said, hefting one in each hand like gold-sculpted barbells. "They're heavy!" We inspected his collection of Civil War swords, the ones he sometimes swirls over his head while verbally decapitating visiting journalists. We looked at engravings detailing the great naval battles of history, marveled at the glittery, mind-boggling collection of silver yachting trophies that filled an entire wall of his office.

I wanted to see what one friend calls the "fun couch" (excuse me, the *bed* for nights when busy execs can't get away from the office) that's supposed to flip out from behind a bookcase at the flick of a switch. But at the moment I didn't have the temerity to make what might be construed as even a passing reference to Turner's renowned womanizing. The last thing I wanted to do was trigger another eruption. This was supposed to be a serious meeting, I repeat, involving serious discussions of The Subject, which Turner considers to be the most important in the world. A serious discussion about arms control, the population bomb, environmental pollution and Turner's personal answer to those global problems, the Better World Society. The multinational society that Turner started and funded—with $500,000 of his own money, put up at a time when TBS was in danger of foundering—explicitly to help *save the world.*

THE BATTLE CRIES of the sixties. Again. *Save the world. Change the world. Rearra-a-a-ange the world.* Now they're the call to arms of Ted Turner, a man who says he's proud to be a "do-gooder."

Turner is an enthusiast, and it would be easy to mock him. Surely he is one of America's wackier symbols. He's the entrepreneurial folk hero who sprang to fame and riches on the strength of a crazy notion that he could leapfrog the three major TV networks by bouncing signals from his tiny UHF station in Atlanta off a satellite and into millions of homes across the country. He's the no-holds-barred business survivor who pillories NBC, CBS and ABC for their "schlock" programming, yet built up his new TBS "SuperStation" by airing reruns of *Leave It to Beaver* and *Kojak*. He's the farsighted creator of CNN, the twenty-four-hour cable news channel, and the free-thinking opportunist who allied with right-thinking Senator Jesse Helms in trying to take over CBS. Never mind taint by association, never mind Helms's denunciations of CBS's "liberal bias." Turner has his own political philosophy. "I'm a conservative liberal," he says nowadays, "and I'm liberally conservative."

That suits the mind of a man obsessed with The Subject. There's no doubting his seriousness. Turner sees it as literally a matter of life and death. And The Subject, again, is basically the imminent end of the world. Global annihilation by the A-bomb, the H-bomb, the population bomb and ecological disaster.

"You know, in the Christian Book of Revelation, the world is destroyed by fire." We're less than three minutes into our meeting, and already Turner's sounding the note of apocalypse. "Well, the way mankind is going, that's almost certain to be a prophecy. We've got to end the insanity."

Turner has transformed himself into a globe-trotting conscience of the world, a latter-day Cassandra crying from the ramparts that all hell is about to break loose unless we *do something*, fast. While James Rouse is trying to arouse humanity, Steve Jobs to educate it and Ross Perot to moralize it, Turner is out to save it. "We're an endangered species," he tells anyone who will listen, and we've all got to pull together in this time of crisis.

That's what Turner is about these days. That's why he founded the Better World Society: a new not-for-profit organization that aims to promote world peace and understanding by using television to advance population control, ecology and an end to the nuclear arms race. What makes this more than an eccentric millionaire's folly is Turner's position as the country's most influential television executive.

That's what intrigued me, the thing that prompted me to ask Turner for an interview and fly down to Atlanta. Here was yet another mogul talking about changing the world. Power combined with idealism can be a potent combination. But was Turner more than talk? Or was he just another egomaniac?

Turner actually seemed flattered to be asked. Journalists are drawn to him like flies to honey. He's the best copy this side of Ollie North. But how many reporters ever ask about his Better World Society? Or solicit his views on arms control, other than as a joke? A Turner press conference often as not begins: "Hey, Ted. Are we going to win the America's Cup?"

Think about that. I mean, how should he know? Turner won the America's Cup, the Super Bowl for the rich and stuffy, in 1977—and he's still getting asked about it. "Hell," he says today, "I don't even race sailboats anymore."

It's a legitimate gripe. After all, in the change-the-world department, Turner is without question uniquely positioned to focus attention on the issues. Cable News Network is the first truly global television network, watched from Washington to Peking, Moscow to Buenos Aires. TBS reaches nearly 50 million homes in the United States; its programming is shown in fifty-four countries, beamed down from satellites covering virtually every corner of the earth. Along with Rupert Murdoch's News Corporation, Turner Broadcasting is turning television from a primarily domestic enterprise into a genuinely multinational one. And the Better World Society fits neatly into this impressive demonstration of global reach.

"The point," Turner says, as we began to nibble around the edges of The Subject, "is to use this advantage to increase people's awareness of the critical issues of our time: the arms race, the damage we're doing to our environment, the problems of malnutrition, poverty, health care and education—the general condition of humanity. As our name implies, we would like to see a better world. We want to use television to help humanity come together."

So who's "come together" so far, I wanted to know. What support was the Better World Society attracting, or was Turner more or less out on his own?

"Hell, no," Turner replies. No one ever gets anywhere going it alone. For one thing, he says, "we've got a hell of a board of directors. We have three former heads of state—Jimmy Carter of the United States, Rodrigo Carazo of Costa Rica and Olusegun Obasanjo of Nigeria—and one current one, Gro Harlem Brundtland, prime minister of Norway. There's Lester Brown, head of the Worldwatch Institute in Washington, Georgi Arbatov, the Soviet Union's leading expert on the United States. We've got Jacques Cousteau, the underseas explorer, and Yasushi Akashi, undersecretary-general of the United Nations.

"I mean, we've got allies all over the world! There are literally hundreds of concerned groups and millions of individuals. Anyone who's concerned with the environment is an ally of ours. Anyone concerned with the danger of nuclear war or the hole in the ozone layer is an ally of ours. Anyone who's hurt when they see a starving child in Ethiopia or cares about the slaughter of rhinos in Africa is a friend of ours. Anyone that's offended about oil being dumped in the ocean, or nuclear waste. It's a varied group, and it's a welcome group. All these people are allies of ours!"

Turner has always been more than a little manic, a "zealot in search of a cause," as *The New Republic* once put it. Daniel Schorr, a former CNN correspondent, described his old boss in a *Washington Post* article as a "bundle of contradictions, fitting no ideological stereotype." Tom Belford, executive director of the Better World Society, calls him "two-thirds do-gooder, one-third businessman," with perhaps just a touch of Don Quixote in him.

Or maybe more than a touch. Certainly there's a starry-eyed naïvité to Turner, at least insofar as it applies to his role as Peacenik Extraordinaire. It began showing up in earnest in 1982, when he flew down to Cuba for some duck-hunting with Fidel Castro. The pair killed lots of ducks (some 150; so much for "ecology"), apparently drank lots of rum and, to hear Turner tell it, fast became friends ("I expected him to be some horrible person, but he was a great guy"). More recently he's said the same about Mikhail Gorbachev and the Soviets in general. ("They're just like us!") Communism, Turner now says, is fine by him. ("It's part of the fabric of life on this planet.")

Ted Turner is a prophet of brotherly love?

"You bet," says Ted. Why, you've got to *love* your fellow man.

"If you treat people with dignity and respect, the way they want to be treated, regardless of race, creed or color, then you don't have hostility. It's the same for friends. It's the same for family. It's the same for international relations."

Maybe this is one of those contradictions Schorr was talking about. A whopper, in fact, if you know anything about Turner's stormy relations with his friends, colleagues and family.

At work, as on a sailboat, Turner is a hard master. In Atlanta, he sums up the secret of management success: "Treat everyone the way you would like to be treated yourself," just as Ross Perot says, just as international relations is supposed to work.

Well, maybe Ted Turner *likes* to be screamed at, chewed out for blunders, trampled underfoot when his views run counter to his boss's. LEAD, FOLLOW OR GET OUT OF THE WAY, trumpets a plaque on Turner's desk. And maybe family life is meant to be, shall we say, *charged.* Turner's first marriage ended in divorce, his second in separation after more than twenty years. The split couldn't have been brought on by some extramarital fling, or at least not by any single fling, since Turner's reputedly had so many. ("That's the little girl I took to Cuba with me," he told one visitor, pointing to a snapshot of a pretty girl about to explode from her swimsuit.) So, if he's now set up house on a California beach with a shapely young helicopter pilot, that can't be the real cause of discord.

No, the rupture evidently occurred because *that's just the way Ted is.* The man's on edge, so focused on fame and destiny that personal relationships lose out along the way.

How many Christmases did Turner spend away from home, for instance, chasing yachting trophies? His wife, "Janie," knows all too well; Turner himself probably doesn't have a clue. As Schorr says, Turner is a bundle of contradictions. He loves his children, he loves his wife. Yet there's always that edge. One minute he's the normal, competitive, aggressive, ambitious man on the go, driven but with time for things like kids or a cocktail. The next he's the obsessive-compulsive—mercurial, erratic and nearly out of control in his impatience to *get on with it.* Curry Kirkpatrick, a writer for *Sports Illustrated,* once accompanied him to a Braves game, where Turner, full-fledged American folk hero, watching America's Game, treated his company to some good old Family Living, Turner-style. Kirkpatrick was talking to "Ted," as he insists on being called, about his lust for Fame—how he got it, and whether he could ever write himself as large in New York as in Atlanta. Ted's in full-screed reply in the affirmative when his wife chimes in with a little support.

"Jimmy Carter did it," she says, sweetly.

Turner apparently doesn't relish help from his womenfolk. "Shut up, Janie," said Turner the Famous Southern Gentleman, the man who grew a mustache in honor of Rhett Butler in *Gone With the Wind*, a man who admires the Southern Code of Honor so much that he wishes dueling could be restored. "Nobody asked you. I'm doin' the talkin' here. You just quiet your yap. If you can't keep your mouth shut," he winds up, "get the hell outa here."

LET'S SEE. WHERE were we? Oh, yes. Turner. In Atlanta. Talking about the Better World Society and the gospel of brotherly love. How to solve the world's problems? All you have to do is treat other nations *just like family*.

Turner figures that if you beam this touchy-feely message around the world, people will respond. (Or at least they will if you don't call them "numbnuts" or tell them to *get the hell off this planet.*) And the reason, he says, is that people by nature want to *like* each other. If Russians and Americans, Moslems and Christians, only got to know one another, there wouldn't be any more fighting. They would be "friends," and nobody (well, hardly anybody) wants to kill his friends. Friends don't nuke one another; they de-nuke. *Voilà*, arms control! End of the threat of nuclear winter!

"I look at the positives in life," says Ted. "Getting rid of nuclear weapons and ending the arms race is positive. And I believe the arms race is going to end in the next few years. But let's look ahead one step further. Think about cooperating with the Soviets. Let's talk about pooling our resources—for example, cutting back on our expenditures on missiles and bombers and working together on the joint exploration of space. That's an adventure all humanity could share in.

"We've got to start thinking globally. The walls between us can come down, just as they are beginning to come down with China. The fact that the Soviets are communists is no big hurdle. The Chinese are communists, and we get along fine with them. So why can't we be friendly with the Soviet communists?"

On a trip to Moscow, Turner walked up to a Soviet official, cocked his thumb and pointed a forefinger at the man's head. "Now, point your finger at my head," he commanded. The Russian obliged. "Can we talk like this?" The Russian agreed that they couldn't. Never mind that other Russians, when Turner wasn't looking, were twirling their fingers around their heads in another universal sign: "Is he crazy?" The moral of this little conversational standoff, Turner said later, was the obvious solution to the arms race, as any fool could see. Just . . . stop . . . building . . . weapons.

Ted Turner has the do-good bee in his bonnet. He returns to the theme again and again as he crisscrosses the country, talking at high schools and colleges and professional groups, delivering the message. "This is war. This is a struggle for survival." Turner is pacing his office as he talks, fretting about the fragility of our world. "The Soviets have twenty thousand nuclear warheads pointed at us; we have twenty thousand pointed at them—on hair triggers. If we continue our current course, sooner or later there will be a mistake. There always is. Look at Chernobyl and Three Mile Island. We're just lucky we haven't blown up the world already!"

IT PROBABLY SOUNDS as though I'm making fun of Turner, setting him up for a fall. Journalists tend to do that. No doubt about it, we're a cynical, naysaying lot, and it's easier and a lot more fun to take cynical, naysaying potshots at idealists like Turner than it is to take them seriously. I mean, just think of all the cheap laughs you could score. World harmony through *Leave It to Beaver* reruns! Wally for UN ambassador!

But I've tried to curb the impulse, however tempting, because it really would be unfair. For while I'm skeptical about Turner's save-the-world fervor, his naïve generalizing about "love" and "international understanding," I don't think he's at all wrongheaded. In fact, I think he's a hero.

What is a hero, after all, but someone who persists against great odds? Who dreams big, sticks to his guns, runs downfield with flashy abandon to Win One for the Gipper? Whether that One is winning the America's Cup, breaking the networks' stranglehold on the communications industry or promoting world peace, you can't help but admire Turner's pluck and his tenacity.

What's more, he persists even though he secretly may be just as skeptical about the ultimate results of his do-gooding as I am. As a businessman, Turner is a tough-minded realist who doesn't expect (or at least doesn't always expect) immediate or necessarily grand results. And I'm convinced that he isn't merely on a galaxy-sized ego trip. In our conversation about the Better World Society, I asked Turner why he thought he could make a difference. I expected him to say something about the global role of television, which would have been true enough. Instead, he took the question more personally. "Well, Ted Turner can't make a difference," he said with some irritation, ticked off that I'd presume that he thought he could change the world on his own. "Ted Turner is only one man. All Ted Turner can do is do what he has been doing—join with lots of other people who are aware of these problems and are trying to change things."

Not that any doubts about ultimate results or Turner's own intentions would matter. After all, there are the facts to consider. Like those forty thousand warheads poised for flight across the North Pole. Or famine in Africa. Or illiteracy in the schools. They're serious problems, deserving serious attention. Somebody's got to do something about them. Someone has to take responsibility, try to get people together and build momentum for change. Why not Ted Turner? At least that's the way he sees it, he and a few people like him. Maybe he can make something ("just a little teensy something") happen.

That's a heroic attitude toward life. Turner's success, in fact, hinges on it. He is, after all, an American folk hero, vested in an odd way with society's unarticulated hopes and yearnings. Secretly we are all urging him on. We cheered his campaign against the networks. We were delighted when he showed up deliriously drunk at the stodgy America's Cup awards ceremony. And now we hope his optimism can once again carry his ideals, that the Better World Society will take off and make a difference where cynical governments (and cynical journalists) have failed.

And as I said, you can't doubt Turner's sincerity.

Not long after he started the Better World Society, he delivered a widely reported speech at John Denver's Windstar Foundation in Colorado. It was a rambling talk, full of fatuous enthusiasm ("Well, I've never spent two days in one place and it's been really great") and liberal guilt neuroses ("*We* are the greatest problem in the world"). But it was vintage Turner, and when it came to the gospel, the man knew his stuff. It was a rapid-fire staccato of startling facts, eloquent in their brevity.

"We're in a war," Turner declared, sounding his familiar theme. "A war that will determine whether the human race, or any forms of higher life, will exist on this planet past the next few years. Today, as we sit here, one hundred square miles of Africa became a desert. Over five thousand acres of the Amazon alone were cut down. It's the same everywhere else in the Third World. Twenty years ago, fifty percent of Haiti was forest; today, it's less than five percent."

And take the population explosion: "China's doing a good job. But in most parts of the world there's been very little progress. In Africa, the average family has six children. The situation in Central America is even worse. At three percent annual population growth, we'll have twenty times as many people in a hundred years. We're already overgrazing and overusing much of the land we have. The massive use of fertilizers, pesticides and intensive farming techniques required to feed our growing population is depleting the nutrients in the world's topsoil at a very rapid rate. We lose several inches of topsoil a year now to erosion alone. Gradually it will become harder and harder to feed all the earth's people. And how does that affect other species of life on this planet? In Africa, less than one percent of the wildlife that was alive a hundred and thirty years ago is alive today."

Deforestation. Famine. They ineluctably lead to Turner's main hate—the arms race, the root of all evil. "We're raping the world economically to pay for this loaded military machine," he tells his audience, to thunderous applause. "And what for? So we can blow ourselves to kingdom come? We must be nuts! I mean, maybe we've built all these weapons just so we can kill ourselves if the poison doesn't work. You know, the poison and the chemicals that we're dumping into our atmosphere and our oceans." Maybe the world won't end with a bang after all, Turner suggests. Maybe there will just be a high-tech chemical sizzle. "Yeah. It will be just as if we went out and took an overdose of some kind of drug and passed from the scene. Yes, sir. That's one hell of an epitaph!"

You can't help but be impressed. Turner does his homework. ("I've got access to more information than anyone on this planet!") He talks to experts in ecology, arms control and sociology. He laces his conversation with pithy factlets. A quick reference, say, to a new book, *America the Poisoned.* An oblique flick at the lunacy of the "dense pack" basing system that not long ago was being considered for U.S. strategic missiles. (Remember? That was Defense Secretary Caspar Weinberger's stellar idea for protecting MX launchers from a Soviet first strike. You'd pack them all together in a tight little site in the expectation that so many Russian missiles would be targeted at the base that they would commit "fratricide" by running into one another and exploding in midair.)

Turner, not surprisingly, finds a lot in the world that's chilling. ("I mean, who's running this place, anyway?") Still, it's not Turner's sincerity that's convincing. Actually, it's his record.

Money talks. Turner put half a million dollars into the Better World Society at a time when he really couldn't afford to. Sure, you could shrug that off. What's half a million when you're in debt by $2 billion? In fact, Turner has turned his financial troubles into a not-so-dubious mark of distinction. "I've got more debt than any man in history!" he has crowed on more than one occasion. Even so, I think it would be a mistake to discount Turner's financial contribution, for he didn't give only money. The whole concept was his. He got the Better World Society started by bringing together a prestigious board that could raise money and help make things happen. And over the objections of TBS directors, he guaranteed that TBS would air the society's documentaries—in itself a substantial commitment of expensive airtime.

Nor is the Better World Society Turner's first *cause célèbre.* In fact, it's just getting off the ground. "We've run documentaries on the dangers of nuclear war and the state of U.S.–Soviet relations. We've finished an eleven-part ecology series, *Only One Earth*, that will run through 1988 in some twenty countries, and another on nuclear terrorism, *The Terror Trade: Buying the Bomb*. That isn't much," Turner says, "but it's only our second year. We'd like to expand as quickly as possible." More important, he believes, are the documentaries that TBS airs. To be sure, most of the network's fare is distinguished by its mediocrity: a dreary mélange of sitcoms, baseball games, B-grade movies and game shows. On the other hand, Turner from the very beginning insisted that TBS make at least some commitment to public service, however loosely defined, and Turner often points out that that's more than the major networks offer.

He launches into a denunciation of the networks at the slightest provocation. "The critical issues never get decent treatment on normal television. By that I mean network television," he says contemptuously. "They're not in the news or information business. They're in the entertainment business. The whole point of their existence is to win in the ratings, and so they play to the lowest common denominator. Programming that's serious, thoughtful or complicated is not normally high rating, and so it isn't run. Do you know how much documentary programming the majors will do this year? I'll tell you: CBS has scheduled sixteen hours of documentaries, NBC fifteen hours and ABC five hours. Most of those are on real controversial issues, like wife-beating. CNN will have literally hundreds of hours of discussion on the critical issues. So will TBS."

Like professional wrestling and *Kojak*?

Ooops. Sorry, there I go again. It's just that Turner's arrogance is so overwhelming. CNN, with its twenty-four-hour news broadcasts and talk shows, may with some justification call itself "the world's most important network." But eight years ago, when it took up that self-congratulatory tag line, it was barely a blip on the world's radar. And while TBS indeed has a reputation for underwriting documentaries that would not otherwise be aired—*National Geographic Explorer, The Undersea World of Jacques Cousteau*—many of its more politically ambitious films are often so one-sided, if not outright treacly, as to be almost worthless to Turner's cause. How much footage of the A-bomb bursting over Nagasaki does it take to convince people that they're against nuclear war, for instance? Who isn't against nuclear war?

Turner says that's not the point.

Jacques Cousteau may not stop the Japanese from hunting whales or do much to clean up the oceans. A documentary on the trade in spent nuclear fuel may not spur effective international police action. But you have to start somewhere. Anything that changes the climate in which we see the world's problems helps. "We live in an interdependent world," Turner says, echoing a cliché that's become a staple of newspaper editorials. "If we can see that the world's problems are shared, maybe we can come together to solve them."

The 1986 Goodwill Games, a fifteen-day pseudo-Olympics in Moscow, was Turner's most ambitious international bridge-building extravaganza to date. When Jimmy Carter pulled the United States out of the 1980 Olympics in Moscow, and the Soviets returned the favor in 1984, Turner walked into the office of TBS executive vice-president Robert Wussler, his pinstriped aide-de-camp. "Hey, Bob," he said. "We've got to do something. . . . The Russians should be in the Olympics." A few days later, Wussler was on a plane for Moscow, bearing an odd proposal. How about staging an alternative Olympics? Turner's people suggested to a top Soviet broadcasting official. An Olympics that would be genuinely apolitical and put the United States and the Soviet Union back into direct international athletic competition for the first time in ten years.

It's hard to tell whether the Goodwill Games were a triumph or a disaster. Hardly anyone in the United States watched them, partly because the vast time lag meant that "live" events were shown at home well after midnight. Turner worked hard to attract such world-class athletes as Carl Lewis, the track star, and figure-skating champion Debi Thomas, along with teams from seventy-nine other nations. But many top international stars didn't show. Worse, the Games' main goal—getting "the East and West back together"—quickly took second place as the Soviets turned the competition into a huge propaganda-fest.

During the opening ceremonies, the Soviets treated spectators to a series of colorful card displays. First a huge picture of Lenin flashed on-screen, ricocheting from satellite to satellite across the world, then a representation of a U.S. cruise missile blocked out with an *X*. Or was it a skull and crossbones? Orbiting cosmonauts delivered a homespun little pitch for Moscow's latest arms-control proposal, and choirs of fresh-faced Soviet youths sang the praises of socialism and world unity. Washington got into the act by banning U.S. military teams from the Games—"There goes the boxing team," wrote *The New Republic*—and the Soviets pulled back from a promise to let South Korea and Israel compete. Predictably, advertisers were wary. When the final bill was tallied, Turner lost $26 million on the venture.

Did he mind? Evidently not. The man who keeps a miniature of Walt Disney's Jiminy Cricket on his desk ("Accentuate the positive, eliminate the negative!" he chants in a weird uplifting incantation) insists that the Goodwill Games were a "terrific" investment. "It's like start-up expenses. You always lose money at the start of a new business." Turner is confident that the next Games, to be held in Seattle in 1990, will be profitable. Since they'll take place on U.S. prime time, they'll be much more widely viewed—perhaps even more so than the Olympics in Seoul. Besides, Turner adds, almost as an afterthought, a loss of $26 million is only money. "How do you put a price tag on human understanding?" he asks. "What good is it to be a billionaire if a nuclear bomb is going to hit? What good is money in a burned-out world?"

Turner's love of hyperbole hurts him. No one, except possibly Turner himself, really believes that the Goodwill Games are a force against war. They're not the only alternative to a "burned-out world." Yet to suggest otherwise to him is to invite ridicule.

In Dallas, some months after talking with Turner, I asked Ross

Perot how he went about enlisting in causes. Did he volunteer to upgrade the Texas school system? Tell anyone who would listen that we had a big problem and we'd better fix it?

No, Perot replied. The only thing to do was to wait for people to come to you. You can see a zillion things wrong with the world, he said, but if you go out and tell people how to change things, you'll be dismissed as a "zealot" or a "crackpot." So Ross sits in Dallas, speaking his mind when it concerns him, but for the most part waiting for the phone to ring.

Is Ted Turner, then, a crackpot? I asked Perot. For some reason that touched a nerve, and he bristled. "It's his right to say what he thinks," Perot said. More than that, it's his obligation. "If he feels strongly, it's his obligation to speak out."

At his headquarters, Perot keeps a bronze sculpture of Teddy Roosevelt, with a saying from the old Rough Rider himself: "It's not the critic who counts, who points out how the strong man stumbled. The credit belongs to the man who is actually in the arena, who errs and comes up short again and again, who knows the great enthusiasms, the great devotions, who at the worst, if he fails, at least fails while daring greatly."

Or, as Perot puts it, "The activist is not the man who says the river is dirty. The activist is the man who cleans up the river."

In that dare-to-be-great spirit, let's suspend skepticism for a moment. Turner's in the arena, the man who's trying to clean up the river. So, let's take him and his Goodwill Games at face value. It seems to me that you really have to hand it to the guy. What are the Olympics but a dream, the fantasy of every sandlot athlete in the country? And here's Turner, creating a new Olympics that may in time become every bit as prestigious—and noble—as the original. Think of the wonderful naïvité it takes to even consider such an undertaking. And the brassy, tough-minded management chutzpah required to bring it off.

Maybe Ted Turner, peacenik, is no joke either. Maybe the Better World Society really can make a difference. In that case, Citizen Ted ("I am first and foremost a citizen of this planet!") might prove himself a man of history.

GLORY

People who know Turner well say that is his ultimate ambition. That begs a question: why?

JULY 1988. The Democratic Convention in Atlanta. A coming-of-age, of sorts, for Ted Turner.

Eight years earlier, on the same occasion in New York, Turner's fledgling Cable News Network was the new kid on the block. Which is to say, in the lofty world of network news, Nowheresville.

ABC, NBC and CBS cornered all the best camera angles. CNN was consigned to a spot so far from the podium that its newscasters needed binoculars to see what was going on. The networks' star correspondents garnered interviews galore with Democratic luminaries. Those who sat down with Turner's people, recalls one CNN wag, did so as a way of "meeting their commitment to charity." Walter Cronkite, John Chancellor and Frank Reynolds covered the convention from soundproof newsrooms packed with the latest technological wizardry. CNN anchor Bernard Shaw made do in an echoing cubbyhole little better equipped than a broom closet. Every time the band struck up a tune, he had to switch to a commercial—or otherwise be drowned out by the noise.

Times have changed. When the media magnates from CBS, NBC and ABC converged on Atlanta in 1988, they faced a tricky dilemma. They wanted to capture the full sweep of the convention's activity, from the speeches to the rallies of the crowds to the balloons flying and confetti cascading from the rafters. But they risked a troubling confrontation with reality. The Omni Convention Hall, where all the hoopla took place, is owned by Ted Turner. Worse, dominating any decent camera shot of the Atlanta skyline is another Turner property: the $75 million CNN Center, a sprawling glass-and-steel hotel and office complex topped by an eight-foot set of iridescent blue lights signaling: CNN . . . CNN . . . CNN.

If you read that Turner . . . Turner . . . Turner, it's easy to understand why the movers and shakers among the Big Three were none too pleased. They weren't about to give their nemesis ("The world's most important network!") any free advertising. But how to avoid it? Everywhere their cameramen turned, they encountered another reminder that they were on enemy turf. Yet hardly a sign of CNN's overwhelming presence crept into the telecasts, and the effort taken to ensure that is a measure of how far CNN and Ted Turner have come. Once disparaged as the "Chicken Noodle Network," CNN started in June 1980 with a string of financial losses and fewer than 2 million viewers. Today, it is healthily in the black with an audience of 46 million. The Big Three have become the Big Four, and it's the latest entry whose influence, profits and prestige are fastest on the rise.

There's a metaphor here. By rights, the Atlanta convention should have been a pinnacle of Turner's success. Yet he was strangely disengaged. He gave parties and played the celeb. He talked to the press. He touted his company's prospects. ("The best network, the best hotel, the best convention ever!") But there was a feeling of make-believe, as if Turner's movements were all motion without substance. As if his heart wasn't really in it and his attention was already turning elsewhere.

Does Turner find success empty? Or merely boring? The man who loves winning can barely abide having won. Even as he celebrates victory, he's already thinking about how to move on.

CNN Center. Visiting conventioneers call it the "House that Ted Built," and it's full of clues to Turner and his restlessness. The complex was built to be chic, but it looks more like fifteen Howard Johnson motels stacked one on top of another around a huge atrium. Several hundred hotel rooms all have little balconies overlooking this central, glassed-in canyon. Far below, playing to the void, a chamber orchestra renders something vaguely Mozartian. In the empty, echoing marble lobby, in a Parisian-style café, tables "shaded" with jolly yellow-and-white umbrellas wait for someone, anyone, to come by for an apéritif.

There was a spot of activity in a Ye Olde British Pub, so in I went. ("Hey, mate. A pint o' bitter?") A clutch of people sat at the bar, talking baseball. Bob Horner, an Atlanta Braves star, had just left the team. "Who's Ted going to get?" wondered a fat man perched on a thin stool. After a time, it dawns on me. *Who's Ted going to get?* When you talk sports in Atlanta, you're talking

Turner. He owns the Braves. He owns the Hawks, Atlanta's basketball team. Across the pedestrian thru-fare, late into the night, a little boutique offers Braves and Hawks mugs and pennants, along with I ♡ ATLANTA T-shirts. More "Ted."

It's as if the whole place were a stage, waiting for the star and his supporting cast, the lights ready to be dimmed. At CNN Center, Atlanta's most visible downtown landmark, the focus whether in business or pleasure is always "Ted." *Ted's Place. The House that Ted Built.* The looking glass.

Of course, it's an illusion. CNN Center and the network it houses are more than a set for Ted Turner's historical playacting. CNN has grown larger than its founder, as has TBS, and their operations run smoothly in the hands of capable deputies. But the metaphor fits nonetheless. Turner seeks fame, lusts after the limelight. When he's not there, it's as if the stage were abandoned, as indeed it is once his attention has shifted. And no one doubts that it has shifted. These days Turner merely presides over his communications kingdom. He's less and less the activator.

That role does not suit Turner. In fact, it's outright dangerous. One body of opinion suggests that Turner grabbed MGM not merely to get new programming for TBS, but simply to do it. To get on to something bigger and better, to create a new challenge.

I wonder whether this isn't the thing that drove him to set up the Better World Society as well. That, too, is a new challenge, a bigger and bolder way of acting on the world and getting Turner's own name in lights. After all, the larger the problem, the larger the solution—and the larger the solution, the larger the rewards of fame and fortune.

Let's talk about those rewards. Turner says he doesn't care about money, and I don't really doubt him. "I mean, just look at the time I've spent sailing," he says. "Until a few years ago, I spent twenty-five percent of my time racing. I would have made four times more money if I'd stayed and worked that extra twenty-five percent, because it was at a critical time in my business, when I could have made it really big."

The choice of words is unconsciously revealing. *I could have made it big.* In his heart of hearts, Turner really thinks he hasn't made it big. For him, there's no such thing as "enough." He can never be "big," because he can always think of how to be bigger. The word *enough* barely figures in his vocabulary, except as a sort of joke. "Success is like having sex fifteen times a day," he once said. "There's such a thing as too much of a good thing."

Which, without getting into Turner's sexual lexicography, is just a locker-room way of saying there's no such thing as "too much."

Is there a theme in all this lusting and commotion and self-promoting bravado, apart from blind ambition?

Of course, say Ted and his aides. Part of the plan is to build TBS into the first global network. Another part is to use television to solve the world's problems. Well, okay. But perhaps the "plan" is just as much to solve the problem of Ted's overwhelming appetites, his glory-lust.

When Turner leaped into the public eye, during his first run at the America's Cup, he wanted to be the world's top yachtsman. Then he proclaimed that he would become the world's richest man and, after that, president of the United States. Now, the goal, some CNN staffers joke, is to become Czar of the World, or at least win a Nobel Peace Prize.

James Roddy, a Turner broadcasting executive and former sailing crony, told one interviewer that his boss's ambitions are "all part of a progression. Ted just keeps moving to larger and larger arenas. In the old days, he wasn't satisfied until everyone in a room listened to him. Then it became everyone in town, then the state, then the country, and now the world."

The obsession shows up in family life as well. Home is never "enough" either, it seems. It's not just the girls, or the fits of irascibility, that make living with Ted tough. It's his driving need to elevate every aspect of life to the level of the mythic. He buys historic southern plantations, the better to recreate the world of his favorite movie, *Gone With the Wind.* Remember that Rhett Butler mustache? Turner didn't grow it just to look like Rhett Butler; in his mind's eye, Turner *is* Rhett Butler. It's no coincidence that he named his sons Rhett and Beauregard, or that it reportedly took all his wife's efforts to keep him from naming his daughter

Scarlett. Nor is it any coincidence that the Oscar for *Gone With the Wind* occupied a special place of honor on his desk after he acquired MGM.

Heroism and fame. They go hand in hand with Turner. And how to be a hero without battles, the swordplay of business and sports and romance? As a boy, packed off to military school by his taskmaster father, he dreamed of leading dangerous missions and fighting glorious battles. Alexander the Great, Napoleon and Lord Nelson peopled his imagination. Lots of kids dream such dreams; the difference with Turner is that he still dreams them. In high school, he wrote a poem on Alexander's great victories; today, he'll quote them and compare those battles to his own. His collection of Civil War swords and rifles is merely the physical expression of the clashing of arms he hears within. A little doll of his hero, Lord Nelson, occupies a niche in his office, its right sleeve hanging limp.

Turner is in that office now, pacing, working off restless energy. If money doesn't motivate him, what does? I ask. "Concepts! Adventure! Variety in life!" Turner bursts out, as if to say, "What else?"

"What else," in this case, might well be answered, "strife," "blood" and "competition." Turner considers struggle to be the natural law of life on earth. It's another of those contradictions: Ted Turner, peacenik, is Ted Turner, warrior. Anyone who knows him well will tell you how much Turner loves to fight, and how central struggle is to his worldview. Christian Williams, a reporter for the *Washington Post* and author of a Turner biography, thinks that love of competition might just be *the* driving force in Turner's makeup.

He tells how he watched one day as Turner walked up to a placid pond on his Hope Island plantation and spat a wad of tobacco juice into it. Suddenly the still waters roiled. Alligators. "This may seem like a sleepy place," explained Turner, "but things aren't what they seem. All around us you see the survival of the fittest going on. Every little animal competing for what's his. It's natural. You can learn a lot from it."

And what has Turner learned? Survival of the fittest. The law of natural selection. At the alligator pond on Hope Plantation, he tells how 'gators catch ducks: They grab them from below and drown them by holding them underwater. He has made that a metaphor for life. You can either be a duck or an alligator, he says, and a man must choose.

Survival of the fittest. In his wars against the networks, Turner sees himself and his TBSers as business-world guerrillas, prevailing on the strength of quick lightning strikes and sneak attacks. He has a thousand slogans:

"When you're the little guy, you have to be fast."

"Hit 'em before they know what is happening, no holds barred."

"The rabbit can get away from the fox, but he better get on his hind legs and hop."

There's real ruthlessness in that frenetic, freewheeling style. At the Better World Society, Turner talks of saving the world, making thine enemy thine friend. In business, he sings another refrain: Kill the bastards! There's Turner the romantic, the college classics student who remembers enough literature to quote from Conrad's *The Nigger of the "Narcissus"* in commemorating one sailing victory, and there's Turner the brutal, unyielding infighter.

During the 1979 Fastnet Race off southern England, when a sudden, hurricane-strength gale tore the fleet apart and killed fifteen sailors, Turner suffered as severe a lashing in the media as he and his crew experienced on the seas. The reason was his utter lack of contrition in winning. Dozens of ships in a fleet of 306 were sunk or damaged in the worst ocean-racing disaster ever. Turner himself was reported lost. Under the circumstances, a more modest or less competitive man might have lain low and spoken in somber tones about the tragedy.

Not Turner. He was all hard-edged defiance: "The king is dead, long live the king. It had to happen sooner or later. We won because we had a good crew and a strong boat and lots of experience, and the people who didn't have those have gone to the big regatta in the sky. I'm not going to say I'm sorry I won. I'm not going to say it."

Never say die. "Never give in. Never, never, never." Turner quotes Churchill, too.

He props his feet up on the edge of a glass coffee table. Ever the contradiction, his craggy, jutted-jaw looks make him every inch the "Man in the Hathaway Shirt," as he once was. But something doesn't quite jibe. Maybe it's the voice. He speaks in a shout, but it's a bit like listening to Donald Duck—a little too high-pitched, a little nasal, a little like a "quack."

The subject by now has turned to The Other Subject—Ted Turner and the secret of his success. And on this occasion that secret is tenacity, like the name of his boat, *Tenacious*. "Nothing ever came easy for me," Turner's saying. "Most people don't realize this, but I started sailing because I wasn't good at sports that required any kind of physical ability. I just stuck with it. For my first eight years of racing, I never won the club championship. I was second, but I never came in first. I just kept working on it, like a marathon runner. By sheer force of practice and stick-to-itiveness, you can eventually run twenty-six miles. Just stick to it, and one day you find you've run the Boston Marathon."

Ted tells that to lots of journalists. There are lots of "secrets" to his success, lots of variations on a theme. To a group of reporters and businessmen, not long after my own meeting with him, Turner spoke thus:

"The secret of my success is that I never quit. Winners never quit, and quitters never win. You might go bankrupt, you might lose everything, but as long as you're out there still dukin' back, as long as you haven't given up, you're not beaten. And remember this. A lot of people from time to time have written me off, said I've done something real stupid. But you've got to remember: A lot of battles in history were won in the eleventh hour of the battle. It might have looked like it was over. But the old saying is true: It's never over till it's over.

"If you ask me what I really enjoy, what makes Ted Turner run, it's that I really do enjoy a difficult situation. It's the challenge of life that's most appealing. I mean, we're all dead, aren't we? We're only here for seventy years at most, and half of us have lived most of our lives already. If you're fifty years old, as I am, you've only got twenty or thirty more years to go. If you're lucky. I mean, try thinking about that. I remember one time when I was really depressed a few years ago, everybody I looked at was this skeleton.

I didn't even see their faces. They were all dead! The most beautiful woman in the world, all she is going to be is bones.

"And against the backdrop of history, how long has man been on this planet—ten million years? Our span on earth is short! Compared to that, we're dead already! So why be afraid? Why worry about financial security? What is there to lose? If you say, 'Well, I'm dead already,' the answer is: 'There's nothing to lose.' I mean, I'm going to try to hang on to life as long as possible. But what I'm trying to say is this: 'Since I'm dead, don't be afraid, don't be a coward. Be brave.' That's easy to say, but it's important. Have courage. In your business, in your life, have courage. And that's a matter of psyching yourself up. Enthusiasm can carry you a long way."

ALL THAT STRUGGLING, striving and lusting. All that talk of death and glory. Turner is obsessed with dying. There's so much to do, and so little time.

The fear of death came to him early. You can pinpoint the date exactly: March 5, 1963, the day Robert Edward Turner, Jr., his father, calmly thanked the cook for breakfast, asked what was for lunch and then went upstairs to his study. There he put a .38 pistol to his head and pulled the trigger.

Turner was then twenty-four, and the shot still echoes. The father, a demanding, driven, complicated man, could by turns be charming, kind and warm—and just as suddenly turn with fury on the world. Often he would return home in the early morning hours, perhaps drunk and scarred by barroom brawls, perhaps to beat his son with a coat hanger for some real or imagined infraction of the rules. He would double the punishment if the boy cried.

A self-made millionaire who started his own outdoor billboard business in Cincinnati before the war, Ed Turner wanted his son to be as tough and self-reliant as he was. He loved his children dearly. Perhaps he felt he loved them too much, for their good or his. Love could turn bitter; things you loved too much could be lost. One room of the family house was occupied by Ted's younger sister. The family listened helplessly as she screamed her life away, ravaged by a rare and untreatable form of lupus that ate at her for years before finally letting her pass.

Perhaps because of that, the elder Turner kept his distance from his son. Better not be too close. Better not love too much. It might make the son weak; worse, he, too, might be lost. And so he sent his son away to military school from the fifth grade on. To help him along on his enforced march to manhood, the father one summer charged Ted rent to live at home—twenty-five dollars a month out of his earnings of fifty dollars. When Ted objected, his father told him that if he could find someplace cheaper, he was welcome to move out. Another summer he rewarded his son for his high school graduation by giving him a new Lightning sailboat. But there was a catch. It was a gift, yes, but Ted had to come up with half the purchase price—which the father deducted from his son's summer pay.

Nothing the son could do was good enough. "Ted strained to measure up," recalls one boyhood friend, "but frequently he didn't." When he got a B on an exam, his father demanded to know why he hadn't gotten an A. When Turner completed a household chore, his father would invariably make him do it over. "Not good enough," he would say, deriding the son for his weakness and lack of self-discipline. Some of Turner's friends suggested that he was being too hard, that Ted would be crippled in later life by self-doubt and insecurity. Nonsense, the father replied. Insecurity is the "best motivator" there is. He wanted Ted to be insecure, he told his son's first wife, because insecurity breeds competitiveness, and competitiveness makes for greatness.

Those lessons showed up many years later at Hope Plantation, in the little parable of the alligators and the ducks. The law of life is survival of the fittest. Only the strong and the willful survive, and you must choose how you will be. Turner, who kept an alligator in his room at college, made his choice. The day he arrived at Georgia Military Academy, he walked into his dorm room and beat up the biggest of his three roommates. "Who's the boss here?" he demanded. "You are," they all agreed. The next day Turner walked into the adjoining room, thinking to repeat the previous night's success. "I'm the boss here, too," he declared—whereupon four guys jumped him and knocked the daylights out of him.

Turner went away to college. He wanted to go to the Naval Academy at Annapolis, but his father said he should be trained in business. He feared as well that his son's growing success as a sailor—he was creaming the fleet with the Lightning his father had given him—would prove too great a distraction. Besides, the family put great stock in an Ivy League education. So off Ted went to Brown. To his father's chagrin, he didn't get into Harvard.

Perhaps in rebellion against the enforced routine of military school, and his father's expectations, Turner at Brown became the Southern Playboy—drinking, chasing girls, getting embroiled in scrapes to the point of being suspended, not hitting the books very hard. That bothered the father. Worse was Turner's choice of studies: Classics, literature, poetry—the stuff, at the time, of a traditional liberal arts education. Turner Senior thought it would make his boy a softie. What a waste, he said, and one day sent a letter:

"My dear son," it began. "I am appalled, even horrified, that you have adopted Classics as a major. As a matter of fact, I almost puked on the way home today. I am a practical man, and I cannot possibly understand why you should wish to speak Greek. With whom will you communicate in Greek? These subjects might give you a community of interests with an isolated few impractical dreamers, and a select group of college professors. God forbid!

"It would seem to me instead that what you would wish to do is establish a community of interests with as many people as you possibly can. With people who are moving, who are doing things, and who have an interesting, not a decadent, outlook.

"I suppose everybody has to be a snob of some sort, and I suppose you will feel you are distinguishing yourself from the herd by becoming a Classical snob. If I leave you enough money, you can retire to an ivory tower and contemplate for the rest of your days the influence that the hieroglyphics of prehistoric men had upon the writings of William Faulkner. Incidentally, he was a contemporary of mine in Mississippi. We speak the same language—whores, sluts, strong words and strong deeds."

The father concluded: "You are in the hands of the Philistines, and dammit, I sent you there. I am sorry. Devotedly, Dad."

TURNER'S RESPONSE WAS to publish the letter, in full, in the college newspaper. He eventually switched to economics, but apparently that did not placate the father. He refused to send the money to pay for his son's senior year. Not that it mattered. At a party in his room one night, Turner entertained friends with tales of the less-than-exclusive love life of his dorm-mate's steady girlfriend. Not long after, the guy got revenge by calling the campus cops when Turner had a girl in his room. Those were the days before the sexual revolution, and Brown was not amused. He was expelled, for good.

Back home, all was not well. Turner's parents divorced. Business pressures were mounting. Turner's father had aggressively expanded the family billboard business, and now he worried that he was overextended, that he had gone too far. He began working seven days a week, took no time off and gave up all outside activities. Seemingly on the verge of a breakdown, the elder Turner lost his nerve. He began talking about selling out.

His son was furious. He had worked at the business for ten summers, and knew it from the ground up. He didn't understand why it couldn't be saved, let alone prosper. He said so, often and bitingly. Without mincing words, he asked where his father's vaunted toughness had gone.

Survival of the fittest. Ed Turner taught his son well. And here, now, he found himself locked in battle with the child he had so painstakingly trained for greatness. What a shock it must have been, to suddenly find himself unable to carry off his new business venture. And then to see his son, so full of willful confidence, fight him so fiercely to take over, and with such utter disregard for the blood ties between them.

Was it the pressure that took Ed Turner's life, or the shame at coming up short? Roger Vaughan, author of *The Man Behind the Mouth*, suggests it was something more complicated: an act that was at once a token of the father's own guilt in raising a son who could fight so ruthlessly against him, and that was a gift as well, given out of pride in the sheer purity of his son's competitiveness—the trait the father valued above all else. A last gift that, when given, would remove the obstacle to his son's ambitions.

It's impossible to say, and perhaps not even fitting to speculate. All that can be said is that Ed Turner never left anything to chance, in life or death. As for the son, Ted Turner has said more than once that, deep in his heart, he believes he killed his father. That just as the father drove him, he later drove the father. Drove him to suicide.

TALK ABOUT TURNER'S penchant for the mythic. The blood of the father on the hands of a son. The sins of a father visited on the child. It has all the elements of a Greek drama, right down to Oedipal guilt.

Let's talk about Oedipus, the Greek king of legend who, cast off by his parents in toddlerhood, ended up marrying his mother and killing his father. The classics are full of such familial contretemps. Theseus, another mythic Greek, accidentally-on-purpose killed his dad when he "forgot" to take down some black sails on his yacht. Interpreting that as a signal that he was dead, his father (a king, conveniently) hurled himself from a cliff. And consider the real-life legend of Alexander the Great, Turner's hero. The shadow that King Philip II of Macedon cast over his son was considerable. Philip was a formidable empire builder in his own right, and Alexander, as Plutarch tells it, was forever complaining to friends that his father "would anticipate everything and leave him and them no opportunities for performing great and illustrious action." Alexander was thus not overly dismayed when his father was murdered (By whom? some historians darkly wonder), leaving the twenty-year-old heir to follow his ambitions freely.

Such unusually intense father-son rivalries, often unconscious, may be the most important force in the Alexander Complex. They represent a craving for autonomy that can propel the son into a solitary, winning orbit. "Even though a child might show a great deal of affection for his father," writes New York psychologist Harold Levinson, "he is struggling to defeat him by showing his independence and starting his own business."

Did Turner feel suddenly freed when his father died?

On one level, no. The death clearly haunts him. "It was the greatest tragedy of my life," he says today. Yet Turner wasted little time in seizing the opportunity. As his wife of the time, Judy Nye Hallisey, puts it, "He felt challenged. Now he was in a position to carry on, to outdo his father."

Ed Turner willed his billboard company to his son, but it was nearly a worthless bequest. Turner had signed an agreement to sell the company shortly before his death, and the buyers wouldn't undo the deal—despite the younger Turner's pleas. How Turner broke apart that deal has become part of Turner's personal legend—and a symbol of his no-holds-barred business style. He would go to any length to keep hold of the business, he informed the new owners. If he couldn't have it, neither could they.

His first move, a day or two after his father's death, was to transfer all the leases for the billboard company to a separate firm, established in his own name. Then he hired all his father's old employees and put them on the new company's payroll. That done, he called up the new owners and started to threaten. He would go out and build new billboards in front of theirs, he told them. He would burn the company's records. He would kill the business, even if he had to destroy himself in the process. Appalled, the would-be owners of Turner Outdoor Advertising pulled out.

That Turner won is almost beside the point. The episode was a harbinger of the future. When the odds were against him, he played to the hilt, gambled everything and won. Turner never forgot that lesson.

After all, it was himself that he was fighting for. The billboard business was his identity, the only way of proving himself to the only audience that counted: his father. "I came out of that tragedy the same way I've come out of every other. I didn't quit. I went to work the next morning and said, 'If my father were here today, he'd want me to work and try to pull this company out of the morass it's in.' "

That it was his father's "morass" made it all the better. How better to prove yourself, to outdo your father, than to make good on a deal that had beaten him . . . and after doing that, to go further, to keep building the business?

Turner's career since then has been an odyssey of bigger and bolder ventures, bigger gambles and ever-greater debts. It wasn't merely confidence in his own instincts that gave him the courage to undertake great risks; it was fear of failure. Not the failure of betting wrong and losing money, but rather the fear of not betting enough and therefore falling short in the race to measure up to what he imagined were his father's expectations.

Turner went deeply into hock to get his own billboard company back on its feet, and then bought another. And then another and another. He branched into radio and television. When he paid $2.5 million for Channel 17, a financially troubled Atlanta UHF station, his accountant quit, declaring that Turner couldn't carry the debt and would quickly go bankrupt. Three years later, Turner had the money-losing operation safely in the black. Within six years, the station had become WTBS—the SuperStation that now reaches more than 40 million homes. Meanwhile, Turner snatched up the Atlanta Braves baseball team. Then the Atlanta Hawks. He won the America's Cup, started CNN, took aim on CBS and, suddenly, Ted Turner was *famous*.

People sought his autograph. Pretty girls flocked to him. There were interviews in *Playboy*, on *60 Minutes* and on the Phil Donahue show. Money flowed in. Despite the bath he took on MGM, *Forbes* last year rated Turner high on the list of the country's richest men, with TBS stock valued at roughly half a billion dollars.

Oh, to be rich and famous. How better to banish the ghosts of the past than to be *the* Ted Turner, "the most indebted man in history," rich and colorful to boot—the folkloric "Captain Outrageous." It would seem that Turner's cup runneth over.

But has it?

In literature and in life, even in TV miniseries, heroes are always cursed by a fatal flaw. For the Greeks, it was usually hubris, the sin of aspiring to be like the gods, and the penalties could be stiff. Oedipus, upon discovering his sins, put out his eyes. Alexander consumed himself. He died after a wild debauch, burned out at age thirty-three.

If Turner is similarly cursed, what penalty might fate exact? Turner's ruthless competitiveness, his restless ambition to always be bigger and better, certainly conceal a deep inability to love.

Gary Smith, a reporter for *Sports Illustrated*, has gathered some telling insights.

"I don't think Ted Turner loves anything," sailing buddy James Roddy told him about Turner's racing days. "His hands were on the wheel of the boat, but his mind was on the finish line and the headline that said, TURNER WINS."

"I was a fairly disturbed child," said Turner's son from his first marriage, a CNN cameraman. "Dad didn't have time for me."

"I never really enjoyed sailing that much," said Turner himself.

That's a stunning statement from a man who spent decades chasing yachting trophies around the world. But it makes sense. So long as his father was alive, sailing was the only way Turner could win. And he just *had* to win. He had to win so badly that during the America's Cup he would throw up on the walk down to the docks at race time.

He had to win in the Fastnet Race, too, the one that took place in a gale off the English coast. At the height of the storm, over the crashing of the waves, one crew member recalls how he heard a man screaming. He looked toward the stern and saw Turner, spitting salt water and howling. "This'll show who has the stuff!" he screamed. "This'll show who has the stuff!"

It's probably no surprise that a man obsessed with showing "who has the stuff," who's got so much to prove, doesn't have much time for entangling emotional commitments. Hence the rocky family life—the divorce, the separations, the distance from the kids.

Like father, like son. Turner, too, packed his boys off to military school. He, too, doubled the punishment when they cried. He, too, insisted that they earn their keep and docked their summer's pay for working in the family business.

And he, too, has now experienced the pressures that drove his father to break down: the endless hours, the frenetic globe-hopping, the sudden and unexpected bouts of vulnerability.

So much to do, so little time.

And no end to the demands or easing of the need to win. Try living with that sometime. Try living with something that, even in the moment of victory, allows no more than a flicker of rest or satisfaction. Because it's time to be moving on, to get on to the next thing. To have more glory. To banish the ghost.

Several years ago, when CNN had established itself as a sure winner and its founder was being acclaimed as an energizing force in the moribund television industry, *Success* magazine put Turner on its cover. It was a moment of public triumph, perhaps the first time that he had been so recognized for his business rather than sailing accomplishments. He was, as the magazine said, at last a success. And what did he do? As he told a group of Georgetown University students, Turner held the cover photo upward toward heaven and cried, "Is this enough for you, Father? Is this enough?"

BIG DAY AT the Harvard Club. Ted Turner is in town, and a boisterous crowd of New York businessmen, ad execs and journalists have come for the show.

"This is the finest turnout we've ever had," boasts the MC. "People have come from all over—Boston, Portland, Chicago, Washington." No doubt about it. Turner is a big draw.

He's supposed to deliver a talk on entrepreneurship: how I got where I did, the secrets of my success, et cetera. And Turner gamely tries to explain. He's got some tips.

"You know," he says, "the golden rule of life is the golden rule of business: Do unto others as you would have them do unto you. The reason I've had success in sailing and business was that I treated my employees and partners the same way I would have liked to be treated."

The crowd's a little quiet. Maybe he's said that once or thrice too often. Maybe they've heard the stories about working with Ted, and know better. Turner tries again.

"Another thing I've learned from experience: hard work. You know, get to work early, don't watch the clock."

Some pinstriped banker types exchange glances at a table near the podium, smirking into their water glasses. A faint buzz of conversation grows at the back of the room.

"And honesty. You have to be honest. You've all read about Ivan Boesky. Well, I haven't lost any sleep over that, because I know I've never done anything wrong. It's a big temptation to cut corners, particularly when the situation is a little dicey, a little bit desperate. You can make a lot of money when you're dishonest. But don't; it's not worth it."

Turner rambles on. "You got to take vacations, got to have variety in life. Otherwise you go stale. I mean, even God takes weekends off. When He made the world, why, He rested the seventh day!"

That gets a laugh, but it's clear things aren't going terribly well. The crowd's tuned in, but not exactly thrilled with the pearls of wisdom so far. And neither is Turner. He doesn't really like the subject. A hint of impatience creeps into his voice; you can almost sense him thinking, What is this, the Dare to Be Great Lecture Series? *Let's get real.*

"Death," says Turner. "We're all dead."

Sudden silence in the hall. Then a big laugh.

Barely five minutes into his speech, and Turner has already jettisoned the program notes. He's back to his long view of history, about 10 million years back.

"I mean, how long have we been around, anyway? And how long do we have? *Homo erectus*, our common ancestor, appeared on the plains of Africa some ten million years ago. Mankind has been using fire for four hundred thousand years. We've been able to read and write for five thousand years. And modern civilization has really only been around for two hundred years.

"What I'm trying to say is that we've made lots of progress, there's lots to be cheerful about. But there's also a lot to be terribly ashamed of, problems that we have not been able to fix even if we call ourselves 'modern.' People in the Middle East are struggling to exterminate themselves. People in this country throw trash and bottles out of their car windows. The world's population is growing out of control.

"We've got to get in control. That's why I'm a strong believer in the philosophy of Jesus Christ, Mahatma Gandhi and Martin Luther King—that we should love each other, that we should work very hard to get along. And just because our grandfathers hated a certain group of people and nailed them to crosses or sent them to the gas chambers doesn't mean we have to keep doing it, any more than we have to keep slaves today just because our great-great-great grandfathers may have. We have to continue to progress, as a species. Protecting the environment, controlling population, banning the bomb—those are the things that interest me most."

Turner's onto the themes of the Better World Society. This isn't a fund-raiser. He's talking about them because he's decided to talk about something other than business and money. He wants to talk about something he thinks is more *important*, and he does so with evangelical fervor.

"That's why money has never really been my prime motivation in business. Why, when my father shot himself, at age fifty-one, he was the richest he'd ever been. I've met a lot of people who are extraordinarily wealthy, and they never seemed any happier than people of more modest means."

Turner and his father. He mentions how his dad started from nothing. How he taught his son the billboard business. How he emphasized the importance of honesty and a man's word. ("Son, every morning in your life, except maybe on weekends, you're going to be looking in a mirror as you shave. If you like what you see there, you're a success. If you've done something you're ashamed of, you'll have to see it in your face every day.") How his death was the greatest tragedy in Turner's life.

Turner and his father. He will talk about him before an audience of several thousand, but not one-on-one. Perhaps he can do so because he's confident that he's finally beaten him, or put his father behind him. Perhaps he feels that he's finally satisfied him.

And how? By becoming a folk hero. By working to save the world. By having all the money he could wish and being able to say that money doesn't count, except as a tool to do bigger and more important things. Like *saving the world.* When you're working for the welfare of millions, how can you be haunted by ghosts?

How can it be said that you didn't shoot high enough, that you didn't measure up?

Is this enough for you, Father?

Turner pauses for a moment, as if to catch his breath before plunging into a new topic. Who knows what it will be? Not Turner, at least not until he starts talking.

Then, from way back in the audience, comes a faint voice, the first question from the entrepreneurs' club:

"Hey, Ted! *Are we going to win the America's Cup?*"

Normally that would be really irritating. This time it's a gift, a no-brainer, a fast and easy segue from the personal past to the impersonal and less-threatening future.

A few more quickies come Turner's way, like "What's next for TBS?"

"I don't know," he answers. "It's like *Dallas*. Tune in next week. Hey! Maybe we'll colorize *Casablanca*!"

A man asks, "What were the circumstances of your coming to terms with your destiny?"

Turner's taken aback. Big ego or not, that's too much. He grabs the opportunity to veer back to his preferred turf, the general state of the world.

"I don't like today's organized religions," he says, "and I used to be very, very religious. But I'm not anymore. So, I'm not sure there is anything as your destiny. Man's responsible for his own fate.

"We need a whole new philosophy of religion. Think about Christianity. You got to remember, Christ lived at a time when his people were slaves of the Romans. They wanted to be free, just like they do today. Everyone wants to be free to determine his own destiny. But for the Jews, freedom was militarily impossible. Christ couldn't throw the Romans out. So he invented a new philosophy. He created a dream world for his people. He said, Make the most of your suffering in this world. Know that you'll be persecuted in this life, but also know that you'll go to heaven in the afterlife and take satisfaction in the knowledge that the Romans will be thrown in hell. This made people feel better; it was like giving them drugs. It was the opium of the masses."

Turner's beginning to roll now. The audience is laughing, applauding, rewarding his provocations and dramatic poses. Which only eggs him on. It sounds as if he's just ambling from laugh-line to laugh-line, but he's actually leading up to something essential.

"It all gets back to original sin," he says, "the idea that we're all sinners. That we're all damned. That we're so bad that we're going to burn in hell forever. And because we're so bad Christ had to come down and die on a cross so that his blood could make us clean. Think about that. I mean, that's human *sacrifice*. Personally I think it's okay to run around a little bit, have a few beers. Man, I wouldn't burn *anyone* in hell forever for that! We don't even do that to our murderers. We just fry them once. Or give them life imprisonment, with cable TV, I might add!

"The point," Turner shouts, gesticulating over the hoots and applause, ". . . the point is that I think *we're all good*!

"Maybe we raise a little hell, do some things we're not proud of, but that burn-in-hell-forever . . . the whole thing is just out of whack. If Christ were alive today, he would have a whole different agenda. He'd be talking about nuclear weapons, environmental degradation, population control. He wouldn't have any truck with these dyed-in-the-wool religious fundamentalists—you know, Genesis, Exodus, Leviticus, those 'flat earth' people who think that maybe *Voyager* never flew around the world. If Christ were alive today, he wouldn't make distinctions between Christians and heathens. He wouldn't set rules about who gets into heaven and who doesn't.

"Personally I don't believe there is a heaven. I think we're in heaven right now, and we're only around for seventy years. So we got to make this our heaven. We've got to make the most of life. Yes, sir. Next question."

"Aren't you playing God?" calls a man in the back of the room.

Turner sounds a little pained. "No, I'm certainly not *playing God*," he says.

"I'm just trying to live in a world where we all get along together, so that we cooperate more with one another. And we'd better learn to do that, otherwise we'll all be dead. I've said it before and I'll say it again: We're an endangered species. Very,

very endangered. It's kind of like the time of Noah. I don't guess there were any signs of the Flood, but Noah had insider information. He was the Ivan Boesky of his time. But there's no way to build an ark to get off this earth, and that's why I'm trying to change the world, make it more intelligent and forward-thinking.

"Who knows? Maybe mankind will come together. Maybe one day we'll all have the same government. Maybe we'll all speak the same language. Maybe we'll all be integrated to the point where there are no blacks and no whites and we're all *brown*. It may not be as interesting a world. Maybe there will be no more competitive sports. We'll all be buddies and do 'we' things instead of 'me' or 'you' things. Shit, I don't know. But the way we're going now, with hatred and prejudice and you're no damn good and your religion is no good, and I'm the only one that's right and if you don't agree, well, hey, I'm a redneck and I'll blow your damn head off with my .357 magnum, make my day! There ain't much future going that way!"

By now it's bedlam in the audience. The decibel count has risen steadily as Turner's oratory heats up, and now people are clapping, whistling and cheering. The bankers who were mugging to one another earlier are now pounding on the table. This is "the Mouth of the South" on a roll, "Captain Outrageous" living up to his name. So what if he's declared, "I'd rather be Red than dead." So what if he's announced to the world that "Gorby's" his boy.

Says Turner, "I don't think I'm a Commie, for Christ's sake. I'm worth half a billion dollars!"

With that, Turner makes his good-byes, then strides from the podium. He's had another hour in the limelight. He's charged up and ready to go. Across town, appointments are waiting. There are calls to make, people to see, a never-empty reservoir of anxiety to work off. Time's awasting. He has to be in California for dinner, or maybe Atlanta, and probably there's that morning meeting in Washington followed by dinner in London.

You have to move fast to better the world and meet that final deadline, the last line of his autobiography.

Turner's memoir is semifictional, or rather it's reality as Turner wishes it to be. It's about an enlightened mogul who, in a time of crisis, is called upon by the president to negotiate a peace. The superpowers are on the brink of war, and only he can save the world. And of course he does—the business mogul as intergalactic Catcher in the Rye.

Turner's telling me all this in his office in Atlanta. The mogul-hero is sitting on a sofa, leaning toward me, hands on his knees. The picture of focused earnestness. "You want to know how my book ends?"

I nod.

"Well, the last line is . . . 'And they all lived happily ever after.' They all lived happily ever after."

Turner repeats it like a mantra, then juts out his square, dimpled jaw as if to say, "Well, how do you like that!" It's a quintessential bit of Turner: the naïvité, the ego, the confidence.

And just suppose one man could bring peace to the world's 5 billion people. Would he, too, live happily ever after?

I wanted to ask, but Turner was already up and out of his chair, heading for the door. He's delivered his message; the interview is over. No more idle chitchat. He bellows to Dee Woods, his secretary in the next office, and grabs a sheaf of papers off his desk. There's no handshake, no polite good-bye.

I'm left standing there, shifting from foot to foot, and so wander away to find my own way out. I'm halfway down the hall when the door to Turner's office snaps open and a bushy head pokes out, as if someone had just told him it might be politic to say good-bye. "Hey! So long. I enjoyed meeting you."

Bang! Before I can respond, the door slams shut. And even before it closes, Turner's once again barking orders into his telephone.

CHAPTER NINE

OBSESSION

◆

DANIEL LUDWIG treated the Amazon jungle as if it were his own backyard. He was the world's richest man. His shipping fleet girdled the globe. He owned mines, plantations and resorts around the world.

One day Ludwig had a vision. He dreamed that he could corner the world's timber market. The dream was very specific. It obsessed him, he once said, a recurring image of "trees planted like rows of corn"—trees that could be harvested, turned into wood pulp and shipped to hungry markets aboard his private navy. Where better to grow trees than in a rain forest? Ludwig reasoned, and so he bought a huge chunk of Brazil's Amazon jungle.

Imagine it. The colonial era ended a hundred years ago. Yet here was a man—in the 1960s—contriving to create a personal fiefdom in a foreign country. It was the biggest land grab since Hitler marched into Czechoslovakia. In a stroke, Ludwig became the largest private landowner in the Americas, if not the world. His aim was to build a forestry and agricultural complex of unrivaled scope and productivity. He bulldozed the rain forests, laid down three thousand miles of roads and set up towns, plantations and factories. He called it Jari, after the muddy tributary that flowed through the heart of his jungle kingdom more than four hundred miles from the ocean. He spent hundreds of millions of dollars, never imagining he could fail. But he did fail, utterly. In 1982, fifteen years after going to Jari, the octogenarian adventurer called it quits. The project that started as one of the twentieth century's greatest feats of venture capitalism became one of its most spectacular flops. And it cost Ludwig nearly half his $2 billion fortune.

The Amazon has a long tradition of swallowing up would-be empire builders. In the early 1900s, an intrepid Brazilian Army commander named Cândido Mariano da Silva Rondon strung a telegraph line nine hundred miles through Brazil's wild northwest jungles. It was what Teddy Roosevelt called a "Cyclopean" feat, comparable to building the Panama Canal. Then along came radio telegraphy. The anthropologist Claude Lévi-Strauss, retracing Rondon's route years later, found the obsolete transmission stations in ruins amid a sordid landscape of "madmen, starvelings and adventurers."

In the 1920s, the auto czar Henry Ford dreamed of planting forests of rubber trees in the Amazon to supply his assembly lines in Detroit. He built a town, shipped in men and equipment and planted thousands of trees. He lost hundreds of millions of dollars for his effort. A devastating blight and the invention of synthetic rubber killed off "Fordlandia." Today, hardly a sign of it remains.

Ludwig was by far the most ambitious. All those trees planted in straight lines. What convinced him that he could succeed where so many others had not? What persuaded him that he, Daniel K. Ludwig, could tame nature itself? The other men in this book are still at the top of their games. Ludwig, beaten by forces larger than himself, is a prime example of "divine restlessness" gone wrong. When the Alexander Complex spins out of control, sheer willfulness overwhelms vision. The dream becomes an obsession. The empire builder, who distorts the reality of others so that he may lead, loses his own sense of reality. His money, power and past success blind him to his limits. A false sense of omnipotence takes hold, as if literally anything under the sun were possible. Like conjuring a civilization out of the wilderness.

PICTURE THE TYPICAL shipping magnate. Greek. Sleek. Grasping. A Zorba of finance. A lion of the international social limelight.

Now meet Daniel Ludwig. Or, rather, try to meet him. Chances are you can't.

You might try calling his public relations man. Good idea, but forget it. The guy has been hired to keep people like you away, to keep Ludwig out of the news. Call it unpublic relations. You might also hang around the lobby of his office building in New York. You would then get to know the security guards pretty well. Ludwig never seems to make an appearance.

As a last resort, you could lie in ambush on the street outside his tony Fifth Avenue apartment building, perhaps even for weeks on end, as a photographer for *New York* magazine did back in 1977. Unlike most other paparazzi bushwhackers, he finally caught a glimpse of Ludwig and snapped a photo. Ludwig, spry as a cobra at eighty, heard the click of the shutter, whirled and threw an armlock around his adversary's neck. The photographer, vastly younger but apparently not much stronger, broke the hold and beat a retreat. Ludwig, poised to shuffle in hot pursuit, thought the better of it and continued on his way. He never uttered a word.

Nearly a decade would pass before Ludwig allowed another photographer to snap his likeness. The occasion was a sunny day in 1985, when the mayor of Jersey City, a gritty port town with spectacular views of the Manhattan skyline, called a press conference to make an unprecedented announcement. Choice waterfront property would be opened for development for the first time this century. At the mayor's side, smiling genially, was Ludwig. As the cameras whirred, Ludwig excitedly stood by as the mayor disclosed the magnate's plan: to build a small town of 1,500 townhouses and some 750,000 square feet of offices on a sprawling tract of marshland and abandoned railroad yards directly across the Hudson from New York's World Trade Center. The money involved: $700 million.

Ludwig's sudden, and fleeting, leap into the limelight only underscores his reclusiveness. After the debacle at Jari, Ludwig seemed to retreat even further into himself, as if to hide his embarrassment and humiliation. The veil of secrecy is so complete that, to this day, most people have never even heard of him.

PERSONALLY I KNEW little about Ludwig until just a few years ago, when *Newsweek* assigned me to update the Jari story. What I found made it seem incredible that Ludwig should be so obscure. Ordinarily his accomplishments would make him a man of history.

For much of the seventies, he was the world's richest man, a self-made multibillionaire in the best rags-to-riches tradition. His $2 billion fortune made him wealthier than his better-known contemporaries Howard Hughes and J. Paul Getty. And Ludwig made his stash as a true visionary. He was among the first big-time shipping magnates to tap into the cheap-labor markets of Asia to build his vessels. He was the father of the modern supertanker, the ship that revolutionized the oil business. He built luxury resorts in Mexico and the Caribbean before the great tourist boom began. He owned shipyards in Taiwan, South Korea and Japan, coal mines in Australia and South Africa, citrus plantations in Panama, a refinery in Indonesia and a string of savings and loan institutions in the American Southwest. Not to mention his fleet of seventy-plus ships.

With assets like that, you'd think Ludwig would revel in celebrity. But he does not, nor does he seem to enjoy his money, at least as others would. *New York* magazine once figured that Ludwig's wealth, stretched end-to-end, would encircle the globe twelve times. Yet Ludwig, who made his fortune at sea, has never owned a pleasure boat and to this day takes public transportation when, as he once put it, "the distance is too far to walk." Even at the height of his power, he lived almost invisibly with his wife in a suburban bungalow in Darien, Connecticut. "We hardly ever saw them," a next-door neighbor told one reporter. "Nobody knew exactly who they were. I always thought he was some kind of bank executive—nobody very important."

As far as I can determine, Ludwig has been interviewed only twice in his life. He will doubtless die an enigma. Perhaps that's what intrigued me about his last truly great undertaking, his misadventure in the Amazon. What drew such a retiring man to such an Olympian effort? Was he trying to bring civilization to the jungle? Or was he merely trying to tame it?

Surely Jari counts among the brashest of brash ventures, an act of cowboy capitalism that harks back to frontier days when railroad tycoons opened up the American West. When a Brazilian banker and former Cabinet minister visited Jari some years ago, one of the few Brazilians Ludwig ever allowed to set foot on his turf, he wryly commented that it was an impressive project—for the nineteenth century.

As Ludwig saw it, though, Jari was pure twenty-first century. His 4 million Amazon acres would become the hub of a new world's forestry industry, supplying the world's paper mills and, almost incidentally, producing enough rice to feed a hungry planet. He intended that everything Jari imported and exported would be carried in his own ships—allowing him, it seemed at the time, to build a private merchant marine that in sheer numbers would exceed the navies of some great powers. Incredibly this entire stratagem centered on an exotic tree that Ludwig had discovered by accident and thought no one else knew about. It was called the gmelina, an Asian hardwood that grew as much as seventeen feet a year and reached maturity in five to seven years.

At Jari, Ludwig sowed hundreds of thousands of gmelinas, millions even. American forestry executives, catching wind of what he was up to, flew down to Jari for a look. They left shaking their heads, unimpressed with the scraggly gmelinas that seemed so sickly next to the towering pines of the Pacific Northwest. But Ludwig was never one to be put off by scoffers. He built the first thirty-thousand-ton tanker in his Norfolk, Virginia, shipyard at a time when the largest oceangoing cargo ship was but half its size. Against respected engineering advice, he dredged the great Orinoco River in Venezuela, opening up this Amazon tributary to seafaring traffic. At age seventy, when other magnates would be content to sit back and let their money make money, he plunged into Jari with blinding—and often blind—fervor.

And so he ordered the bulldozers to move in. He imported thousands of workers and engineers. He paid a Japanese shipyard $250 million to build a giant floating pulp mill, and then hired a fleet of tugboats to tow it merrily through the Indian Ocean, around the tip of Africa, across the South Atlantic and up the Amazon River to Jari. What a jarringly surrealistic vision that must have been, a spanking-white industrial complex with all its towers, ducts and conveyors floating silently through the primeval jungle. During the

Second World War, primitive Pacific islanders worshiped the warplanes that passed overhead and the gods who flew them. To the Amazon Indians, what a god—a terrible god—Ludwig must have seemed.

His crews smashed the virgin forest into muddy wastelands of broken stumps and burned-out brush. Species of wildlife were wiped out. And the devastation was for nothing. Nearly forty thousand workers labored day and night. The giant pulp mill, put into operation almost immediately, belched billows of yellow smoke from its seventeen-story smokestacks. Freight trains chugged through the jungle; a steady caravan of tractor trailers and trucks beat up and down Jari's network of roads, veiling them in perpetual clouds of swirling red dust. The once-impenetrable wilderness was cross-cut into a tidy grid of plantations, threaded through with miles of roads linking well-kept towns and villages, complete with neat little bungalows, supermarkets, hospitals and churches.

Yet for all its humming, thrumming activity, Jari always hovered on the edge of disaster. From the beginning, it was beset by technical blunders and management missteps, often compounded by Ludwig's hubris and imperious ways. One problem was land. In 1967, Ludwig paid a group of Portuguese landowners seventy-five cents an acre for the Jari spread, a bargain price by any measure. The trouble was that the boundaries of the property had never been properly established. Ludwig soon became entangled in a hornet's nest of lawsuits and conflicting ownership claims, many of which were never resolved.

Then there was Ludwig's arrogance in assuming that he could beat down the Amazon itself. The prize gmelina, which was to supply Ludwig's pulp mills, was indigenous to Asia. It had never been grown in South America's tropics, and it did not take to the sandy soil around Jari. Worse, it was prone to blight. Ludwig refused to acknowledge the environmental miscalculation, partly because the whole enterprise hinged on it. Instead, he insisted that more and more acres be planted. The tree *would* take; he decreed it. Against his boss's explicit orders, one enterprising manager secretly planted a stand of Caribbean pine, another fast-growing tree, albeit a softwood. It responded well, and when confronted with the results Ludwig grudgingly added the new timber—but only because it offered Jari its sole chance for success.

While Ludwig battled the elements, political resistance rose up against him. In some ways, Ludwig was an easy mark. As an American and one of the world's wealthiest men, he was a natural target of criticism and suspicion. Some Brazilians imagined he was establishing a private fiefdom, armed to the teeth and independent of Brasília. Others swore that he trafficked in everything from gold and uranium to human slaves. A few suggested that he was harboring former Nazis; SWASTIKA OVER THE AMAZON, trumpeted one newspaper exposé at the time.

The secrecy surrounding Jari only encouraged such fantasies, and Ludwig didn't help matters. Convinced that he had a direct line to Brazil's ministers and ruling generals, he characteristically refused to respond to the mounting allegations against him. Even the most senior government officials could not visit without permission; journalists were banned altogether. "For many years," says Lucio Flavio Pinto, author of a book on Jari, "Brazil's presidential palace was popularly thought to be an extension of Daniel Ludwig."

Resentment peaked in 1979, an especially difficult year for Jari. Ludwig had just brought his pulp mill on line, yet only a third of the acreage needed to supply it had been planted. Global timber and paper prices were about to collapse. Production costs at Jari were twice their projections. To survive, Ludwig decided he had to expand. At the precise moment that newspapers were clamoring for his ouster, Ludwig turned to the Brazilian government for help. He summoned top officials and suggested it was in their interest to finance a whole slate of expensive infrastructural projects, including a major Amazon dam. That was the breaking point. "Brazil is not a colony where a big businessman can impose orders," bristled the Ministry of Industry at the time. The government refused to back Ludwig financially. Worse, it used the occasion to rule on the conflicting land claims swirling around Jari. The verdict: that Ludwig legally owned only about 40 percent of the territory he had paid for.

The double blow was the end for Ludwig. He invested virtually nothing for the next two years and cut costs ruthlessly. The pulp mill never stopped, but thousands of workers were let go, projects were abandoned and equipment was left to rust in the open. Ludwig was forced to liquidate assets to keep Jari going; he sold his hotel in Acapulco where Howard Hughes held fort, along with some Australian mines. By 1982, Ludwig wanted out altogether. He sold Jari to the Brazilians for $88 million, less than a tenth of what he had invested. With that, Ludwig closed a chapter of his life. He never went back.

DESPITE THE ALMOST unimaginable magnitude of his loss, Ludwig remained an extraordinarily rich man. One billion dollars subtracted from $2 billion, a conservative estimate of his fortune at the time, leaves $1 billion. And that almost inexhaustible cache of money, perhaps, is the reason the grand venture called Jari went bust. Ludwig failed because he succumbed to the illusion of his own omnipotence, the illusion that his wealth made him too powerful to fail.

Ross Perot, one of America's two or three richest men, has strong opinions on the subject of money. Too much, he says, is almost as bad as too little. When you've got lots of money, you're inclined to throw it at problems rather than think them through and solve them. Too much money saps your discipline, "fuzzes" your goals. Your company ceases to be lean and mean. Instead of being partners and members of a team, your fellow workers become employees, whose psychic stake in the venture is invariably less than your own. Your ability to multiply your own efforts by working through others is vastly reduced. Worst of all, you're blind to all this. You begin to lose touch with reality and the necessities of the market. When that happens, Perot concludes, "you're dead."

Steve Jobs started NeXT on a relatively Spartan budget, partly with that in mind. "We're not scrounging enough," he would admonish coworkers time and again. If NeXTers were content to go out and simply buy the best equipment and technology available, without demanding price discounts and cutting every corner on costs, how could they be psychologically primed to discover better and cheaper ways to build their new minisupercomputer? How could they be fast and hungry enough to outsmart and outhustle bigger and more established competitors?

We've heard Ted Turner on this point. "If money is your god," he says, "you can never be full. No matter how much money you have, you'll never be happy, because you will never have enough. I mean, it's like trying to corner the silver market. Money has never, never been my god. One reason I've been successful is that I don't even care about money. God, no!"

It's hard to argue with someone who makes his case as forcefully as Turner. Somewhere along the line, he learned to value money for what it can accomplish—how it translates into opportunity and, most of all, how it translates into power.

Surely Daniel Ludwig counted every penny as he started out. He was born in 1897 in South Haven, Michigan; his father was a ship's captain, real estate broker and swashbuckling speculator-of-all-trades. His grandfather had built a modest shipping and timber empire on the Great Lakes, and though he subsequently lost much of his fortune, the Ludwig family remained comfortably well-off until Ludwig was a teenager. When he was fifteen, his parents were divorced. His father, smelling opportunity in the Southwest oil boom, took his son along but, as Ludwig told *Fortune* magazine more than twenty years ago, more or less ignored him afterward. Young Daniel dropped out of high school, knocked around the waterfront of Port Arthur, Texas, for a few years, drifted from one odd job to another. After a time, he found his way back home to Michigan, where he worked as a ship chandler's assistant and, later, as a marine engine repairman. He began moonlighting, and by the time he was nineteen had enough private contracts to quit his job. It was the last time he ever worked for anyone other than himself.

Money was always a problem. For the next twenty years, Ludwig looked for his big break in one venture after another. During Prohibition, he allegedly got involved in leasing ships to at least one company involved in illegal bootlegging. He started a business repairing and chartering ships; more often than not, it seemed on the verge of bankruptcy. Ludwig was nearly forty when he achieved his first real success. With war on the horizon, Ludwig wanted to buy an old cargo freighter and convert it into an oil tanker. He approached Chase Manhattan Bank for a loan, but got nowhere. His frayed shirt cuffs inspired little confidence; he had hardly any assets to put up as collateral. He did, however, have an ingenious plan: A company had already offered to charter the ship, he told the bankers. If Chase would loan him the money to buy it, he would assign the charter to the bank. The charter fees would be large enough to cover his mortgage—and leave him a modest profit.

The Chase bankers, though startled by the novelty of the proposition, accepted. As long as the ship stayed afloat, their money was safe. For Ludwig, the deal was even better. He had to put up no money of his own to buy the vessel; yet by the time the loan was repaid in a few years, he would own it, free and clear of debt. This bit of financial wizardry, then unknown in the shipping business, became the basis of his fortune. Going out and chartering ships that had yet to be built, then using the charter to win the financing to build them, he quickly created a private navy. During World War II, he prospered. By the 1950s, he was the biggest shipowner in the world. He was the first Western shipping magnate to open yards in Japan and South Korea, effectively launching those countries' postwar shipping industries. He built oil tankers, ore carriers, container ships and oceangoing barges. He diversified into oil, coal, raw materials. He bought hotels, banks and Latin American plantations.

All along the way, he husbanded his resources. He was abstemious to a fault. "I have no hobbies," he once said. Work was all, and that, too, was a model of parsimonious efficiency. When he borrowed, he made sure the cash flowing from the project would cover his payments. He rarely relied on his own money to finance a venture, and he always owned his companies outright. He never issued stock; he evidently didn't want to deal with pesky shareholders—or pay a dividend. Before investing, he always made sure that he had won every special concession and tax break he could. Unless he had a financial edge, the deal wasn't for him.

Ludwig's system worked beyond his wildest expectations. It worked, that is, until he went to Jari.

The Ludwig who built fancy schools for Jari executives and

threw away millions without testing either the political or ecological climate was not the shrewd, miserly executive who built a shipping and financial empire. Nor was the Ludwig who hired capable managers and gave them free rein the same man who, in the Amazon, fired lieutenants by the dozen and issued edicts that were inviolable—even when they were transparent prescriptions for disaster. Somehow Ludwig lost his perspective. It's impossible to say precisely why, but I suspect that money at some point lost its value. There was so *much* of it. It became so tempting to solve problems by throwing cash around. What's a million here, a million there, when you've got two thousand or three thousand million?

My high school economics teacher, a survivor of Auschwitz whose respect for food was legend, used ice cream cones to illustrate this point. Discussing the law of diminishing returns, he would treat us to the vision of a scrawny boy savoring an ice cream cone. Many ice cream cones—or millions of dollars—later, the kid is a chubby, squint-eyed slug. Somewhere along the line that little boy ate more than he really wanted or needed. This isn't to say that lots and lots of money automatically turns you into a slug. But if you haven't led a life filled with "concepts, variety and adventure" (as Ted Turner would put it), if you don't have clean, clear goals for putting your money to work, then it becomes nothing but so many ice cream cones. "Money is a way of keeping score," Carl Icahn frequently tells reporters, trotting out this chestnut as if it were the wisdom of the ages. In fact, it isn't. Money keeps score in the game of life only if you're playing for ice cream.

Ludwig never was. His foray into the Amazon may have been motivated at least partly by greed and ego, but it's also clear that he wanted to mark himself as a man of history, to do something that no one else had been able to do. It was Ludwig's methods, not his reach, that brought about his downfall. He succumbed to the seduction of money, not as a "way to keep score," but more in the contempt for sufficiency that the phrase implies. When you've got so much money that you can't count it, the temptation is to think that you can operate outside the natural laws that bind us. Great wealth confers great freedom and power; in the ordinary world, Ludwig could do anything. But the Amazon was no ordinary world. All the regular rules were meaningless. Ludwig, blinded by his past success, either overlooked this fundamental fact or believed it did not apply to him. Money would get him over any unforeseen hurdle. It never occurred to him that those hurdles might prove too big.

Which, of course, they were. Godlike, Ludwig looked upon the Amazon and thought to impose order on chaos. He dreamed of "planting trees like rows of corn." The jungle offended him—all that confusion, darkness, haphazardness. "He had a passion for straight lines," writes biographer Jerry Shields in *The Invisible Billionaire*. "He was compulsive about getting rid of every extraneous detail. Pare it down. Chop off the fat. Do away with non-essentials. He had done that with ship design and with his personal life. He had a knack for locating the fine line between function and economy. This was his genius. It was also his downfall."

Shields suggests that Ludwig failed because he did not understand that nature had its own economy, one that "stresses proliferation, not reduction." That's true enough. Ludwig did not see that in the jungle you cannot just cut one thing down and plant something else to replace it. The Amazon ecology is too complex and interdependent for that. Even so, the enterprise was more than that; it was more a failure of vision than of understanding. But that, too, is only part of an explanation. It was Ludwig's impatience that caused the greatest problems.

His age had something to do with that. Ludwig started Jari when he was well into his seventies. He chafed at delays; he was angry that there was so much to do and so little time left. And so he turned peremptory. With every visit, he'd tear up the budget and draft a new one. Don't cut a road there, cut it here, he'd order—even if the new route led through a swamp. Instead of the methodical, painstaking Ludwig of old, one former employee told Shields, the new Ludwig was always leaping before he looked. "Mr. Ludwig always goes immediately from idea to execution," the manager complained. "It was hit or miss."

Ludwig's willful refusal to see things as they were showed up in other ways. Consider his pure blind faith in his prized gmelina, for example. World Bank forestry experts warned Ludwig that his expectations for the tree were too optimistic. The timber would grow at only half the rate he believed, they said; other advisers suggested that he would be better off planting another variety of tree, such as the Caribbean pine. Ludwig wouldn't listen. He preferred to believe his own people—who, it turned out, deliberately inflated their numbers for fear of angering their boss. To his peril, Ludwig also ignored warnings that the Brazilian government was tiring of his autocratic ways. He could have defused the political tensions that ultimately brought him down—had he sensed the signals and acted early.

By the end of the venture, Ludwig was metaphorically blinded. He believed only what he wanted to believe. At this point, as Perot might put it, Ludwig was "dead." He was jolted back to reality only when it at last became inescapably clear that, if he persisted, he would be bankrupt. How extraordinary, how inconceivable, for the world's richest man to find himself running out of money, the one resource that had seemed inexhaustible.

Ludwig is hardly the only empire builder to become obsessed to the point of unreason. Steve Jobs fought so strenuously against what he saw as the commercialization of Apple that he was forced out of the company he created. James Rouse tried so hard to develop Wye Island, a remote island in Chesapeake Bay, that he almost bankrupted his company. Ted Turner's desire to "own" MGM blinded him to the financial pitfalls.

Perhaps such crises are inevitable. An empire builder would not measure up if he failed to keep pushing the frontiers of the known and the possible. Arguably, there's an element of latent self-delusion in such compulsive self-confidence. It's the gambler's faith that because he has beaten the odds before, he can do so again. It's the maverick general's faith that because he's proved his generals wrong in the past, he can safely flout them in the future. The empire builder's best friend, his own ego, in time becomes megalomaniac. No one else can see as well or as clearly as he.

Perhaps it's only fitting that the Alexander Complex, that "divine restlessness," should contain the seed of self-destruction. After all, before obsession comes the dream, and those who dream are the great creators. The empire builders operate in a world removed from the rest of us, driven by forces that, most often, we cannot fully comprehend. A fortunate few are swept up as employees, fellow campaigners on a great adventure, empowered by their energy and grand designs. The rest of us are touched indirectly; their work changes our lives and the way we see the world.

But do we ever really know them? Daniel Ludwig came to grief in the Amazon, a recluse and, to the end, a mystery. There's Lord Jim standing on a beach, silhouetted against the jungle. You can know the empire builder at least partly by his dreams. But you can only glimpse, fleetingly, his double-edged divinity.

INDEX

INDEX

INDEX

INDEX

INDEX

INDEX

INDEX

INDEX